Google Scholar and

Google Scholar and more : new Google applications and tools

In only a few years, Google has become an authoritative provider of multiple products which have changed the digital information landscape. This book discusses how libraries can go beyond Google's basic search and Scholar functions to expand services for their patrons. Respected authorities reveal the expanding variety of new Google applications developed in the past few years, many of which have not received wide attention and are as yet not often used in libraries. Applications explored include Google Co-op, Google News, Google Docs & Spreadsheets, Google Calendar, and Google Talk.

This book also discusses different important aspects of the company's expansion of functions, such as the failure of the Google Answers experiment, the broad variety of free Google applications that librarians can use to collaborate, and the success of Google's Blogger, among others. A helpful chronology of Google's growth is provided, as well as comparative analyses between various Google functions and other functions that are currently available. The book is extensively referenced.

This book is an invaluable resource for academic librarians, public librarians, school librarians, library science faculty, and special librarians.

This book was published as a special issue of the *Journal of Library Administration*.

William Miller is Dean of Libraries at Florida Atlantic University. He is Past-President of the Association of College and Research Libraries, has served as Chair of the *Choice* Editorial Board, and is a frequent contributor to professional journals, as well as being a contributing editor of *Library Issues*. He was named Instruction Librarian of the Year in 2004 by the ACRL Instruction Section.

Rita M. Pellen is the Associate Director of Libraries at Florida Atlantic University. She has served on committees in LAMA, ACRL, and ALCTS, as well as the Southeast Florida Library Information Network, SEFLIN, a multi-type library cooperative in South Florida. Honor society memberships include Beta Phi Mu and Phi Kappa Phi.

Google Scholar and More

New Google Applications and Tools for Libraries and Library Users

Edited by William Miller and Rita Pellen

Routledge
Taylor & Francis Group

LONDON AND NEW YORK

First published 2009 by Routledge
2 Park Square, Milton Park, Abingdon, Oxon, OX14 4RN

Simultaneously published in the USA and Canada
by Routledge
270 Madison Avenue, New York, NY 10016

Routledge is an imprint of the Taylor & Francis Group, an Informa business

© 2009 Edited by William Miller and Rita Pellen

Typeset in Times by Value Chain, India
Printed and bound in the United States of America on acid-free paper by IBT Global.

British Library Cataloguing in Publication Data
A catalogue record for this book is available from the British Library

ISBN10: 0-7890-3614-2 (h/b)
ISBN10: 0-7890-3615-0 (p/b)
ISBN13: 978-0-7890-3614-8 (h/b)
ISBN13: 978-0-7890-3615-5 (p/b)

CONTENTS

Introduction:
Using Google Applications:
Expanded Tools for Libraries

Our previous volume, *Libraries and Google* (Haworth Press, 2005) included an article by Michael J. Krasulski and Steven J. Bell entitled "Keeping Up with Google: Resources and Strategies for Staying Ahead of the Pack." Anyone who has not, in fact, been keeping up with Google since 2005 has missed a lot, as this new volume illustrates, including a whole slew of new applications introduced since that time, as Google moves beyond simple search. The astounding evolution and fast pace of change and growth is chronicled in the first item in this collection, Richard Robison's "Google: A Chronology of Innovations, Acquisitions, and Growth." As Robison points out, Google has either purchased or developed in-house a whole slew of Web 2.0 applications, many of which are treated in detail elsewhere in this volume. Robison also chronicles the growth of the company from a graduate student research project to one of America's largest corporations.

Google's Web applications, by and large, have all the strengths and weaknesses that one would expect from the creator of the one-size-fits-all search box, including concerns about spotty coverage, noise, false drops, redundancy, security, and privacy, but nevertheless all of the newer services have a potentially important place in library services, though some are so new that most librarians have yet to explore them.

The first service explored in this volume, Google Scholar, is the most well-known, and is the focus of four articles here. Many have previously noted the unevenness of the coverage in this tool, and the lack of documentation, but there are strengths also, and the tool is especially useful for those libraries which cannot afford the expensive megasearch science reference tools. In "Thinking Inside the Box: Comparing Federated Search Results from Google Scholar, Live Search Academic, and Central Search," Rachel Cooke and Rebecca Donlan indicate that Google Scholar was, at the time they did their investigation, clearly superior to Microsoft's Live Search Academic, and in a few cases even to the library's own Central Search software offered by Serials Solutions. They conclude that although both Google Scholar and Live Search Academic produce partial and/or irrelevant results on occasion, they occasionally also produce something not found by the traditional search resources, and can be helpful in verifying citations or providing the full text of an item.

Lyle Ford and Lisa Hanson O'Hara, in "It's All Academic: Google Scholar, Scirus, and Windows Live Academic Search," come to similar conclusions, pointing out that in certain subject areas, Google Scholar actually provides more relevant citations than the fee-based Scirus. Ford and O'Hara counsel libraries to "enable Open URL and other link resolving systems" to better enable users to take advantage of the free tools.

In "Join the Conversation: Show Your Library's Google Scholar and Book Search Expertise," Luke Vilelle counsels librarians to offer workshops on these tools and embrace them, even though they have not been traditionally developed by librarians or traditional library vendors. Doing so, he says, will enhance our stature and increase use of our collections. Somewhat less positively, David Ettinger suggests acceptance of the inevitable in "The Triumph of Expediency: The Impact of Google Scholar on Library Instruction." He recognizes that Google Scholar is competing with the more traditional resources but knows that the population as a whole has a "predilection for easily navigable Web resources" which we must accept and work into our approach to instruction.

Most of this volume looks beyond Google Scholar, to the many other applications developed in the past few years by Google. Especially interesting is Kay Cahill's examination of a failed experiment, Google Answers, in her article "Worth the Price? Virtual Reference, Global Knowledge Forums, and the Demise of Google Answers." Cahill compares this tool, in which independent contractors were paid a fee to answer questions, with the free global forums in which people voluntarily offer responses to questions, and concludes that even though the quality of the Google Answers responses was superior, the economic model was ultimately unsustainable.

In "Google and Collaboration," Carrie Newsom and Kathryn Kennedy discuss a variety of free Google applications that librarians can use to collaborate. Google Docs & Spreadsheets is a "personalized document center," stored online with Google, through which people can collaborate on documents and store the results. The spreadsheet component acts much like Excel, again enabling collaborative entries. The authors wrote their article using Docs & Spreadsheets. They also discuss two other applications that can be used collaboratively: Google Calendar and Google Talk (a VoIP chat service). Google Calendar is also the subject of Sara Davidson's "Scheduling Smorgasbord: Google Calendar and Key Contenders." Davidson compares Google Calendar with Yahoo! Calendar, Windows Live, and 30 Boxes. She finds Google Calendar superior to the other products in most ways, as its growing market share would indicate.

There are 1.4 new blogs created every second, and Google's Blogger is one of its more important and successful applications. In "Blogger: Your Thoughts Here," Tricia Juettemeyer compares this Google tool to competitors Vox and WordPress.com and concludes that while Vox is better for the more sophisticated user, and Wordpress.com is good for the novice, Blogger is preferable in most cases for most users, and is best for those wishing to customize, change the template, and integrate external widgets from the Web. Covering some of the same ground, Robert J. Lackie and John W. LeMasney, in "Blogger, WordPress.com, and Their Pseudoblog Alternatives: A Comparison of Focus, Features, and Feel," compare Blogger and WordPress.com, and also focus on a variety of "pseudoblog" tools such as Facebook, del.icio.us, Flickr, Picasa, Technorati, and popurls. They recommend Blogger for most applications, but WordPress.com for "anything even remotely out of the ordinary."

Google Co-op is "a platform that enables you to customize the Web search experience for users of both Google and your Website." In "Libraries and Google Co-op," Dawn Bassett and Maha Kumaran illustrate the ways in which the components of this tool, custom search engine, subscribed links, and topics, can be used by libraries to create custom search engines and develop "vertical search" which can eliminate noise and limit searching to preferred sources. This tool would be particularly useful in special library applications and for libraries that cannot afford subscriptions to traditional paid search resources.

Finally, in "A Squatter on the Fourth Estate: Google News," Jim Galbraith describes this news service which covers 4,500 news sources and is continuously updated. Galbraith describes it as one of Google's "lesser lights," not as much a potential boon as Scholar or as appealing as YouTube; it is simply an aggregator which has successfully built an audience of millions of users, even though it simply resends the work of other resources rather than doing original reporting itself, and offers no commentary. He finds it to be a "powerful news search engine, useful for keeping up with current events, fact-checking, and light news research," but not as useful for in-depth work or fast-breaking events.

The sampling of Google applications in this collection reveals a vibrant and restless company, unwilling to be left out of any corner of the Web universe, willing to experiment and sometimes fail, and determined to be on the cutting edge. It is remarkable that these applications are available without charge to libraries, and incumbent upon us to experiment with and evaluate them for potential use. Keeping up with Google is certainly not becoming easier as time goes by, but it is more important than ever.

William Miller
Dean of Libraries
Florida Atlantic University

Google:
A Chronology of Innovations, Acquisitions, and Growth

Richard Robison

INTRODUCTION

John Battelle recounts when he first saw Google's Zeitgeist in 2001. This tool shows the top gaining and declining queries for a time period, and the results showed that Google, along with the other major search companies, was building a "database of intentions." This, he explains, is a database made up of all the searches people perform, clearly showing what we as a culture want, desire, or prefer. He exclaims that "Google knows what our culture wants" (Battelle, 2006, 1-4).

Although the capturing of these "intentions" is powerful, the difficult task, as any information professional may attest, is to monetize or assign a value to the satisfying of these "intentions." What is information worth? Google, regardless of its founders' early antipathy towards advertising, has been to some extent successful in answering this age-old question by using targeted, context-based advertising to appear next to one's search results. In fact, Google has been so successful in this regard that, as one journalist observes, "As far as the stock market is concerned . . . Google isn't really a search engine or Web portal company–it's an on-line advertising machine" (Ingram, 2006).

Google's brief history shows that its strategy for growth revolves around increasing its ability to capture and satisfy its users' "intentions" and the continued development of its technology to interpret and target advertising to address these "intentions." Google's strategy has been to build around the initial success of its search technology, which is still by far its most important online property, garnering close to 88% of its traffic (Tancer, 2006). By developing specialized searching, such as through Google Scholar, or acquiring additional content, such as through Google's Library Project, or offering online tools, such as email or word processing, Google seeks to better address its users' "intentions" and thereby increase the size of its advertising audience. As Google's Senior Vice President of Global Sales and Business Development Omid Kordestani once remarked, "A lot of the world's content is not accessible today and thus it is not easily monetizable today. We will figure out how to get more and more content and find the right way to put ads on it" (Hansell, 2005).

With all of its innovations, acquisitions, and success as an advertising company, it is more difficult to see Google simply as a company whose mission is "to organize the world's information and make it universally accessible and useful." A 2007 *Wired* magazine interview asked Google CEO Eric Schmidt this question: "When you joined Google it was just a search engine. It has grown into much more. How should we think about Google today?" Schmidt replied,

> One is as an advertising system. Another one is as this end-user system (the search, email, and other applications Google delivers to users through an Internet browser). A third way to think of Google is as a giant supercomputer. And then a fourth way is to think of Google as a social phenomenon involving the company, the people, the brand, the mission, the values–all that kind of stuff. (Vogelstein, 2007)

This chronology aims to illustrate Google's development and to show that Schmidt and "Wall Street" are correct, that Google is no longer simply a "search engine" but much more. Although it is impossible to capture Google's every move, such as every one of the myriad of companies it has acquired, it is hoped that in reviewing this chronology, libraries, and institutions of higher education in particular, will gain a more thorough understanding of the company that is changing our world.

1989 Tim Berners-Lee proposes and begins work on a global hypertext project, which will come to be called the World Wide Web (WWW). He describes this project as "an internet-based hypermedia initiative for global information sharing" (Berners-Lee n.d., "Tim Berners-Lee").

December 1990 Tim Berners-Lee releases the first hypertext browser/editor, called *WorldWideWeb* (Berners-Lee n.d., "The WorldWideWeb").

October 1994 Mosaic, a graphical web browser, is released for free. This browser, developed by Marc Andreeson at the National Center for Supercomputing Applications (NCSA), revolutionizes the way people access the WWW (Rainie, 2005).

March 1995 Sergey Brin and Larry Page meet for the first time during a tour of Stanford and San Francisco led by Brin for prospective graduate students, who included Page (White, 2006, 24).

September 1995 Larry Page enrolls in the Stanford PhD program in Computer Science. He joins Brin who has been in the program for 2 years (White, 2006, 27).

Fall 1995 Digital Equipment Corporation releases Alta Vista, a "Super Spider" program that can store every word of every HTML page on the Internet into a searchable index. Its index consists of approximately 30 million Web pages (Lewis, 1995).

January 1996 At Stanford, Sergey Brin and Larry Page begin collaboration on a search engine called **Backrub**. Their primary innovation is that this search engine analyzes the "back links" or the links that point to a Website to assist in the value of how a particular site will be weighted in the final results. This approach led to Google's famous PageRank formula, named after Larry Page (Vise & Malsead, 2005, 38). At this time, before the advent of Google, the "Best of the Web" competition names Yahoo! as the most "Important Concept" and the "Best Navigation Aid" in 1996 followed by the AltaVista Search Engine ("The best of the web" 1996).

1998

January 9, 1998 Patent application filed for "Method for node ranking in a linked database" (Google's **PageRank** algorithm) by Larry Page and The Board of Trustees of the Leland Stanford Junior University. In order to commercialize this patent, Google agrees to pay an undisclosed amount of royalties to Stanford University until 2011 (Page U.S. Patent No. 6,285, 999; Blumenstyk, 2004).

April 14-18, 1998 Brin and Page present their original paper for Google at the 7th International World Wide Web Conference. They include an appendix titled, "Advertising and Mixed Motives," wherein they express their skepticism and concern over the current business model of search engines allowing advertising dollars to influence their search results. They conclude by writing, "we believe the issue of advertising causes enough mixed incentives that it is crucial to have a competitive search engine that is transparent and in the academic realm" (Brin & Page, 1998).

August 1998 Andy Bechtolsheim, Sun Microsystems co-founder and technology investor, writes a $100,000 check made out to "Google Inc." (Vise & Malsead, 2005, 48).

September 7, 1998 Google is incorporated. It begins operations in a garage in Menlo Park, California. Google maintains a special search link on its homepage for Stanford University. At this time, Google answers about 100,000 search queries a day (Vise & Malsead, 2005, 58-59). Google's original business model was to sell its search technology and did not sell its first advertisements until the first quarter of 2000 (Google Inc., 2004a).

1999

February 9, 1999 Google, still referred to as a Stanford University project, is named one of the Top 100 Web Sites by PC Magazine (Willmott, 1999).

June 7, 1999 Google secures $25 million in funding from two Silicon Valley venture capital firms, Sequoia Capital and Kleiner Perkins Caufield and Byers (Google Inc., 1999).

June 25, 1999 Google, along with AOL and Netscape, begins experimenting with incorporating recommended Websites from the volunteer-run "Open Directory Project" (DMOZ) into its search algorithms (Henry, 1999).

November 4, 1999 Google handles over 4 million searches a day and employs about 50 people according to Sergey Brin (Walker, 1999).

2000

March 11, 2000-October 9, 2002 Era of the dot-com crash. This is a fortuitous event for Google's growth because it has access to a surplus of engineers and programmers (*Investopedia* n.d.; Vise & Malseed, 2005, 93-95).

June 26, 2000 Google's index reaches **1 billion pages** making it the largest search engine on the Internet (*Google Newsletter*, 2000). Google answers over 18 million search queries a day making it the busiest search engine on the Web (*USA Today*, 2004). Yahoo! selects Google to provide its search results. Although undisclosed, the contract is the biggest in Google's brief history and helps solidify the company's business (Kopytoff, 2000).

August 2000 Google begins offering searching for Web-enabled cell phones (Katz, 2000).

October 2000 Google introduces **AdWords.** This service allows Websites to sign-up with Google to display Google's advertising. Using an algorithm, Google scans each site and then selects relevant ads to display on the Website (*Advertising Age,* 2000).

December 2000 Google answers more than 100 million searches a day (Google Inc. n.d., "Google milestones").

December 31, 2000 Google generates total revenues for 2000 of $19,108,000 mostly from the text-based advertising introduced in the first quarter of the year. Google is still not profitable, though (Google Inc., 2004a).

2001

February 2001 Google acquires **Deja.com**, a company that made posting and archiving messages to electronic bulletin boards (known as

Usenet newsgroups) easier. One of the first efforts to collaborate online, Deja's database contains over 650 million messages. Deja.com will morph into Google Groups, Google's own bulletin board service (Stellin, 2001).

June 2001 Google begins showing results from **Google Zeitgeist**, which documents the top 10 gaining and declining queries of the week (Google Inc., 2001a). It will be replaced May 27, 2007 by **Hot Trends**, a service that shows the top 100 queries by day (Google Inc., 2007a).

July 2001 Google introduces **Image Search** (Zipern, 2001).

September 4, 2001 Patent awarded for "Method for node ranking in a linked database" (the PageRank algorithm) to Larry Page and The Board of Trustees of the Leland Stanford Junior University (Page U.S. Patent No. 6,285,999).

September 20, 2001 Google acquires **Outride, Inc.**, a spin-off of Xerox PARC and a developer of online information retrieval technologies, in particular, in the "field of relevance technology" (Google Inc., 2001b).

December 2001 Index reaches **3 billion pages** ("Google Offers," 2001).

December 31, 2001 Google generates $86,426,000 of revenues and records its first annual profit of $7 million (Google Inc., 2004a).

2002

In **2002**, Larry Page and Marissa Mayer begin investigating the feasibility of digitizing massive collections of text. According to Mayer, their initial experiment took place in Larry's office with Larry controlling the scanner and Marissa turning the pages of a book to a metronome. They managed to digitize a 300-page book in a little over 35 minutes (*Spiegel Online*, 2006; Google Inc. n.d., "History of Google Book Search").

February 2002 Introduction of **Google Search Appliance**, a hardware solution that allows organizations to index and search their internal and external Webpages (Google Inc., n.d., "Google milestones"). This is one of the few revenue streams that doesn't completely rely on advertising.

April 5, 2002 Overture, Inc., the leading pay-for-placement search engine, sues Google for patent infringement (Kopytoff, 2002). This is potentially a major threat to Google's business model and ability to grow. Overture will be purchased by Yahoo! in 2003 and this lawsuit will be resolved just before Google goes public in 2004.

April 18, 2002 Google Answers starts. Google uses live researchers to answer questions users post. Users indicate the amount they are willing to spend for an answer to their query (Olsen, 2002).

September 2002 Google News begins. Over 4,000 leading news sources from around the world are included. Google's innovation is that what appears on the page is determined by an algorithm and not a human editor (Walker, 2002).

December 2002 Google Catalogs is launched. This service initially provides searching to over 600 companies catalogs (Sullivan, 2002).

Froogle is introduced. This service focuses on products for sale and allows for price comparisons (Sherman, 2002).

December 31, 2002 Google generates $439,508,000 of revenue, of which 94% are from advertising. Of these advertising revenues 75% are generated from Google Websites and 25% from the Google Network, that is Websites that participate in Google's AdSense program and display Google's advertising. Google records a profit of almost $100 million (Google Inc., 2004).

2003

January 2003 Google surpasses Yahoo! as the number one search destination. Google's share of the search audience reaches 29.5%, followed by Yahoo at 28.9% (Jansen & Spink, 2004, 5).

February 2003 Google, Inc. gains first U.S. patent for a method of determining the relevance of Web pages in relation to search queries (Olsen, 2006).

February 16, 2003 Google acquires **Pyra Labs**, developer of software for creating Weblogs at Blogger.com (Harmon, 2003).

April 23, 2003 Google buys **Applied Semantics**, a text processing software company that makes applications for online advertising and managing domain names. Applied Semantics' flagship product is AdSense (*ComputerWire*, 2003; Bishton, 2003).

July 2003 Google **AdSense** program begins (Festa & Olsen, 2003). One part of this program, AdSense for Content, allows Website owners, including bloggers, to include Google's advertising on their site. The site owner is paid when someone clicks on the ad. Sergey Brin claims to have created this program "after he became worried that the Internet crash would keep people from creating interesting Web pages for Google to index." Many believe that this program created an economic foundation for the increase of blogs (Hansell, 2005).

September 7, 2003 Google is 5 years old. It is estimated to answer 200 million search requests a day (Graham, 2003).

September 30, 2003 Google acquires **Kaltix Corp.** Kaltix develops personalized and context-sensitive search tools (Google Inc., 2003).

October 2003 OCLC opens 2 million WorldCat records for Google's spiders to crawl. The pilot project is called **Open WorldCat** (Quint, 2003).

Google contracts to be the sole provider of contextual advertising for **PRIMEDIA's** About.com and most of its Consumer Media and Magazines Group. It also purchases PRIMEDIA's contextual advertising system, **Sprinks**, thereby integrating and eliminating another competitor (*WebAdvantage.net Internet Marketing News,* 2003).

December 2003 Google begins displaying **WorldCat** records in its search results (O'Neill, 2004).

A 2003 report by OCLC, **Environmental Scan: Pattern Recognition**, suggests that Google is "disintermediating" the library, that some library data shows Google handles more requests in a day and a half than all the libraries in the U.S. do in a year, and that, overall, studies find information consumers to be satisfied with information provided by search engines (De Rosa et al., 2004).

December 31, 2003 Google generates almost $1.5 billon of revenue, of which 97% is from advertising. Of these advertising revenues 56% are generated from Google Websites and 44% from the Google Network. Google records a profit of almost $106 million (Google Inc., 2004).

2004

January 20, 2004 Google launches **Orkut**, a social networking service (Walker, 2004a). Orkut does not seem to catch on much in the U.S. but becomes very popular in Brazil. By the end of 2004, 60% of its users are from Brazil (*The Financial Times,* 2004).

February 17, 2004 Index reaches **6 billion pages**. This includes 4.28 billion Web pages and 880 million images, 845 million Usenet messages, and a growing collection of book-related information pages (Google Inc., 2004b).

Yahoo! ends its relationship with Google, opting to use its own Yahoo Search Technology (Hu & Olsen, 2004).

March 17, 2004 Google introduces **Local Search**. Google sees the demand for better local results that will link consumers to merchants and service in their neighborhoods (*Grand Rapids Press,* 2004).

April 1, 2004 Limited release of new email service, **Gmail**. Gmail offers an unprecedented 1GB of free storage space (Google Inc., 2004c). Privacy concerns abound, though, since Gmail scans email text in order to offer targeted text ads next to messages (Walker, 2004b).

April 29, 2004 Google files for $2.7 billion **IPO**. It chooses to use a public auction process to determine the "fair value" of Google stock rather than investment banks setting the price (Waters, 2004).

Google answers about 400 million searches a day (Graham, 2004).

July 13, 2004 Google acquires **Picasa Inc.**, a digital photo management and publishing company. Picasa's service integrates with Blogger so that users can easily publish photos to their blogs (Google Inc., 2004d).

July 26, 2004 Google updates **IPO** to raise $3.3 billion with a target market capitalization of $36 billion (Weisman, 2004).

August 9, 2004 Yahoo!, which purchased Overture, Inc. in 2003, settles Overture's 2002 patent infringement lawsuit with Google for 2.7 million shares of stock. This means Google can continue its advertising model without fear of royalty payments or further litigation (*San Jose Mercury News,* 2004).

August 18, 2004 Brin and Page's "Letter from the Founders," prior to their IPO, announces that Google "is not a conventional company" and that their purpose in forming Google was to create a service for "instantly delivering relevant information on virtually any topic." They enunciate their business philosophy, including such phrases as "Don't be evil" and "Making the world a better place" (Google Inc., 2004e).

August 19, 2004 Google goes public. Initial shares trade at $85 and reach $100.33 at the close of the first day of trading. At this price, Google's market capitalization stands at about $27.2 billion, making the company more valuable than General Motors Corp., Ford Motor Co., Starbucks, and Amazon.com Inc. (Vise, 2004).

October 7, 2004 Google unveils **Google Print** at the Frankfurt Book Fair (*The New York Times,* 2004).

October 14, 2004 Google releases **Desktop Search**. This downloadable application allows users to index and search information on their personal computer (Olsen, 2004). Desktop Search becomes a major concern for privacy advocates.

October 27, 2004 Google acquires **Keyhole Corp.**, a supplier of online satellite maps (*The Toronto Star,* 2004). Keyhole's technology will become Google Earth.

November 18, 2004 Google Scholar project opens to the public. Anurag Acharya, the engineer who started the project, says his motivation was to give back to the academic world which Google comes from and to assist students in finding more recent materials. He often was frustrated as an undergraduate in India that the library had so many out-of-date materials (Markoff, 2004).

December 14, 2004 Google Print Library Project announces partnerships with **Harvard University, Stanford University, University of Michigan, Oxford University, and the New York Public Library** to digitize parts of their book collections. Harvard holds some 15 million volumes; the New York Public Library has 20 million; Stanford has more than 7.6 million; and the University of Michigan has 7.8 million. Oxford's main library alone has more than 6.5 million books (Carlson & Young, 2004). At Michigan, the plan is to scan 7 million volumes. Larry Page estimates it will take Google 6 years to digitize this many items, a project University of Michigan librarians estimated would take 1,000 years (Coleman, 2006).

December 21, 2004 Google posts its "Ten things Google has found to be true" page. It includes statements such as, "Focus on the user and all else will follow," "It's best to do one thing really, really well," and "You can make money without doing evil" (Google Inc., 2004f).

December 31, 2004 In its first year as a public company, Google generates $3.2 billon of revenue, of which 99% is from advertising. Of these advertising revenues 51% are generated from Google Websites and 49% from the Google Network. International markets account for 34% of total revenues. Google records a profit of almost $400 million for the year (Google Inc., 2004).

2005

January 25, 2005 Google Video is released. At this time, it only searches the captions from TV shows on certain stations, such as PBS and CNN, and provides still images. No actual video is provided (Vise, 2005). YouTube.com will open its doors in November 2005 and quickly become the most popular online video site.

February 1, 2005 Google launches **Google Maps** (Kane, 2005).

March 28, 2005 Google acquires **Urchin Software**, a developer of software that helps Website owners analyze the traffic coming to their sites and the impact of advertisements (*The New York Times*, 2005). Urchin's technology will become Google Analytics.

April 15, 2005 Google Video begins accepting user-generated video content (*The Online Reporter*, 2005).

May 2005 A world-wide survey of over 1,200 academic authors on the practice of self-archiving on the Web finds that 72% use Google to search for scholarly articles. The survey took place before the release of Google Scholar (Swan & Brown, 2005).

May 11, 2005 Google acquires **Dodgeball.com**, a social networking company that uses mobile text messaging. Its technology is thought to aid the integration of several forms of communication, including instant messaging, e-mail and Internet telephony (Gonsalves, 2005).

June 28, 2005 Google Earth released. It allows one to search for any location on the planet and, if available, offers 3D, satellite imagery of that place (Nguyen, 2005).

August 2005 Google Talk introduced. It is a downloadable Windows application for instant messaging and PC-to-PC voice calls (Claburn, 2005). Skype, Google Talk's more popular competitor, was introduced in August 2004.

September 20, 2005 U.S. Authors Guild v. Google. This is the first lawsuit brought against the Google Print project, Google's massive book digitization project. Three authors and the U.S. Authors Guild claim that Google is infringing upon their copyright (Wyatt, 2005).

October 11, 2005 Google forms "for-profit" philanthropic **Google Foundation**. Initially seeded with $90 million, causes include fighting global poverty, global warming, and $2 million for MIT's "One Laptop per Child" program (Sandberg, 2005).

October 19, 2005 Association of American Publishers (AAP) v. Google. The AAP sues Google over its mass digitization of copyrighted works through its Library Project (Carlson, 2005). Emerging from Google Labs, **Google Reader** (Beta) begins. This is Google's attempt to offer a news and blog aggregator.

November 2005 Google Print renamed **Google Book Search** (Grant, 2005).

November 16, 2005 Google launches **Google Base**, a classified ad type of service that allows business and consumers to easily place ads online. Google Base competes with the much more popular sites Craigslist and eBay (Delaney, 2005).

December 2005 An OCLC report, **Perceptions of Libraries and Information Resources**, finds that of the respondents 62% use Google the most among all search engines, 93% agree Google provides worthwhile information, Google is the highest rated "information brand," 72% of college students select a search engine as their first choice to find information, 69% consider information from a search engine at the same level of trustworthiness as a library information source, and that "books" is the library brand (De Rosa & OCLC, 2005).

December 15, 2005 Google launches **Music Search**. This service provides information on a group or artist, including pictures and albums, and links to buy the music (Litterick, 2005).

December 20, 2005 Google acquires a 5% indirect equity interest in **America Online, Inc.** in exchange for $1,000,000,000 in cash. Google gains ad distribution throughout AOL's network of sites and AOL continues to use Google's search technology. AOL also gets about $300 million in promotional advertising for its online properties through Google's AdSense Network (Perez, 2005).

December 31, 2005 Google generates $6.1 billon of revenue, of which 99% is from advertising. Of these advertising revenues 56% are generated from Google Websites and 44% from the Google Network. Revenues from international markets jump to 39% of total revenues. Google records a profit of almost $1.5 billion (Google Inc., 2005).

2006

Feb. 17, 2006 Google completes acquisition of all of the outstanding equity interests in radio advertising firm **dMarc Broadcasting, Inc**. for total up-front cash consideration of $102,000,000. This marks Google's move into the world of radio advertising (Google Inc., 2006a).

February 24, 2006 Google partners with the **National Archives** to digitize historic films and offer them through Google Video and the National Archives Website (Google Inc., 2006b).

March 9, 2006 Google acquires **UpStartle, Inc.,** which makes online word processing software Writely. This software offers free, access anywhere productivity software that emphasizes collaboration (Nuttall, 2006). Writely will become part of the Google "Docs and Spreadsheets" offering.

March 14, 2006 Google acquires **@Last Software, Inc.**, maker of 3D design software **SketchUp**. The software adds additional functionality to

Google Earth. Google offers a version of it as a free download (Johnson, 2006).

March 22, 2006 Google Finance launched. This is an effort by Google to compete with popular financial information sites, such as Yahoo! Finance and SmartMoney.com (Kopytoff, 2006).

April 2006 Google handles 91 million searches a day (Sullivan, 2006).

June 2006 Google is officially added to the **Oxford English Dictionary** as a verb. It is defined as: (1) intr. To use the Google search engine to find information on the Internet; (2) trans. To search for information about (a person or thing) using the Google search engine. Google sends an open letter to the media fearing for its trademark due to "genericization," that is a trademark that has become colloquial or generic (Moshinsky, 2005/2006).

June 29, 2006 Google Checkout begins. This service offers consumers a way to pay securely for transactions online. The service competes with the much more popular PayPal (Petrecca, 2006).

August 7, 2006 Google pays **MySpace.com** $900 million to provide search functions for MySpace and Fox Interactive sites. The deal expires in the 2nd quarter of 2010 but until then it gives Google a large and dedicated audience to view its AdWords (Holahan, 2006). The MySpace, AOL, and PRIMEDIA deals illustrate a major cost associated with Google's revenues, Traffic Acquisition Costs (TAC). TACs are paid to Google Network members and to distribution partners, such as MySpace or Mozilla, that distribute Google's toolbar and/or other products and/or direct search queries to Google's site. Although TACs have steadily increased for Google, they have actually decreased as a percentage of Google's total revenue (Google Inc., 2006b). Therefore, libraries or other organizations that link to Google or Google Scholar or Google Book Search are providing Google with no cost traffic acquisition. For a brief but interesting discussion on the costs of revenue on the Internet see Michael Eisenberg's article, "Will Traffic Acquisition Costs Bite Google Back?" (Eisenberg, 2006).

August 9, 2006 The University of California system joins Google Books Library Project. Approximately 34 million books will be available for digitization and accessible in varying degrees depending on the books' copyright status (Colvin, 2006).

August 25, 2006 Google's rate of digitization to reach 3,000 books a day from University of California system (Carlson, 2006).

August 31, 2006 University of Michigan begins integrating books digitized by Google into its library catalog. Full-text is offered only for out-of-copyright books. Copyrighted books are used to facilitate searching by displaying pages where search terms appear (Young, 2006a).

September 5, 2006 Google unveils **News Archive**. This service allows users to search back over 200 years of news from selected publications. A key feature is its "timeline" approach in displaying results (Sherman, 2006).

September 26, 2006 Google Book Search incorporates WorldCat records using "**Find in a Library**" link (Online Computer Library Center, 2006).

> **University Complutense of Madrid** joins Google Books Library Project. It is the first non-English speaking library to join (Google Inc., 2006d).

October 10, 2006 Google teams with the Frankfurt Book Fair literacy campaign (Litcam) and the UNESCO Institute for Lifelong Learning to launch "**The Literacy Project**," a project that looks to increase literacy around the world (Kothari, 2006).

> Google launches "**Docs and Spreadsheets**," which integrates the Writely word processing software and its spreadsheet application. This product reinforces Google's drive towards creating cross-platform, Internet-ready collaboration applications (Arrington, 2006a).

October 12, 2006 University of Wisconsin-Madison joins Google Books Library Project (7.2 million out-of-copyright only) (University of Wisconsin-Madison, 2006).

October 20, 2006 Google releases its "**Apps for Education**." This is Google's major effort to insert itself into the world of education, and higher education in particular. Arizona State University (65,000 students) is one of the first schools to sign up. Google agrees to take over their email system and offers complete "Apps for Education" suite of programs. The new e-mail system takes 2 weeks to deploy and ASU officials estimate a savings of over $350,000 a year (Young, 2006b; *ASU Insights,* 2006). The "free" service analyzes text in one's documents and matches up AdWords to show advertising within the applications.

October 31, 2006 Acquires **Wiki** software startup **JotSpot**. On its Website, JotSpot's management notes that "Google shares JotSpot's vision for helping people collaborate, share and work together online" (*T+D* 2007).

November 2006 Hitwise data reveals that the primary user demand among Google properties is for Google search, which commands 78.42% of all visits, followed by Google Image Search with 9.2% (Tancer, 2006). This data reinforces the analysis that Google's other products may not be as much of a threat to competitors as previously believed (*Business Week*, 2006).

November 14, 2006 **University of Virginia** joins Google Books Library Project (approximately 5.1 million books) (University of Virginia Library, 2006).

November 15, 2006 Google completes acquisition of **YouTube.com** for $1.65 billion, setting aside $187.5 million to cover copyright legal issues (*Wall Street Journal*, 2006).

December 1, 2006 Google closes **Google Answers**. It is noted that 800 researchers took part in the service. Some speculate that the Google Answers business model was flawed and point to the "Web 2.0" success of Yahoo! Answers, which does not charge for an answer but relies on the questioner to rate the best answers (Arrington, 2006b).

December 13, 2006 **Google Patent Search** released (Banks, 2006).

December 31, 2006 Google generates $10.6 billon of revenue, of which 99% is from advertising. Of these advertising revenues 60% are generated from Google Websites and 40% from the Google Network. Revenues from international markets increase to 43% of total revenues. Google records a profit of over $3 billion (Google Inc., 2006c). A Merrill Lynch report compares Google's $10.6 billion in revenue to the 2007 upfront advertising market of the 4 major television networks, ABC, CBS, NBC, and Fox. It projects the combined revenue of these television networks to be $8 billion (*Television Week*, 2007).

2007

January 10, 2007 The **National Library of Catalonia,** which consists of five libraries, joins Google Books Library Project (public domain books only, approximately 300,000 titles) (Cruz, 2007).

January 19, 2007 **University of Texas at Austin** joins Google Books Library Project (approximately 9 million books) (University of Texas at Austin, 2007).

February 2007 Google acquires video "in-game" advertising start-up, **Adscape Media,** for $23 million (Olson, 2007). This will give Google an advertising presence with video games.

February 5, 2007 **Princeton University** joins Google Books Library Project (public domain books only, approximately 1 million books) (Cliatt, 2007).

February 7, 2007 Google opens **Gmail**, which now provides 2.6GB of e-mail storage space, to the general public. An invitation is no longer needed to sign up (Loney, 2007).

April 2007 Google commands 55.2% of Web searches, approximately 3.8 billion for the month, followed by Yahoo at 21.9% and MSN/Windows Live Search at 9% (Bausch, 2007).

> Google is ranked as the third most valuable Internet property with 119,640,000 unique visits. Yahoo! and the Time Warner Network are ranked one and two, respectively (comScore Inc., 2007).

> Google moves into radio advertising. Google strikes a deal with Clear Channel Radio to provide 30-second ads to 675 of their radio stations using Google's AdSense for Audio (Sayer, 2007a).

> A study of academic researchers finds that 61% use Google frequently and over 90% use it at least occasionally. Likewise, over 35% of researchers use Google Scholar frequently and over 70% use it at least occasionally (Research Information Network, 2007).

April 13, 2007 Google announces plans to buy its arch-rival, **Double-Click**, an online targeted advertising company, for $3.1 billion. This acquisition further consolidates Google's position in the online advertising world but gravely concerns Google's rivals (Sayer, 2007b).

April 20, 2007 Google announce $1 billion in profits for the first quarter of 2007 (Diaz, 2007).

May 10, 2007 At Annual Shareholders meeting, shareholders vote down a proposal to stop Google from displaying censored results in **China** (Larkin, 2007).

> Reuter News Agency claims Google's new corporate tagline is, "Search, Ads and Apps," which reflects a shift into online software applications according to its CEO Eric Schmidt (*Reuters.com*, 2007).

May 16, 2007 University Library of Lausanne joins Google Books Library Project. Google will digitize some 100,000 volumes published in the 17th, 18th and 19th centuries (Bibliothèque Cantonale et Universitaire–Lausanne, 2007).

> Google introduces "**Universal Search**." This is a major redesign of how its results page will appear. The goal is to create a more

"integrated and comprehensive way to search for and view information online" (Google Inc., 2007b). Search results may now include video clips, images, maps, books, suggested search terms, and more.

May 27, 2007 Ghent University in the Netherlands joins Google Books Library Project allowing digitization of out-of-copyright books only (University of Ghent, 2007).

May 29, 2007 Google acquires **GreenBorder Technologies Inc.**, a Web security company. GreenBorder protects e-mail and Web users from malicious or unwanted computer code and offers "virtualization" technology that separates physical computer hardware from the software used to run the machine. This technology "creates a secure zone, called a sandbox, for online interaction" (Auchard, 2007).

June 1, 2007 Google buys **Feedburner**, an RSS management firm that has over 430,000 RSS feeds. This opens a new area for Google to use its AdWords and AdSense technology and allows advertisers access to many more RSS feeds (Mills, 2007).

June 9, 2007 Michigan universities agree to let Google host their e-mail systems and to participate in Google "Apps for Education" (Morath, 2007).

June 11, 2007 Google takes over e-mail systems for Trinity College, Dublin and for universities in Egypt, Kenya, and Rwanda. Google "Apps for Education" service is also included (Coughlan, 2007).

June 15, 2007 Google makes agreement with the 12 university library consortium, the **Committee on Institutional Cooperation**, to digitize up to 10 million volumes. The libraries are: University of Chicago, University of Illinois, Indiana University, University of Iowa, University of Michigan *(existing agreement not superseded),* Michigan State University, University of Minnesota, Northwestern University, Ohio State University, Penn State University, Purdue University, University of Wisconsin-Madison *(existing agreement not superseded).* Google Books Library Project has agreements with 25 university libraries. This project will allow the consortium to create a **"Shared Digital Repository"** of out-of-copyright books. The repository will be hosted by the University of Michigan (Carnevale, 2007; Committee on Institutional Cooperation, 2007).

June 19, 2007 Acquires **Zenter,** a company that provides software for creating online slide presentations. Google plans on incorporating this software into its "Docs and Spreadsheets" service. A true "Google Office" service is now possible (Schillace, 2007).

July 10, 2007 Keio University in Japan joins Google Books Library Project. Google will digitize up to 120,000 public domain books. Keio is the 26th library to join Google's Library Project (DeBonis, 2007).

Of course, a chronology such as this can never be complete, and by the time this article is published, the reader will undoubtedly be well aware of many important developments that have occurred since the last entry here. Given Google's dynamic nature, such change is inevitable.

REFERENCES

Advertising Age. 2000. Breaking news, October 23.

Arrington, Michael. 2006a. Google "Docs and Spreadsheets" launches. TechCrunch. com. October 10. <http://www.techcrunch.com/2006/10/10/google-docs-spreadsheets-launches/> (accessed June 14, 2007).

Arrington, Michael. 2006b. Yahoo's big win. *TechCrunch.com*. November 30. <http://www.techcrunch.com/2006/11/30/yahoos-big-win/> (accessed June 18, 2007).

ASU Insights. 2006. ASU, Google offer Google Apps for Education. October 10. <http://www.asu.edu/news/stories/200610/20061010_asugmail.htm> (accessed October 26, 2006).

Auchard, Eric. 2007. Google acquires Web security startup GreenBorder. *Eweek.com,* May 29. <http://www.eweek.com/article2/0,1895,2138338,00.asp> (accessed June 2, 2007).

Banks, Doug. 2006. Now you can search for U.S. patents. *The Official Google Blog*. December 13. <http://googleblog.blogspot.com/2006/12/now-you-can-search-for-us-patents.html> (accessed June 22, 2007).

Battelle, John. 2005. *The search: How Google and its rivals rewrote the rules of business and transformed our culture*. New York: Portfolio.

Bausch, Suzy. 2007. Nielsen//NetRatings announces April U.S. search share rankings. *Nielsen//NetRatings*, May 21. <http://www.nielsen-netratings.com/pr/pr_070521.pdf> (accessed June 9, 2007).

Berners-Lee, Tim. N.d. *Tim Berners-Lee.* <http://www.w3.org/People/Berners-Lee/> (accessed June 7, 2007).

Berners-Lee, Tim. N.d. *The WorldWideWeb browser.* <http://www.w3.org/People/Berners-Lee/WorldWideWeb.html> (accessed June 7, 2007).

The Best of the Web Awards. N.d. <http://botw.org/1996/awards.html> (accessed June 2, 2007).

Bibliothque Cantonale et Universitaire–Lausanne.2007. Google numrise 100'000 livres. June 13. <http://www.unil.ch/Jahia/site/bcu/cache/off/pid/16159?showActu= 1179242022222.xmland actunilParam=news> (accessed June 16, 2007).

Bishton, Tamsin. 2003. A place for everything. *Revolution*, June 11.

Blumenstyk, Goldie. 2004. Search result for Google and Stanford: Windfall.edu. *Chronicle of Higher Education*, July 16. <http://chronicle.com/weekly/v50/i45/ 45a02503.htm> (accessed January 26, 2007).

Brin, Sergey & Lawrence Page. 1998. The anatomy of a large-scale hypertextual Web search engine. *Computer Networks and ISDN Systems* 30, nos. 1-7 (April): 107-117.

Business Week. 2006. So much fanfare, so few hits. July 10. <http://www.businessweek. com/magazine/content/06_28/b3992051.htm> (accessed June 15, 2007).

Carlson, Scott. 2005. 5 Big publishing houses sue Google to prevent scanning of copyrighted works. *Chronicle of Higher Education,* October 20. <http://chronicle. com/daily/2005/10/2005102001t.htm> (accessed June 8, 2007).

Carlson, Scott. 2006. U. of California will provide up to 3,000 books a day to Google for scanning, contract states. *Chronicle of Higher Education,* August 25. <http:// chronicle.com/free/2006/08/2006082501t.htm> (accessed September 15, 2006).

Carlson, Scott. & Jeffery Young. 2004. Google will digitize and search millions of books from 5 leading research libraries. *Chronicle of Higher Education,* December 14. <http://chronicle.com/daily/2004/12/2004121401n.htm> (accessed June 8, 2007).

Carnevale, Dan. 2007. Google strikes deal with 12 universities to digitize 10 million books. *Chronicle of Higher Education,* June 7. <http://chronicle.com/daily/2007/ 06/2007060705n.htm> (accessed June 18, 2007).

Claburn, Thomas. 2005. New apps keep Google pushing beyond search. *InformationWeek,* August 29. <http://www.informationweek.com/story/showArticle.jhtml?articleID= 170100948> (accessed June 20, 2007).

Cliatt, Cass. 2007. Library joins Google project to make books available online. News@Princeton, February 5. <http://www.princeton.edu/main/news/archive/S16/ 84/71S02/index.xml> (accessed June 8, 2007).

Coleman, Mary Sue. 2006. Google. the Khmer Rouge and the public good. Address to the Professional/Scholarly Publishing Division of the Association of American Publishers. February 6. <http://www.umich.edu/pres/speeches/060206google. html> (accessed June 10, 2007).

Colvin, Jennifer. 2006. UC libraries partner with Google to digitize books. <http:// www.universityofcalifornia.edu/news/2006/aug09.html> (accessed June 11, 2007).

Committee on Institutional Cooperation. 2007. CIC/Google Book Search Project frequently asked questions. <http://www.cic.uiuc.edu/programs/CenterForLibraryInitiatives/ Archive/PressRelease/LibraryDigitization/FAQ6-5-07finalREV2.pdf> (accessed June 12, 2007).

ComputerWire. 2003. Google buys semantic search firm for context ads. April 24.

ComScore Inc. 2007. comScore Media Metrix releases April top 50 web rankings and analysis. <http://www.comscore.com/press/release.asp?press=1429> (accessed June 8, 2007).

Coughlan, Sean. 2007. Google's e-mail for universities. *BBC News,* June 11. <http:// news.bbc.co.uk/2/hi/uk_news/education/6741797.stm> (accessed June 22, 2007).

Cruz, Maria. 2007. National Library of Catalonia joins Google Book Search Library Project. *Criticas.* <http://www.criticasmagazine.com/article/CA6408359.html> (accessed June 22, 2007).

DeBonis, Laura. 2007. Keio University Joins Google's Library Project. *Inside Google Book Search.* <http://booksearch.blogspot.com/2007/07/keio-university-joins-googles-library.html> (accessed July 14, 2007).

Delaney, Kevin. 2005. Google widens reach to product listings; Consumers, businesses post items for sale; company denies Base is a move on eBay. *The Globe and Mail,* November 16.

De Rosa, Cathy, Lorcan Dempsey, & Alane Wilson. 2004. *2003 environmental scan pattern recognition : a report to the OCLC membership.* Dublin, Ohio: OCLC.

De Rosa, Cathy and OCLC. 2005. *Perceptions of libraries and information resources : a report to the OCLC membership.* Dublin, Ohio: OCLC.

Diaz, Sam. 2007. Google makes $1 billion 1st-quarter profit. *The Washington Post*, April 20.

Eisenberg, Michael. 2006. Will traffic acquisition costs bite Google back? *Seeking Alpha*, May 28. <http://internet.seekingalpha.com/article/11288> (accessed June 28, 2007).

Festa, Paul & Stefanie Olsen. 2003. Google ads now self-serve. *CNET News.com*, August 6. <http://news.com.com/Google+ads+now+self-serve/2100-1024_3-5060917.html?tag=item> (accessed June 12, 2007).

The Financial Times. 2004. Google learns how to samba. December 3.

Gonsalves, A. 2005. Google acquires mobile social-networking company Dodgeball. com. *InformationWeek*, May 12. <http://www.informationweek.com/story/showArticle. jhtml?articleID=163101669andtid=5979> (accessed June 22, 2007).

Google Inc. N.d. Google milestones. <http://www.google.com/corporate/history.html> (accessed January 30, 2007).

Google Inc. N.d. History of Google Book Search. <http://www.google.ca/googlebooks/ newsviews/history.html> (accessed January 26, 2007).

Google Inc. 1999. Google receives $25 million in equity funding. June 7. <http://www. google.com/press/pressrel/pressrelease1.html> (accessed June 9, 2007).

Google Inc. 2001a. Google Zeitgeist archive. June 5. <http://www.google.com/press/ zeitgeist/weeks-june.html> (accessed June 20, 2007).

Google Inc. 2001b. Google acquires technology assets of Outride Inc. September 20. <http://www.google.com/press/pressrel/outride.html> (accessed June 20, 2007).

Google Inc. 2001c. Google offers immediate access to 3 billion web documents. December 11. <http://www.google.com/press/pressrel/3billion.html> (accessed June 7, 2007).

Google Inc. 2003. Google acquires Kaltix Corp. September 30. <http://www.google. com/press/pressrel/kaltix.html> (accessed January 30, 2007).

Google Inc. 2004a. 2004 Annual Report. <http://www.sec.gov/Archives/edgar/data/ 1288776/000119312505065298/d10k.htm> (accessed May 26, 2007).

Google Inc. 2004b. Google achieves search milestone with immediate access to more than 6 billion items. February 17. <http://www.google.com/press/pressrel/6billion. html> (accessed June 16, 2007).

Google Inc. 2004c. Google gets the message, launches Gmail. April 1. <http://www. google.com/press/pressrel/gmail.html> (accessed June 20, 2007).

Google Inc. 2004d. Google acquires Picasa. July 13. <http://www.google.com/press/ pressrel/picasa.html> (accessed June 9, 2007).

Google Inc. 2004e. Letter from the founders. <http://investor.google.com/ipo_letter. html> (accessed July 22, 2007).

Google Inc. 2004f. Our philosophy. <http://web.archive.org/web/*/http://www.google. com/intl/en/corporate/tenthings.html> (accessed June 22, 2007).

Google Inc. 2005. 2005 Annual Report. <http://www.sec.gov/Archives/edgar/data/ 1288776/000119312506056598/d10k.htm> (accessed May 26, 2007).

Google Inc. 2006a. Google to acquire dMarc Broadcasting. January 17. <http://www. google.com/press/pressrel/dmarc.html> (accessed June 10, 2007).

Google Inc. 2006b. National Archives and Google launch pilot project to digitize and offer historic films online. <http://www.google.com/intl/en/press/pressrel/video_nara. html> (accessed June 21, 2007).

Google Inc. 2006c. 2006 Annual Report. <http://www.sec.gov/Archives/edgar/data/ 1288776/000119312507044494/d10k.htm> (accessed May 26, 2007).

Google Inc. 2006d. University Complutense of Madrid and Google to make hundreds of thousands of books available online. <http://www.google.com/intl/en/press/ annc/books_madrid.html> (accessed June 12, 2007).

Google Inc. 2007a. Zeitgeist: Search patterns. trends. and surprises. <http://www. google.com/press/zeitgeist.html> (accessed June 20, 2007).

Google Inc. 2007b. Google begins move to Universal Search: Google introduces new search features and unveils new homepage design. May 16. <http://www.google. com/intl/en/press/pressrel/universalsearch_20070516.html> (accessed June 17, 2007).

Google Newsletter. 2000. GoogleAlert #1: Google launches world's largest search engine. June 26. <http://www.google.com/googlefriends/alert1_2000.html> (accessed June 12, 2007).

Graham, Jefferson. 2003. The search engine that could. *USA Today*, August 26. <http://www.usatoday.com/life/2003-08-25-google_x.htm> (accessed June 12, 2007).

Graham, Jefferson. 2004. Tech titans emulate Google's success. *USA Today*, April 30. <http://www.usatoday.com/money/industries/technology/2004-04-30-google-search_x.htm> (accessed June 12, 2007).

Grand Rapids Press. 2004. Close to home; Google rolls out local search options. March 17.

Grant, Jen. 2005. Judging book search by its cover. *The Official Google Blog*, November 17. <http://googleblog.blogspot.com/2005/11/judging-book-search-by-its-cover. html> (accessed June 24, 2007).

Hansell, Saul. 2005. Google wants to dominate Madison Avenue, too. *The New York Times*, October 30. <http://www.nytimes.com/2005/10/30/business/yourmoney/ 30google.html?ex=1288324800anden=b0684c6ec54b2467andei=5090> (accessed June 21, 2007).

Harmon, Amy. 2003. Google deal ties company to weblogs. *The New York Times*, February 17. <http://query.nytimes.com/gst/fullpage.html?sec=technology&res= 9805E6D8113AF934A25751C0A9659C8B63> (accessed June 9, 2007).

Henry, Shannon. 1999. AOL launches web search service. *The Washington Post.* June 25. p. E3.

Holahan, Catherine. 2006. Google gets back into MySpace. *Business Week Online*, August 8. <http://www.businessweek.com/technology/content/aug2006/tc20060808_ 601868.htm?chan=technology_technology+index+page_internet> (accessed June 16, 2007).

Hu, Jim & Stefanie Olsen. 2004. Yahoo dumps Google search technology. *CNET News.com*, February 17, <http://news.com.com/2100-1024_3-5160710.html> (accessed June 19, 2007).

Ingram, Matthew. 2006. Mathew Ingram. Globe and Mail, November 9. <http://www. theglobeandmail.com/servlet/story/RTGAM.20061109.gtwingram09/BNStory/ einsider/einsider?page=rssandid=RTGAM.20061109.gtwingram09> (accessed November 30, 2007).

Investopedia. N.d. Crashes: The dotcom crash. <http://www.investopedia.com/features/crashes/crashes8.asp> (accessed June 22, 2007).

Jansen, Bernard & Amanda Spink. 2004. *Web search: Public searching of the Web.* Boston: Kluwer Academic Publishers.

Johnson, Kimberly. 2006. Boulder firm, Google click: The search-engine giant buys the startup @Last Software to work on Google Earth. *The Denver Post,* March 15. p. C8.

Kane, Margaret. 2005. Google finds its map service. *CNET News.com,* February 8. <http://news.com.com/Google+finds+its+map+service/2100-1024_3-5567274.html?tag=item> (accessed June 21, 2007).

Katz, Marty. 2000. Google offers mobile web service. *The New York Times,* August 11.

Kopytoff, Verne. 2000. Google Is Yahoo's new search engine. *The San Francisco Chronicle,* July 27.

Kopytoff, Verne. 2002. Overture sues Google over patent infringement. *The San Francisco Chronicle,* April 6.

Kopytoff, Verne. 2006. Google Finance hits web; New services to compete with Yahoo, other sites. *The San Francisco Chronicle,* March 21.

Kothari, Brij. 2006. The literacy project. *The Official Google Blog,* October 4. <http://googleblog.blogspot.com/2006/10/literacy-project.html> (accessed June 21, 2007).

Larkin, Erik. 2007. Google shareholders vote against anti-censorship proposal. *PC World,* May 10. <http://www.pcworld.com/article/id,131745-pg,1/article.html> (accessed June 22, 2007).

Lewis, Peter. 1995. Digital Equipment offers web browsers its 'Super Spider.' *The New York Times,* December 18.

Litterick, David. 2005. Google jumps on bandwagon with musical search service. *The Daily Telegraph,* December 16.

Loney, Matt. 2007. Google opens Gmail to all. *CNET News.com,* February 7. <http://news.com.com/Google+opens+Gmail+to+all/2100-1038_3-6157101.html?tag=nefd.top> (accessed June 19, 2007).

Markoff, John. 2004. Google plans new service for scientists and scholars. *The New York Times,* November 18. p. C6.

Mills, Elinor. 2007. Google buys RSS company FeedBurner. *CNET News.com,* June 1. <http://news.com.com/Google+buys+RSS+company+FeedBurner/2100-1030_3-6188275.html?tag=item> (accessed June 19, 2007).

Morath, Eric. 2007. Google. colleges click: Michigan schools to test free cutting-edge e-mail systems. *The Detroit News,* June 9. <http://www.detnews.com/apps/pbcs.dll/article?AID=/20070609/BIZ04/706090339/1001/BIZ> (accessed June 18, 2007).

Moshinsky, Ben. 2005/2006. Google ready to fight genericization. *Managing Intellectual Property* 155 (December/January): 14.

The New York Times. 2004. Technology briefing Internet: Google begins book-excerpt technology. October 7.

The New York Times. 2005. Google acquires Urchin Software. March 29. <http://www.nytimes.com/2005/03/29/technology/29urchin.html?ex=1269752400anden=f115aa8f7550abd8andei=5090andpartner=rssuserland> (accessed June 21, 2007).

Nguyen, Dan. 2005. Google goes gaga on maps: The 3-D imagery is flexible–and out before Microsoft. *The Sacramento Bee.* June 30. p. D1.

Nuttal, Chris. 2006. Google buys online word processor. *The Financial Times*, March 10. p. 17.

Online Computer Library Center. 2006. Google Book Search features links to WorldCat. September 26. <http://www.oclc.org/news/announcements/announcement197.htm> (accessed June 9, 2007).

Olsen, Stefanie. 2002. Google gives some advice . . . for a price. *CNET News.com*, April 19. <http://news.com.com/2100-1023-887360.html> (accessed June 21, 2007).

Olsen, Stefanie. 2004. Google unveils desktop search. *CNET News.com*, October 14. <http://news.com.com/Google+unveils+desktop+search/2100-1024_3-5408765.html?tag=item> (accessed June 18, 2007).

Olsen, Stefanie. 2006. Google lands web search patent. *CNET News.com*, February 23. <http://news.com.com/2100-1024-986204.html> (accessed June 4, 2007).

Olson, Ryan. 2007. Google agrees to buy Adscape. *Red Herring*, February 15. <http://www.redherring.com/Article.aspx?a=21323> (accessed June 14, 2007).

O'Neill, Nancy. 2004. Open WorldCat Pilot: A user's perspective. *Searcher* 12, no. 10: 54-60.

The Online Reporter. 2005. Google's Video service open for submissions. April 16. <http://www.onlinereporter.com/article.php?article_id=747> (accessed June 18, 2007).

Page, Lawrence. 1998. U.S. Patent No. 6.285.999. Washington. D.C.: U.S. Patent and Trademark Office. <http://patft.uspto.gov/netacgi/nph-Parser?Sect1=PTO1andSect2=HITOFFandd=PALLandp=1andu=%2Fnetahtml%2FPTO%2Fsrchnum.htmandr=1andf=Gandl=50ands1=6.285.999.PN.andOS=PN/6.285.999andRS=PN/6.285.999> (accessed June 4, 2007).

Perez, Juan Carlos. 2005. Update: Google pays $1 billion for 5 percent of AOL. *InfoWorld*, December 20. <http://www.infoworld.com/article/05/12/20/HNgoogleaol_1.html> (accessed June 12, 2007).

Petrecca, Laura. 2006. Google wants to handle your online checkout; search giant to be keeper of customers' credit info. *USA Today*, June 29. p. 1B.

Quint, Barbara. 2003. OCLC project opens WorldCat records to Google. *Information Today*, October 27. <http://newsbreaks.infotoday.com/nbreader.asp?ArticleID=16592> (accessed June 10, 2007).

Rainie, Lee. 2005. Internet librarians own the future. *Information Today* 22, no. 1: 42-43.

Research Information Network and the Consortium of Research Libraries. 2007. Researchers' use of academic libraries and their services. April 2007. <http://www.rin.ac.uk/researchers-use-libraries> (accessed June 4, 2007).

Reuters.com. 2007.Google focus on software, not just search/ads-CEO. May 10. <http://www.reuters.com/article/technology-media-telco-SP/idUSN1018550820070510> (accessed June 22, 2007).

San Jose Mercury News. 2004. Google to settle Yahoo patent suit for more than $300 million. August 10. (accessed June 20, 2007).

Sandberg, Sheryl. 2005. About Google.org. *The Official Google Blog*, October 11. <http://googleblog.blogspot.com/2005/10/about-googleorg.html> (accessed June 22, 2007).

Sayer, Peter. 2007a. Google, Clear Channel team in radio ad pact. *CIO*, April 16. <http://www.cio.com/article/104056/Google_Clear_Channel_Team_in_Radio_Ad_Pact> (accessed June 12, 2007).

Sayer, Peter. 2007b. Rivals complain about Google-DoubleClick deal. InfoWorld, April 16. <http://www.infoworld.com/article/07/04/16/HNgooglerivals_1.html> (accessed June 12, 2007).

Schillace, Sam. 2007. More sharing. *The Official Google Blog*, June 19. <http://googleblog.blogspot.com/2007/06/more-sharing.html> (accessed June 19, 2007).

Sherman, Chris. 2002. Online shopping with Google's Froogle. *SearchEngineWatch. com*, December 12. <http://searchenginewatch.com/showPage.html?page=2161381> (accessed June 16, 2007).

Sherman, Chris. 2006. Google debuts 200 year News Archive Search. *Search Engine Watch.com*, September 6. <http://searchenginewatch.com/showPage.html?page=3623345> (accessed June 21, 2007).

Spiegel Online. 2006. Was die suchmaschine plant: "In der Zukunft wird Google noch mehr ber Sie wissen." April 3. <http://www.spiegel.de/netzwelt/tech/0.1518.409431. 00.html> (accessed June 18, 2007).

Stellin, Susan. 2001. New economy: Google's revival of a Usenet archive opens up a wealth of possibilities but also raises some privacy issues. *The New York Times*, May 7.

Sullivan, Danny. 2002. Google launches Catalog Search. *Searchenginewatch.com*, January 2. <http://searchenginewatch.com/showPage.html?page=2161381> (accessed January 24, 2007).

Sullivan, Danny. 2006. Searches per day. *Searchenginewatch.com*, April 20. <http://searchenginewatch.com/showPage.html?page=2156461> (accessed June 17, 2007).

Swan, Alma & Sheridan, Brown. 2005. Open access self-archiving: An author study. Technical Report No. 10999. The University of Southampton. School of Electronics and Computer Science. <http://eprints.ecs.soton.ac.uk/10999/01/jisc2.pdf> (accessed June 22. 2007).

T+D. 2007. Google buys a Wiki company. 61, no. 1: 12.

Tancer, Bill. 2006. Google properties–The extended list. *Hitwise.com*, November 30. <http://weblogs.hitwise.com/bill-tancer/2006/11/google_properties_the_extended. html> (accessed June 16. 2006).

Television Week. 2007. Clicks. May 28. 26, no. 22: 6.

The Toronto Star. 2004. Google buys Internet map provider. October 28. p. D6.

University of Ghent. 2007. Google and Ghent University Library to make hundreds of thousands of Dutch and French books available online. May 23. <http://lib1.ugent. be/cmsites/default.aspx?ref=ABAFBB&lang=NL_BO> (accessed June 21, 2007).

University of Texas at Austin. 2007. Frequently asked questions FAQs about the University of Texas-Google Books Library Project. <http://www.lib.utexas.edu/google/ faqs.html> (accessed June 17, 2007).

University of Virginia Library. 2006. Frequently asked questions (FAQs) about the University of Virginia-Google Books Library Project. <http://www.lib.virginia. edu/press/uvagoogle/faqs.html> (accessed June 8. 2007).

University of Wisconsin-Madison. 2006. UW-Madison joins massive Google Book project. <http://www.library.wisc.edu/digitization/press.html> (accessed June 10. 2007).

USA Today. 2004. The rise of Google. April 30. <http://www.usatoday.com/money/ industries/technology/2004-04-29-google-timeline_x.htm> (accessed June 15, 2007).

Vise, David & Mark Malseed. 2005. *The Google story*. New York: Delacorte Press.

Vise, David. 2004. Investors greet Google with a $27 billion smile; market value tops giants Ford, GM. *The Washington Post*, August 20.

Vise, David. 2005. Google to release TV search service; Yahoo launching video venture. *The Washington Post*, January 25.

Vogelstein, Fred. 2007. Text of Wired's interview with Google CEO Eric Schmidt. *Wired*, April 9, <http://www.wired.com/techbiz/people/news/2007/04/mag_schmidt_trans?currentPage=all> (accessed June 22. 2007).

Walker, Leslie. 1999. com–Live. Interview with Sergey Brin. *Washington Post.com*, November 4. <http://www.washingtonpost.com/wp-srv/liveonline/business/walker/walker110499.htm> (accessed June 15. 2007).

Walker, Leslie. 2002. Google News: Untouched by human hands. *The Washington Post*, September 26.

Walker, Leslie. 2004a. What are your friends searching for? *The Washington Post*, January 25.

Walker, Leslie. 2004b. Gmail leads way in making ads relevant. *The Washington Post*, May 13.

Wall Street Journal. 2006. Google Inc.: YouTube deal is completed with set-aside for suits, fees. November 15.

Waters. Richard. 2004. Google in plan for dollars 2.7bn flotation. *The Financial Times*, April 30.

WebAdvantage.net Internet Marketing News. 2003. Google buys Sprinks from PRIMEDIA. October. 24. <http://www.webadvantage.net/tip_archive.cfm?tip_id=306anda=1> (accessed June 12, 2007).

Weisman, Robert. 2004. Google sets sights on a $3.3B IPO: Web search giant expected to be left with value of $36B. *The Boston Globe*, July 27.

White, Casey. 2006. *Sergey Brin And Larry Page: The founders of Google*. New York: Rosen Publishing Group.

Willmott, Don. 1999. Top 100 websites. *PC Magazine*, February 2.

Wolff, J. 2007. Princeton library joins Google Book Search. *The Daily Princetonian*, February 6.

Wyatt, E. 2005. Writers sue Google, accusing it of copyright violation. *The New York Times*, September 21.

Young, Jeffrey. 2006a. U. of Michigan adds books digitized by Google to online catalog, but limits use of some. *Chronicle of Higher Education*, August 31. <http://chronicle.com/free/2006/08/2006083101t.htm> (accessed November 30. 2007).

Young, Jeffrey. 2006b. Google Expands Its Bid to Run Student E-Mail Systems. *Chronicle of Higher Education*, October 20. <http://chronicle.com/weekly/v53/i09/09a03702.htm> (accessed November 30, 2006).

Zipern, Andrew. 2001. A Quick Way to Search For Images on the Web. *The New York Times*, July 12. p. G3.

Thinking Inside the Box: Comparing Federated Search Results from Google Scholar, Live Search Academic, and Central Search

Rachel Cooke
Rebecca Donlan

INTRODUCTION

Ever since Google debuted in 1999, Web searchers–students in particular–have come to expect clean, simple, one-box search engines.[1] We don't necessarily decry the trend–far from it–as we have written in a previous article describing our experience as beta-testers of Google Scholar.[2] We appreciate the simplicity and power of Google searching and use it every day, often as the first resort. But as information professionals, we note our users' fixation on one-box searching with some concern. How much pertinent, scholarly information can our students retrieve when they only "think inside the box?"

Since Google Scholar was introduced in 2005, other Internet service providers have tried to follow its lead and offer search interfaces to the scholarly literature. We decided to re-examine Google Scholar, and compare it to its only serious open-Web competitor, Microsoft's Live Search Academic. We also wanted to see how well the free federated search engines worked in comparison to Serials Solutions' Central Search, to which we subscribe. How much scholarly information do the free search engines bring up? How well do the open Web services work with our licensed full-text sources? How do those results stack up against the fee-based service? And above all, how well does just one box work?

First, some background about the differences among these search engines. Neither Google Scholar nor Live Search Academic reveal much about how their search engines work, though both describe what their search algorithms are designed to examine. Live Search Academic, which is still in beta, looks at "the quality of the match between the search term and the content of the paper" and "the authority of the paper," though neither is expressly defined. It does not use citation ranking.[3] Google Scholar "aims to sort articles the way researchers do," by weighing full text, author, publication, and number of citations.[4]

Central Search uses Z39.50, XML Gateway, and HTTP connections to mine metadata for search terms, specifically, title, author, keyword (within the metadata), subject, abstract, ISSN, and IBSN. It can also search for a term within the full text of an article or other publication.[5]

Table 1 shows the search types available for each option.

Note that Live Search is still in beta testing, so the number of search options may increase. None of the three search engines offers the option to limit to peer-reviewed publications, a feature that many individual databases offer. Our students are often assigned the task of reading articles in peer-reviewed publications, so this would be a very popular and useful feature for these search engines to add.

Table 2 shows the retrieval options available for each interface.

In this case, Live Search Academic offers much better sorting than Google Scholar, though it is not as good as Central Search. Essentially, Live Search and Google scholar are polar opposites. In Live Search, the user performs a very simple search and spends more time sorting and filtering hits. In Google Scholar, users can perform a much more complex search, so they will spend less time sorting and filtering (although they may do a lot of scrolling to view all of the hits!). Central Search has the most searching and retrieval features of the three, although we have

TABLE 1. Comparative Search Features of Central Search, Google Scholar, and Windows Live Search Academic

Features	Central Search	Google Scholar	Windows Live Search Academic
Title Search	X	X	
Exact Phrase Search		X	X
Boolean Search	X	X	
Author Search	X	X	
Full Text Search	X	X	X
Keyword Search	X	X	X
Subject Search	X		
Abstract Search	X		
ISBN Search	X		
ISSN Search	X		
Limit to Peer Reviewed			
Limit to publication		X	
Limit to Date	X	X	
Limit to Subject Area	X	X	

TABLE 2. Comparative Retrieval Options of Central Search, Google Scholar, and Windows Live Search Academic

Features	Central Search	Google Scholar	Windows Live Search Academic
Academic Journals	X	X	X
Full Text	X	X	
Filter by Full Text	X		
Sort/Cluster by Relevancy	X		X
Sort by Date	X	X	X
Sort/Cluster by Author	X	X	X
Sort by Journal	X		X
Sort by Conference			X
Export Records	X	X	X
Limit by language		X	

found that more features can be a turn-off for student users, who tend to prefer a simple interface.

All three search engines include the option to limit search to academic journals, but there is no way to limit a search to, or sort results by, those that are peer reviewed. This is unfortunate since many instructors specify that they require (or at least prefer) results from peer-reviewed journals. Central Search and Live Search Academic do offer the "Sort by Journal" feature, which does a decent job of removing such grey literature as conference reports, poster sessions, government documents, and working papers. This is helpful for students, since most of the assignments we see at the reference desk require articles published in academic journals, and discourage students from using grey literature. Live Search does allow users to limit to conference proceedings, which is useful, particularly in the sciences, where new research tends to appear in conference proceedings before it does in journals.

This raises an important question: *What*, exactly, are these interfaces searching? A search engine, as important as it is, is only a gateway to content. A fee-based service like Central Search allows the library more control over which sources will be grouped together for users to search. Not every database is compatible with a federated search interface, although as the technology matures, more databases are searchable than used to be the case. The free online federated search engines are in a similar position. Windows Live Search Academic lists the publishers with whom it works, but Google Scholar does not, although users can infer which publishers are included in the Scholar "knowledge base" from search results. In any case, both fee and free federated search engines permit users to indicate that they are affiliated with a particular library so that they can retrieve full text from their library's licensed databases.

So, knowing something about how (and *what*) Central Search, Live Search Academic, and Google Scholar search, we ran some queries to compare results. (These tests were done in December 2006; any features that have subsequently been upgraded are not reflected here.) The sample searches given below are real questions taken from the reference desk. Because we have the "student user" in mind, the search strings are very simple with little Boolean manipulation. This also allowed greater consistency across interfaces. Naturally, many irrelevant hits were retrieved. However, it was noted several times that the title search feature in Central Search and Google Scholar did not always perform well. For example, in Google Scholar, despite searching for "marching band" as the exact phrase in the title, not one of the 39 hits had this phrase in the title. Central Search's title search performed much better, since 11 out of 14 hits had the words "marching" and "band" in the title. Live Search does not have a title search feature, although relevancy did seem to increase when the search terms were put in quotes.

Below the summary table are some additional, interface-specific comments. The terms that we use in our descriptions of the results are defined as follows.

Very Relevant results means that the article's title contained all of the search terms or a very similar term or idea. Abstracts and full text were not analyzed.

Relevant results means that the article's title was "related" in some way to the idea of the search term. For example, general articles on animal conservation were considered relevant to the Florida Panther search. Abstracts and full text were not analyzed.

Journal Articles includes any material published in a journal. These can include book reviews, conference proceedings, and opinion pieces in addition to what one would consider a "typical" article.

SEARCH #1: HIGH SCHOOL MARCHING BAND CULTURE

The student's assignment was to choose any type of social group and describe the members' beliefs, attitudes, and/or group culture. Table 3 shows a summary of the search string and results.

TABLE 3. Search Results for "Marching Band Culture"

Interface	Search String	Total Hits	Journal Articles	Full Text Links	Total Relevant	Very Relevant
Scholar	"marching band" (2006)	39	26	18	5	0
Live	"marching band" (any date)	16	14	0	2	0
Central	"marching band" (2006)	14	6	6	11	1

Best Interface for This Particular Search: Central Search

In the marching band search, Live Search Academic retrieved the fewest relevant hits. There were two relevant hits about student groups, hazing, and marching band students, which might be useful. Google Scholar performed a bit better; though none of the 39 hits retrieved articles with "marching band" in the title, there were five articles on extra-curricular activities of students, which might be of interest. Google Scholar allows the user to limit a search to databases in the social sciences, arts, and humanities, which helps.

Central Search was the only interface to retrieve 11 relevant and one very relevant title, "Attitudes and beliefs in a marching band: stereotyping and accentuation in a favorable intergroup context," from the *European Journal of Social Psychology*. As in the Google Scholar search, we limited the date to 2006 and narrowed the search to databases in the social sciences, arts, and humanities. (Without a date limitation, Central Search retrieved 2,071 hits.)

SEARCH #2: FLORIDA PANTHER

The student's assignment was to research the Florida Panther's environment, behaviors, or endangered status. Table 4 shows a summary of the search string and results.

Best Interface for This Particular Search: Central Search

As in the previous search, Live Search Academic retrieved the fewest relevant hits. There were four hits related to animal conservation in general,

TABLE 4. Search Results for "Florida Panther"

Interface	Search String	Total Hits	Journal Articles	Full Text Links	Total Relevant	Very Relevant
Scholar	"Florida Panther" (2005-2006)	75	69	41	15	7
Live	"Florida Panther" (2005-2006)	13	13	0	4	2
Central	"Florida Panther" (2005-2006)	6	6	4	6	6

two of which were very relevant, with the exact phrase "Florida Panther" in the title. Although Google Scholar had the highest number of relevant hits (15 related to animal conservation in general and seven with the phrase "Florida Panther" in the title), the user would have to review 75 hits to discover the relevant citations. Furthermore, we knew how to narrow our search to the subject areas of biology, life science, and environmental science. One can imagine how much stuff the average user would retrieve, pertinent or otherwise.

Central Search proved to be the best choice for students in this instance. Although it produced fewer relevant citations overall, it included a higher percentage of relevant citations among its results, so a student would not need to sort through so many off-topic hits to find the useful results as he or she might with Google Scholar. We limited the search to general, physical & earth sciences and life sciences databases, sorted results by date, and analyzed only the 2005-2006 hits. Although there were only six hits, all of these were very relevant, with the exact phrase "Florida Panther" appearing in the title. Furthermore, all of these results linked successfully to full text holdings in FGCU's licensed databases.

SEARCH #3: COLLEGE STUDENTS AND SUICIDE

The student's assignment was to research the cause of suicide among college students and/or related issues, such as suicide rates compared with the general population. Table 5 shows a summary of the search string and results.

TABLE 5. Search Results for "College Students and Suicide"

Interface	Search String	Total Hits	Journal Articles	Full Text Links	Total Relevant	Very Relevant
Scholar	"college students" and "suicide" (2005-2006)	1	1	1	1	1
Live	"college students suicide" (2005-2006)	2	2	0	2	0
Central	"college students" and "suicide" (2005-2006)	25	25	10	25	17

Best Interface for This Particular Search: Central Search

In this particular search, all three search engines had very few irrelevant hits, probably due to the more complex string. Here, Live Search Academic and Google Scholar performed about the same, retrieving one or two relevant hits. The Google Scholar search string was "suicide" and "college students" (exact phrase in the title), and limited to "Medicine, Pharmacology, and Veterinary Science" and "Social Sciences, Arts, and Humanities." The search was limited to 2005-2006. Live Search Academic's string was "college students suicide" (in quotes) in search box. Results were sorted by "Date–Newest" and only the 2005-2006 articles were analyzed.

Central Search is the clear winner in this search. The search was limited to databases in education, medicine and health science, and social science. Only the 2005-2006 hits were analyzed. The search retrieved 17 articles that were very relevant, featuring the words "college students" and "suicide" in the title. Better yet, 24 of the citations retrieved linked successfully to full text available through FGCU's licensed databases.

Here are some general comparisons among these three federated search engines.

Google Scholar Advantages:

- Fast retrieval rate.
- More search options than Central Search.
- Most citations were from journal articles, books, dissertations, and theses; most were appropriate for college research.
- Clean-looking retrieval page.

- "Recent Articles" link helpful for sorting results.
- Bibliography manager allows creation and export of citations to a variety of programs, including BibTeX, RefWorks, and EndNote.
- Free online service.

Google Scholar Disadvantages:

- Many irrelevant hits. Despite using an exact title phrase search, not one of the 39 hits actually had this exact phrase in the title.
- Cannot sort hit list by title, or source (as in Central Search).
- Does not usually display the database source; user must click on full-text link first.
- Cannot limit results to full-text.

Live Search Academic Advantages:

- Fast retrieval rate.
- Most citations were from journal articles, books, dissertations and theses; most were appropriate for college research.
- Clean-looking retrieval page.
- Results can be sorted by relevance, date-oldest, date-newest, author, journal, conference.
- Helpful citation manager allows users to click on BibTeX, RefWorks, or EndNote, to produce a text file of the citation for import into citation software.
- Free online service.

Live Search Academic Disadvantages:

- Many irrelevant hits.
- Does not show database source(s) from which citation was derived.
- Full text linking service was not activated for FGCU at the time these tests were run, so we cannot really comment on how well it works.

Central Search Advantages:

- Library specifies which databases are included and can create subsets of databases by discipline.

- "Refine Search to Journals" feature is somewhat helpful. Although the user cannot limit the initial search to journals, he/she can later refine the search by clicking on "Journals." Results of several searches, however, indicate that newspaper and magazine articles are also included.
- "Refine Search by Topic" feature is very helpful. By clicking on "Topics," one can select the link "marching band" which brings up 14 titles with the words "marching band."
- Offers the greatest number of very relevant results.
- Most results were unique titles, though duplicate citations occasionally appear (different databases with the same citation.) Users can sort by title, which is helpful in deduping results.
- "Show Summary" is a useful feature–users can see which databases provide the most hits. This allows users to leave Central Search and search the database separately.

Central Search Disadvantages:

- Retrieval can be painfully slow. The greater the number of databases included in a set, the longer the search takes. We have learned that retrieval time improves when the library groups databases into smaller, more discipline-specific subsets for searchers to choose. Many searches took only a few seconds, but some searches took a few minutes, and in some cases, refining the search took much longer than the initial search. We waited for 45 minutes while trying to refine results to "2000 or later" for the suicide search), before giving up and doing two separate searches for 2005 and 2006.
- Cannot limit search to full text, although many citations did link successfully to full text.
- Cannot limit search to a range of years, only to one year at a time. Results can be sorted by year (though as we have said, this can take a long time).
- The basic screen has one search box, making Boolean searching difficult for the typical user. The default view can, however, be set to advanced search.
- Many important links are not clearly labeled. In general, several helpful links ("journals," "title," "Show Summary") were not prominently placed nor would users easily intuit their significance. For example, the link "Journals" is under the heading "Refine Search." A link that says "View Journals Only" might be more

helpful for the user. The "Topics" link, also under the "Refine Search" heading, was extremely helpful in narrowing down to more relevant searches, but the word "Topics" is not a particularly useful description. "Narrow your topic" would be clearer. "Show Summary" should be renamed "Show Database Source."

In summary, Central Search outperformed its competitors in terms of relevant hits, with Google Scholar performing slightly better than Live Search. Not surprisingly, these results appear to correlate with the number of searching features. Engines with more search features (such as Central Search) retrieve more relevant hits. As search features decrease (as with Google Scholar) there is an increase in irrelevant hits and a general decrease in overall relevancy. When there are virtually no advanced search features (as in Live Search) relevant hits were at the lowest. To be fair, Live Search was in beta testing format and the total number of hits was lower as well.

So what do we do with this information? Florida Gulf Coast University has put a Central Search link on the first page of our homepage. Links to Google Scholar and Live Academic are not on our homepage (yet), but we have registered our IP ranges with both services to allow affiliated users to link to full text in our licensed database holdings. We also use Central Search and Google Scholar at the reference desk. Some of our librarians start with our subscription databases and use Google Scholar and Central Search when they get a particularly challenging question (as in the marching band example). The metasearch engines can "kick start" a stalled search by identifying good sources of pertinent information. The user may see that many hits are coming from JSTOR, for instance, and may then decide to go directly into JSTOR and continue with some advanced searching there. We have also found both Central Search and Google Scholar very useful for confirming citations that are incomplete or incorrect.

Librarians are important partners in promoting, marketing, and teaching the effective use of these products. Thinking inside one box, however, does require a thoughtful search strategy, a point that is counterintuitive to those users who are most attracted to the metasearch engine's apparent simplicity. In a recent article on Google Scholar, Jeffrey Pomerantz points out that resources are only as useful as the researcher's ability to use them. There is a continued need for a librarian's help in discovering and accessing resources.[6] As more one-box search engines appear, librarians will need to focus their efforts on helping users learn how to choose and use these for maximum results.

REFERENCES

1. Callicott, Burton and Vaughn, Debbie. "Google Scholar vs. Library Scholar: Testing the Performance of Schoogle," in *Libraries and Google,* ed. William Miller and Rita M. Pellen, 71-88 (Binghamton, NY: Haworth Information Press, 2005).

2. Donlan, Rebecca and Cooke, Rachel. "Running with the Devil: Accessing Library-Licensed Full Text Holdings through Google Scholar," in *Libraries and Google* ed. William Miller and Rita M. Pellen, 71-88 (Binghamton, NY: Haworth Information Press, 2005).

3. Live Search Academic Beta help pages. Retrieved June 15, 2007, from <http://help.live.com/help.aspx?project=Academic_Search_Help&market=en-us&querytype=keyword&query=stluser&tmt=&domain=live.com>.

4. About Google Scholar. Retrieved June 15, 2007, from <http://scholar.google.com/intl/en/scholar/about.html>.

5. 360 Search Federated Search Service. Retrieved June 15, 2007, from <http://www.serialssolutions.com/ss_360_search.html>. (NB: Serials Solutions re-branded all of its products in early 2007; Central Search is now called 360 Search.)

6. Pomerantz, Jeffrey. "Google Scholar and 100 Percent Availability of Information." *Information Technology and Libraries* 25(2), June 2006, p. 53. Also available online at <http://www.ala.org/ala/lita/litapublications/ital/252006/2502jun/contenta/pomerantshtml.cfm>.

It's All Academic:
Google Scholar, Scirus, and Windows Live Academic Search

Lyle Ford
Lisa Hanson O'Hara

INTRODUCTION

Academic librarians have struggled with the problem of providing users with access to their collections in a "Google-like" manner since Google first arrived in 1998. Because students are familiar with the single search box and often find results that are "good enough," they may begin and end their research with Google. When Google Scholar was released in 2005, some academic librarians hoped for a more scholarly Google search. Much has been written about Google functionality, and in 2006 Neuhaus et al. examined Google Scholar's coverage of the literature in various databases and disciplines. However, Google Scholar is not the only freely available scholarly search engine on the Internet. Microsoft and Elsevier both provide engines to search for science and technology articles–the same material Google Scholar indexes. When Microsoft introduced Windows Live Academic Scholar in early 2006, we wondered how it covered the literature in science and technology compared to Google Scholar. We also wondered about Elsevier's Scirus, which had been around longer than either of the newcomers.

BACKGROUND

In 2005, the University of Manitoba Libraries (UML) received an unexpected invitation from Google to take part in a pilot project. Google engineers wanted to test and develop methods to link Google Scholar search results to licensed library resources. Google's overture, delivered by email, held forth the possibility of making premium scholarly content more accessible to library users. That possibility resonated with the UML; library administration had been positioning the library to take full advantage of electronic resources for five years before Google's offer arrived. The UML accepted Google Scholar's invitation and became the first Canadian library to submit its OpenURL information for testing.

The UML is a large academic research library, with 19 branches serving over 26,000 users at varying stages in their studies, from first year undergraduates to doctoral candidates to medical researchers. The print collection totals just over two million items, and includes more than 15,000 current journal subscriptions. We hold more than 150,000 e-books and 23,000 ejournal subscriptions. Our goal is to make all of our electronic resources discoverable and usable by our users. To that end the UML created a position for an Electronic Resources Cataloguer in 2002, and established an Electronic Resources department to manage licensed resources. Two years later, we implemented Ex Libris' SFX link resolver system. As part of the desire to ease the discovery and use of our e-resources, the UML also set up a task group on metasearch engines to study the efficacy and value of several commercial products in 2004. That group, though unable to recommend the purchase of any particular product, suggested monitoring the commercial products and the newly released Google Scholar.

The task force did not recommend a metasearch product because nothing offered functionality at an affordable price. While Google Scholar did not seem to outperform any other metasearch engines greatly, its price was very attractive. The UML wasn't prepared to promote Google Scholar as our primary metasearch engine, but looked at adding a link to it from our web site. With an eye to effectively presenting it to users and ensuring their access to our print and electronic resources, we considered issues like web site placement, OpenURL and RefWorks compatibility, and promotion within the library. Ultimately, Google Scholar appeared prominently on the UML's webpage. When Google Scholar required libraries to submit electronic holdings rather than using OpenURL technology, the UML complied, driven in part by our earlier decisions, but also because our users appreciated the service.

By 2006, we decided to look at setting up access to Windows Live Academic Search and Elsevier's Scirus, in a similar way. These engines, designed to search the science and technology literature, promise wide-ranging, natural language searching and easy retrieval of full text material. Scirus provides access to scientific, scholarly, technical and medical data on the Web and includes articles from various open access sources as well as ScienceDirect, and the whole Web. Windows Live Academic Search, while in Beta, concentrated on computer science, electrical engineering, and physics. As part of the comparison, we thought it worthwhile to assess all three products in terms of functionality and coverage. We supplied our OpenURL information to Windows Live, including IP addresses for involved staff, in order to examine how our holdings would appear. Scirus, non-compliant with OpenURL, did not require any of our information for us to test it.

METHODOLOGY

In late April 2006, we examined Google Scholar, Scirus, and Windows Live Academic. In terms of coverage, Google Scholar revealed very little information about what sources were indexed. Scirus gave full information on its "About Scirus" page and Windows Live Academic listed the names of twelve publishers along with the information that, while in Beta, they were concentrating on science, computer science, electrical engineering, and physics. In order to judge coverage in these areas against the UML's ejournal holdings, we decided to follow the example set by Neuhaus et al., where they compared 47 different databases indexing a broad range of subject areas to Google Scholar in terms of currency and coverage. In our study, we selected three citations from each of thirteen databases covering science, computer science, electrical engineering, and physics, along with three monographs we found in each of the British Library's database and OCLC's WorldCat. We arbitrarily decided on three citations, based upon the time available for research and the purpose of the study.

To locate citations, we used the native interface of the chosen databases. We chose at random three citations from a range of dates within the last five years since currency of information was one of our local concerns. Titles were searched in Google Scholar, Scirus, and Windows Live Academic as keywords. If no result was found we searched again, adding the surname of one of the authors of the original citation. If the revised search was also unsuccessful, we concluded that the citation was not available in that search engine. We recorded findings including the presence of the citation and whether it linked to the appropriate copy in the University of Manitoba Libraries or whether it located a citation, preprint, or other copy.

In November 2006, we repeated this procedure with the same citations in order to see if coverage had changed or remained stable in the search engines over the previous six months.

FUNCTIONALITY

Google Scholar

The familiar Google search box is available for a basic search in Google Scholar. An advanced search is available from the homepage, offering more advanced keyword searches and exact phrase searching as well as searching by publication date, and publication name. The advanced search also allows a searcher to limit to broad subject areas like "Chemistry and Materials Science," "Physics," "Astronomy and Planetary Science," and "Social Sciences," "Arts," and "Humanities." Google Scholar also offers a "Cited by" link taking the searcher to materials which cite the resource identified in the original search. This service is similar to products like ISI's Science Citation Index. We did not test the functionality of this service since Bauer and Bakkalbasi had already published on this issue. Google Scholar allows OpenURL linking by individual libraries through the submission of their electronic holdings to Google. It does not allow branding of the links by the library, nor does it give libraries control over the placement of the links. Google Scholar's appearance and functionality did not change over the course of this research.

Results sets show an approximate number of hits, which cannot be sorted. There is an option to limit results to recent articles, but no definition of recent is given. Google Scholar does provide some limiting options along the left-hand side of the results screen, but it is unclear how these are generated. Citations can be exported in major bibliographic formats such as BibTex, RefWorks and Endnote, but only singly.

Scirus

Scirus allows searchers to limit their searches to "Journal sources," "Preferred Web sources," or "Other Web sources." In addition to a basic search box allowing searchers to enter search terms, an advanced search is also offered which allows searchers to limit the search to specific parts of the document, limit results by date, format (articles, books, conferences, patents, etc.), file formats, and show results from particular publishers/sources. Searchers may also choose broad subject areas to be searched such as "Astronomy," "Computer Science," and "Earth and Planetary Sciences." Result sets show the number of journal articles, preferred web results and other web results as clickable links to refine the search. To refine the search, keywords are supplied, as well as a search box allowing additional keywords.

Scirus also allows result sets to be sorted by either relevance or date. Multiple citations can be e-mailed, saved or exported in RIS or text format, although this must be done for each page separately. During the November phase of the project, advertising appeared at the bottom of each results page, a change from the April phase when advertising sat at the bottom of the right-hand column. Scirus is not OpenURL-enabled, and therefore has no way of alerting library users to appropriate copies of the journals retrieved.

In April 2006 Scirus listed 19 sources in the "More About Our Information Sources" section of the "About Scirus" page <www.scirus.com/srsapp/aboutus>. In November 2006, the number of sources increased to 23, including new institutional repositories (CURATOR, IISc, and HKUST) as well as the Indian Institute of Science's digital repository of theses and dissertations. Organic Imprints, an open-access project providing papers, abstracts and bibliographic information related to research in organic agriculture is the other new addition. Other sources include SIAM journals, RePEc, PubMed, NDLTD, IoP, Project Euclid, and arXiv, providing access to ETDs, open-access sources, pre-prints, and articles. In January 2007, this number had climbed to 27 sources.

Windows Live Academic Search

Windows Live Academic Search, still in Beta in April and November 2006, offered a single search box on a page titled "Windows Live Academic Search" allowing searchers to enter their search terms. The page gave an introduction to the product and explained that while in Beta the search engine concentrated on computer science, electrical engineering, and physics. Links were set up for librarians and publishers telling these groups how to access the product. Librarians were given information about how Windows Live would work with their OpenURL resolver and information on how to set up OpenURL linking. At this time, branding was not available in Windows Live Academic Search, nor were libraries given control over placement of the links. Twelve science and technology publishers were named as working with Microsoft on this project at the time of its launch, including ACM, IEEE, Taylor and Francis, the American Institute of Physics, the American Physical Society, the Institute of Physics, Blackwell Publishing, Elsevier, Nature Publishing Group, the British Library, OCLC, and John Wiley & Sons Inc.

Once a search was entered in the search box, the results set could be sorted by relevance, date (either oldest or newest), author, journal, or conference. The results set is displayed in a left-hand pane of a two-pane display. There is a "richness slider" which allows the searcher to see more or fewer of the citations in the results set in the left-hand pane. The right-hand pane shows the full citation (including the abstract if available) of the citation being moused over in the left-hand pane. Citations can be exported singly in BibTex, EndNote or RefWorks. No advertising was present in Windows Live Academic Search. RSS feeds were available for searches through Live.com (users need to register with a login and password for this service).

In January, 2007 the introductory page for Windows Live Academic Search disappeared and "Academic Beta" became one of the choices on the Windows Live Search toolbar. The "For Librarians" and "For Publishers" pages could no longer be found at this time, nor could a list of the publishers working with Windows Live Academic. The search mechanisms and results display were the same.

COVERAGE

The following tables show the level of coverage each engine provided when we searched for the 39 citations found within UML-licensed databases. Table 1 is a visual representation of the coverage provided by each engine for each database in November 2006 and Table 2 shows changes in coverage over a six-month period in 2006. The data show that Google Scholar provided the best overall coverage of the three.

TABLE 1. Coverage in November 2006

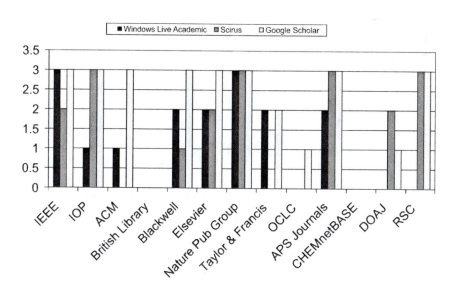

TABLE 2. Change in Coverage

Vendor	Found in Windows Live Academic			Found in Scirus			Found in Google Scholar		
	Apr-06	Nov-06	Change	Apr-06	Nov-06	Change	Apr-06	Nov-06	Change
IEEE	3	3	0	1	2	1	3	3	0
IOP	1	1	0	2	3	1	1	3	2
ACM	1	1	0	3	0	3	3	3	0
British Library	0	0	0	1	0	1	0	0	0
Blackwell	1	2	1	0	1	1	1	3	2
Elsevier	1	2	1	3	2	1	0	3	3
Nature Pub	3	3	0	3	3	0	3	3	0
Taylor & Francis	3	2	1	0	0	0	3	2	1
OCLC	0	0	0	0	0	0	1	1	0
APS Journals	2	2	0	3	3	0	3	3	0
CHEMnetBASE	0	0	0	0	0	0	2	0	2
DOAJ	1	0	1	1	2	1	2	1	1
RSC	0	0	0	3	3	0	3	3	0
TOTAL	16	16	0	20	19	1	25	28	3

That said, we found that Google Scholar often pointed to sources other than the copy licensed by our library. For example, an article found in Elsevier's ScienceDirect by Boxma et al. in the February 13, 2006 issue of *AEU–International Journal of Electronics and Communications* was found in a preprint archive, and not as a licensed journal article. This was true of all three of the ScienceDirect citations searched in Google Scholar. The article was found in Scirus, however, and linked to the copy licensed by the UML.

Coverage in the engines changed from the first searches in April, 2006 to those conducted in November, 2006. While Google Scholar showed a net gain of 3 more citations, Scirus had one less citation in November than in April. Again, Google's net gain was partially due to the retrieval of the ScienceDirect citations which were not retrieved as ScienceDirect links but as links to preprint archives or institutional repositories. We also found that citations appeared and disappeared on an almost daily basis while we were working on the project and demonstrating our findings to various library groups. We noted that ACM citations vanished entirely in Scirus between May and November. A search in January 2007 revealed that the ACM citations could be retrieved again.

CONCLUSIONS

The major observation arising from the research we conducted at UML is that all of these engines are inconsistent in their coverage and performance. At present, we don't feel comfortable recommending any of them to our users unreservedly, but we know that these tools will be used. Of course, any librarian would balk at unreserved recommendation of any single resource. All print and electronic research tools have strengths and weaknesses and should be used in combination with other resources. None of the three search engines advise users of that strategy. In fact, Google Scholar positions itself as the way "to identify the most relevant research across the world of scholarly research" <http://scholar.google.com.intl/en/scholar/about.html>. "Relevant" is a very subjective choice of words on their part. In our study, Google Scholar scored highest in coverage, turning up 71% of the articles we searched, but this is not enough to support its claim.

Scirus bills itself as "the most comprehensive science-specific search engine available on the Internet" <http://www.scirus.com/html/help/advinfo.html>. With only 49% of our articles found in Scirus, it proves less comprehensive than Google Scholar in the areas of science and technology. Scirus behaves most like traditional library databases in terms of search refinement and results management. In the demonstrations we did at UML we found that librarians preferred its search options and results display to those available in both Google Scholar and Scirus. However, no quantitative or anecdotal data has been gathered at UML to see which search engines users prefer. In fact, no quantitative data is available anywhere, so this is one area which is certainly crying out for further research.

Windows Live Academic Search makes the most modest claim of the three, telling us that it "searches content from several publishers in computer science, physics, and electrical engineering" <http://help.live.com/Help.aspx?market=en-US&proect=Academic_Search_Help&querytype=topic&query=Acaemic_Search_Help_PROC_AboutSearchResults.htm>. With only 41% of the articles we searched found in Windows Live Academic Search, Windows Live Academic Search performed the most poorly in terms of coverage.

Librarians can help users by pointing out that these, and similar, search engines shouldn't be relied upon as their sole means of discovering useful material. Providing access to these tools through the UML site gives us an instructional opportunity while giving our users what they want: discovery and easy access to useful resources.

Anurag Acharya says in an interview with Tracey Hughes, "I believe discovery needs to be universal–researchers need to be able to find all that has been done in their area of interest." None of the search engines we looked at achieve that goal. All three engines are useful tools for researchers but, so far, none of them yet replace a systematic, comprehensive search of multiple proprietary databases. Until such a tool is available, librarians are in the same position they have been in for decades: trying to link searchers to the best resources available. That effort has been complicated by promises made by companies such as Google, Elsevier, and Microsoft. Our expectation is that in the near future, academic librarians will be able to demand, and provide, a tool that will far outshine any of the free engines currently available on the Internet.

REFERENCES

Bauer, Kathleen, and Nisa Bakkalbasi. 2005. An Examination of Citation Counts in a New Scholarly Communication Environment (computer file). *D Lib Magazine* 11, no. 9:1.

Hughes, Tracey. 2006. Tracey Hughes interviews Anurag Acharya, lead engineer on Google Scholar. *Librarian Center* Dec. 6, 2006 <http://www.google.com/librariancenter/downloads/Acharya_Interview.pdf>.

Neuhaus, Chris, Ellen Neuhaus, and Alan Asher. 2006. The Depth and Breadth of Google Scholar: An Empirical Study. *portal* 6, no. 2:127-141.

Join the Conversation:
Show Your Library's Google Scholar and Book Search Expertise

Luke Vilelle

INTRODUCTION

Conversations are taking place on your campus. About online re-sources. About free search engines such as Google Scholar and Google Book Search. About their usefulness as academic discovery tools.

Is your library a part of these conversations?

Many libraries show their awareness of Google Scholar, Google Book Search and similar search engines by linking to them from their web sites and/or by integrating library tools such as OpenURL resolvers into them. The adoption of these resources in this manner–making sure your proxy server works with Google Scholar, linking to the resources, and providing descriptions and tips on how to use them–is an important first step.

Just as important, however, is actively engaging the community in discussions about Google Scholar, Google Book Search, and the growing numbers of academic search engines and full-text book search sites on the web.

Engagement requires the library to market the availability of these resources, and instruct on how best to use them and how they integrate with library-subscribed resources. Many academic libraries have created workshops for these purposes, and are now engaged with their communities of users on this topic. Here are a few examples of workshop titles discovered through a web search: at Virginia Tech ("Google Scholar and Google Book Search: their effect on academia"); at the University of California, Riverside ("What is Google Scholar?"); at Dartmouth College ("Using Google for research"); at the University of Manitoba ("Google Scholar: make it a great companion to your research"); at the University of Wisconsin-Madison ("You know you want to Google for academic research"); at the University of California, Berkeley ("Googling to the max"); and at New York University ("Google expert").

By engaging their users through such forums, these and many other libraries have helped their users improve their research skills–and helped themselves become a more credible resource aid in the ever-expanding world of academic research. This paper will explore the reasons for talking to your users about such resources as Google Scholar and Google Book Search, and how the library stands to benefit from such an arrangement.

MOVING FROM AWARENESS TO ADVOCACY

Ask yourself this question: If a campus student newspaper reporter called you today to ask about Google Scholar and its integration with your library's resources, what would your response be? Would the story, when published, read like this?

"Although [the library's OpenURL resolver integration with Google Scholar] has been available since 2005, the assistant university librarian for collection management said little has been done to publicize the service" (Dostal, 2007).

This is not meant to single out this particular library, which is probably representative of many academic libraries. The example is used only to demonstrate the approach that many libraries have taken with such databases as Google Scholar and Google Book Search: the library will link to the database from its web site, provide a few tips, and place its OpenURL resolver in Google Scholar, but then go no further.

It's certainly not for lack of interest in Google's activities among librarians.

Judging by the numbers of people at the Google exhibits at the American Library Association's annual and midwinter conferences, there is no shortage of intellectual curiosity among librarians in regards to the research products Google offers. Google has responded to the interest by creating the Google Librarian Central blog (http://librariancentral. blogspot.com/), complete with a newsletter for librarians, and both Google Scholar (through libraries' article linking services) and Google Book Search (through Open WorldCat) help connect discovered resources to their availability in nearby libraries.

But the use of this information on campus to enlighten students or faculty members, through brown-bag lunches, workshops, or library instruction sessions, is irregular. In the summer of 2005, the University of California library system surveyed each of its campus libraries to find out their attitudes and whether there was new programming in response to Google Scholar. Not surprisingly, reactions to the search engine varied widely. Meltzer summarized in the follow-up report in August 2005:

> The replies indicate a core of respondents do not use Google Scholar at all. Others use it rarely, instead strongly preferring licensed article databases purchased by the libraries for use in specific disciplines. Some are reluctant to use it because they are unsure of what it actually covers.

> Among those who do use Google Scholar, they value it as a way of getting at older, more obscure, interdisciplinary, and difficult to locate materials quickly and simply. It is open access and sometimes

easier to use than traditional resources. It provides another point of entry to the world of scholarship. At public service desks, it is used as an entrée into the use of OpenURL or licensed resources, and as an option for non-UC affiliated users. *Some campuses are beginning to adopt Google Scholar in their teaching* [italics mine].

Google Scholar and Google Book Search are more than aids to reference work. They are more than just two additional resources for librarians to suggest as options for students. They offer opportunities to connect with your library community on a level that both librarians and their users can understand. Students like and understand Google (or, at least, they think they do). Librarians like and understand database searching. What better way to connect the two than through a Google-like search of an academic-like database? What do librarians know more about than searching for books and articles, which is exactly what Google Book Search and Google Scholar offer?

Many librarians have leveraged their search skills to make themselves experts in using Google and other general web search engines. Scholar, Books, and other similar resources offer an even greater opportunity for outreach in academic communities.

By taking partial ownership of these resources, and similar ones developed across the web in the coming years, libraries can remove the perception that librarians only assist with resources subscribed to by their own libraries and the library's print collection.

In the past two years, the Virginia Tech Libraries have hosted two library workshops and sponsored five Faculty Development Institute classes on Google Scholar and Google Book Search, and have incorporated Google Scholar and Google Book Search into some library classes for undergraduate and graduate students.

Through these efforts, the library becomes a credible resource aid for those who wish to use these tools. Though librarians are not responsible for the content and design of Google Scholar and Google Book Search (just like most of the subscription databases employed by librarians every day), we can be experts on their innovations and uses.

The nearly fifty graduate students and faculty who have attended the Faculty Development Institute sessions and the library-sponsored workshops consistently reported that they found the sessions useful. When given the opportunity to try their own searches in Google Scholar and Books, everybody found something of use. They viewed these tools as potentially powerful resources for their work.

Along with the gratification of introducing community members to useful resources, the classes have also offered a great opportunity to highlight similar resources on the web and offered by the library. Lure the faculty member into the conversation with Google Book Search, and then showcase the full-text searching capability of NetLibrary and Safari Tech Books Online. Get the graduate students into Google Scholar, and help them to see the value of your library's article linking service. From both Scholar and Books, showcase how the library's LibX browser extension can route you to library holdings from points across the web.

OBJECTION:
GOOGLE DOESN'T NEED OUR HELP PUBLICIZING ITS SERVICES

This is an excellent point. Google can certainly promote itself. Every search of Virginia Tech's web site (a Google-provided search) results in Google Scholar promotion at the end of the first page of results–"Find academic research papers with Google Scholar." On the campus student newspaper web site, a banner ad for Google Scholar tells students, "Nail that paper with Google Scholar." Several college student newspapers published articles about Google Scholar in the weeks and months after its launch–articles about new library-subscribed databases tend to be much tougher to come by.

So, no, Google doesn't need librarians' help to thrive.

Extending this concept a step further, Cathcart and Roberts (2005, 173) argue that "as with all business ventures, Google's ultimate focus is not providing a service that truly meets the needs of researchers for comprehensive, quality information, but its bottom line."

However, wouldn't Google improve its bottom line by developing a service that meets the needs of researchers for comprehensive, quality information? There does not necessarily seem to be a conflict here.

Second, librarians already spend much of their time promoting commercial products. Think about it the next time you refer someone to an EBSCO database or an Elsevier journal or any of the other commercial vendors librarians work with daily. By doing so, you are increasing the usage numbers for that product, making it more likely your library will re-subscribe, and helping the vendor's bottom line.

Cathcart and Roberts (2005, 173), to their credit, point out that in disagreements with journal publishers about rising costs of serials, "librarians have already experienced conflict with for-profit information providers." However, they then argue that "the potential for further conflict with Google, which would appear to have even less incentive to truly be after the hearts and minds of librarians, appears inevitable."

Does it matter whether Google wins the hearts and minds of librarians? Researchers are the ultimate judge, and progress in improving the results that users receive from any type of Google search should be supported by librarians.

The worthiness of Google Scholar as a research tool has been debated extensively—see Jacso (2005, 2006a) for decidedly negative reviews; Bakkalbasi (2006), Bauer (2005), Gardner (2005), or White (2006) for mixed reviews; and Pauly (2005) for an unabashedly positive review. Much has been written about Google Book Search regarding the associated copyright issues, but less about its value as a research tool—for reviews, see Jacso (2006b), Ojala (2006), or O'Leary (2006).

I do not seek to argue the merits of such reviews. Rather, I assume, based on my experiences teaching these databases, that both Google Scholar and Google Book Search can assist researchers in their work. Further, librarians can help researchers by providing discussion forums and workshops focused on these resources.

CREATING TEACHABLE MOMENTS FOR GOOGLE SCHOLAR AND BOOKS

Upon the debut of Google Scholar in November 2004, the Virginia Tech Libraries wanted to inform its users about the best ways to utilize such an exciting tool. The library decided to offer a two-hour workshop as part of the university's Faculty Development Institute, a series of sessions offered each semester for faculty and graduate students.

By offering and publicizing this session, the library established itself as a campus leader in understanding and using this new resource. In the spring 2005 semester, the library offered two sessions on Google Scholar. In the fall 2005 semester, the library offered two more.

The announcement of the Google Book Search library project (initially called Google Print) took place in December 2004, but the database did not make its debut until November 2005. When it became searchable, Google Book Search became another element in the session—both because of its value as a searchable resource and as a discussion point for copyright issues.

Vidmar, in a 2007 presentation encouraging librarians to teach Google Book Search and Google Scholar, found the following reasons to teach these topics.

- Friendly interface that individuals recognize
- Free and readily available!
- Not a replacement for library databases and catalogs!
- Research madness: Leads to harder resources such as library catalogs and databases!
- If you can complain about it, then you should be able to teach it!

A good list, though Vidmar does not include what may be the most important reason: your users will almost certainly find Google Scholar and Books useful.

The Google Scholar presentation at Virginia Tech takes about 45 minutes, and it covers such topics as source and date coverage, comparisons to native search engines, deciphering the results, ranking of the results, locating the full text of articles (from on- and off-campus), the citation count feature, and best uses.

Examples of prime uses of Google Scholar discussed in the presentation include:

- Easy to search
- One-stop, interdisciplinary searching
- Searching full-text across a broad spectrum of publishers (rare in library databases except for JSTOR)
- Finding papers on the web that have never made it into library databases (e.g., some conference papers, white papers, preprints, etc.)
- Tracing citations

Among the faculty and graduate students taught at Virginia Tech, the citation searching feature was easily the most popular. Participants enjoyed the capability of quickly tracing citations, as well as looking up their own articles to see who Google Scholar found citing their publications. Faculty members were pleased to discover themselves cited in publications they had not previously known existed.

The Google Book Search presentation at Virginia Tech is a 30-minute presentation, and it explains the Google Book Search Library Project and Publisher Program, some of the associated copyright issues, the types of results you can get, and discovering where you can get a copy of the book.

Examples of prime uses of Google Book Search discussed in the presentation include:

- Tracking down a quote that you can't find or quite remember
- Identify relevant sections within books that you never would have previously realized existed
- Allows you to be very specific in your searches
- Cited reference searching–put your article title in to see what books have cited it

Again, the cited reference searching proved popular. In addition, the ability to search the full text of books captured the imagination of many of the attendees. When your prior book searching experience has entailed only searching the spare descriptions in catalogs, the capability of searching full text and being able to better discern what books would actually be helpful is quite appealing.

I found no thorough examination of how Google Book Search and other burgeoning full-text searchable book resources could be used as a tool for information literacy, but the relationship of Google Scholar to information literacy has been explored–notably, by Kesselman and Cathcart and Roberts.

Kesselman (2005, 384) suggests:

> A logical place to start is with Google Scholar's attributes–it is fast and easy to use and can lead students to hundreds of relevant, scholarly articles and other scholarly materials. From there a focus on the research process at large is recommended:
>
> - How does Google Scholar fit in to your research process?
>
> - When should you use Google Scholar or another scholarly search engine?
>
> - When should you search for journal articles using a database that a library subscribes to?

Cathcart and Roberts examine Google Scholar in relation to each of the standards in the ACRL Information Literacy Standards, and find "while Google Scholar has some useful and redeeming qualities, its ultimate value in meeting these standards is limited" (2005, 168). Cathcart and Roberts do suggest that Google Scholar could be turned into an information literacy ally. "Because it offers the familiarity of Google, yet introduces the users to scholarly articles and the concept of a citation index, it could serve as a bridge to the more reliable, comprehensive resources offered by the libraries" (175).

The tone of this suggested comparison is decidedly negative (Google Scholar is portrayed as not as reliable or as comprehensive), but the idea is a good one: create a bridge between Google Scholar and library resources. Instead of limiting the bridge to one-way traffic from Google Scholar to library resources, though, you can establish that the bridge can take users the other way as well. Struggling to get started in library databases? Try Google Scholar, with its broader, deeper database, to see if it can get you over the initial hump.

At Virginia Tech, Google Scholar is introduced–as a database similar to general interest library databases, not as just another web search engine–to freshmen each spring semester in the Communication Skills course, which has 25-30 sections and 600-plus students.

As part of the class, the instructor gives students a citation and requires them to locate the full text of the article. Two methods are demonstrated to locate the article–through Google Scholar or through the library web site. Certainly, it is important for students to know how to search for a library's journal holdings and understand what they find in a bibliographic record–but the easier alternative for many of these articles is for the students to type the title into a Google Scholar search, click on the title (or the OpenURL resolver) and find the full text.

Google Scholar, as an alternative for topical article searching and for cited reference searching, and Google Book Search, as an alternative to traditional library catalog searching, are also both part of orientation sessions for new graduate students at the beginning of the academic year.

As York (2005) suggested in "Calling the Scholars home: Google Scholar as a Tool for Rediscovering the Academic Library," these types of resources may direct users to items provided by the library.

BRIDGING THE GAP TO SIMILAR RESOURCES

No matter how big a fan of Google Scholar you may (or may not) be, all librarians could probably agree that Google's various search engines are not the answer for every research need.

Vine (2006, 99), in a mostly critical review of Google Scholar, sums up her review by asking, "That is where the greatest challenge lies: How can librarians, with far fewer resources than Google, succeed in getting the message out that, in many cases, easy [research] is no substitute for good [research]?"

The funny thing is, the best way to move students outside the Google box may be through Google itself. It's a bit of a paradox, but often you must first begin with Google. Lure them in with Google, then return them to the world with knowledge of Clusty, library databases, and a broader view of the world of research.

Accompanying this shift, though, is a caveat: an emphasis to the students that the librarian is not there to tell them that a particular database or web search engine is always best.

Librarians' traditional role as gatekeepers of information, much like that of newspapers and other forms of mass media, has been challenged for the past decade by the growing reach of the internet. The alternative for librarians, providing people with advice and options for research, empowers patrons and forces them to think critically.

Let's look at Google Scholar as an example of how to provide people with options and introduce them to many resources they never previously knew existed. Although Google did not invent the idea of scholarly web searching with Google Scholar (one older example is Scirus, a Web search engine for scholarly scientific materials, which debuted in 2001), it quickly became the most well-known because of Google's clout. Now, Google Scholar can serve as a base to introduce people to similar engines, such as Windows Live Academic, and more distant relatives, such as Scirus, CiteSeer, and various federated search engines (e.g., ToxSeek).

If your library has a federated search engine of its own, this is a prime time to introduce it and compare the results from multiple library databases to those you can find in a Google Scholar search.

Speaking to a group excited about the citation searching capabilities of Google Scholar? Then also discuss what the Web of Science can do, with its analytical capabilities and impact factor rankings of journals. But the comparison need not be made in a disparaging manner. There is no reason to kill your users' enthusiasm for Google Scholar–there are legitimate reasons why somebody might pick Google Scholar for citation searching over Web of Science (speed, ease of use, not as steep a learning curve). But there is some terrific functionality in Web of Science, not available in Google Scholar, that your users will want to know about.

Google Book Search also can serve as an excellent bridge to similar resources. Discussion of the Open Content Alliance, Live Search Books, and Amazon's Search Inside the Book capability naturally follows from an introduction of Google Book Search. Plus, the library has its own online book collections, which offer the bonus of being able to actually view and read the full text of the books. You can search more books in Google Book Search, but you probably will not be able to view more than a few pages if the book dates from any year since 1925. But in NetLibrary, you can not only search the full text of nearly 50,000 books, but you can also read the entire book.

Perhaps most rewarding, in the case of Google Scholar and Books, is the ability to open faculty and students' eyes to the library's efforts to extend the presence of its resources onto the open Web.

At Virginia Tech, LibX (http://www.libx.org/) directs access to library resources from anywhere on the internet through an open source Firefox browser extension. Installed on all the computers in the two Virginia Tech library classrooms, its ubiquitous shield draws the eyes of users when sitting in a session.

Placing Virginia Tech's OpenURL resolver in Google Scholar (and now also in Windows Live Academic) provides great shock value for users of these resources. Not only is it a terrific tool for users, but it also is a great public relations tool. Realizing that the library has a presence in mighty Google opens people's eyes to the rapid integration of Web resources and traditional library resources.

CONCLUSION

Google Scholar and Google Book Search, though not developed by libraries or traditional library vendors, represent tremendous opportunities for libraries to reconnect with their users (and to connect with non-users for the first time). Such connections will require more work than simply placing a link to Google Scholar and/or Google Book Search on your Web site. They will require actively publicizing these resources, and engaging the community in discussions about how the library's resources have been integrated into Google Scholar and Google Book Search. Through this sort of advocacy, you can open up new worlds of research for your users, both within Google's domain and in the realm of more traditional library resources.

REFERENCES

Bauer, Kathleen & Nisa Bakkalbasi. (2005). An examination of citation counts in a new scholarly communication environment. *D-Lib Magazine,* 11(9). Retrieved March 29, 2007 from <http://dlib.org/dlib/september05/bauer/09bauer.html>.

Bakkalbasi, Nisa, Kathleen Bauer, Janis Glover, & Lei Wang. (2006). Three options for citation tracking: Google Scholar, Scopus and Web of Science. *Biomedical Digital Libraries,* 3(7), Retrieved March 29, 2007 from <http://bio-diglib.com/content/3/1/7>.

Cathcart, Rachael, & Amanda Roberts. (2005). Evaluating Google Scholar as a tool for information literacy. *Internet Reference Services Quarterly,* 10(3/4), 167-76.

Dostal, Erin. (2007). Google gives scholars access to Northwestern U. library resources. *Daily Northwestern,* February 23, 2007.

Gardner, Susan, & Susanna Eng. (2005). Gaga over Google? Scholar in the social sciences. *Library Hi Tech News,* 22(8), 42-45.

Jacso, Peter. (2005). Google Scholar (Redux). *Peter's Digital Reference Shelf*–June. Retrieved March 29, 2007 from <http://www.gale.com/servlet/HTMLFileServlet?imprint=9999&region=7&fileName=reference/archive/200506/google.html>.

Jacso, Peter. (2006). Deflated, inflated, and phantom citation counts. *Online Information Review,* 30(3), 297-309.

Jacso, Peter. (2006). Google Book Search. *Peter's Digital Reference Shelf*–November. Retrieved March 29, 2007, from <http://www.gale.com/reference/peter/google books.htm>.

Kesselman, Martin, & Sarah Barbara Watstein. (2005). Google Scholar and libraries: point/counterpoint. *Reference Services Review,* 33(4), 380-87.

Meltzer, E. (2005). *UC Libraries use of Google Scholar.* August 2005. Retrieved March 29, 2007, from <http://dla.ucop.edu/inside/assess/evaluation_activities/docs/2005/googleScholar_summary_0805.pdf>.

Ojala, Marydee. (2006). Reviewing Google Book Search. *Online,* 30(2), 12-14.

O'Leary, Mick. (2006). Google Book Search has far to go. *Information Today,* 23(10), 41-47.

Pauly, Daniel, and Konstantinos I. Stergiou. (2005). Equivalence of results from two citation analyses: Thomson ISI's Citation Index and Google's Scholar service. *Ethics in Science and Environmental Politics,* 33-35. Retrieved March 29, 2007, from <http://www.int-res.com/articles/esep/2005/E65.pdf>.

Vidmar, Dale. (2007). Challenging your dark side: Teaching Google Scholar and Book Search. Presented at the Online Northwest Conference, Corvallis, Oregon. Retrieved March 29, 2007, from <http://www.sou.edu/~vidmar/onlinenw2007>.

Vine, Rita. (2006). Google Scholar. *Journal of the Medical Library Association,* 94(1): 97-99. Retrieved March 29, 2007, from <http://www.pubmedcentral.nih.gov/articlerender.fcgi?artid=1324783>.

White, Bruce. (2006). Examining the claims of Google Scholar as a serious information source. *New Zealand Library and Information Management Journal,* 50(1), 11-24. Retrieved March 29, 2007, from <http://eprints.rclis.org/archive/00007657/fullmetadata.html>.

York, Maurice C. (2005). Calling the scholars home: Google Scholar as a tool for rediscovering the academic library. *Internet Reference Services Quarterly,* 10(3/4), 117-33.

The Triumph of Expediency:
The Impact of Google Scholar
on Library Instruction

David Ettinger

INTRODUCTION

Holding forth the prospect of immediate gratification with minimal effort, the seductive allure and beguiling simplicity of Google Scholar pose formidable challenges to the librarian providing bibliographic instruction to already reluctant students. When the quest for expedient, serviceable results becomes the driving force of research, librarians face a potentially difficult task trying to convince patrons of the value of learning how to search proprietary library resources such as specialized databases.

As one observer has editorialized, "Is it any wonder that increasing numbers of library clients are deserting their traditional knowledge store for something that is much more user-friendly, and increasingly able to deliver the needed information? . . . Most of us want information now, and we want it fast. And yes, increasingly we want it to work like Google–quickly, simply and without complication" (Gorman, 2006, 98). How can the university library even think of competing with the likes of Google Scholar when the best we can typically offer is a dizzying array of disparate and oftentimes inscrutable resources frequently difficult to search?

Since Google Scholar's inception in November 2004, there has been an ongoing debate among information professionals about its impact. Presaging its appeal, Carol Tenopir was among the first to identify its ineluctable mystique. The subtitle of her article "Google in the Academic Library" presciently (and ominously) declared: "Undergraduates may find all they want on Google Scholar." Its shortcomings notwithstanding, she went on to write, "it will be wildly popular with students," especially since it "seemingly answers their teachers' and librarians' main objections to the web–that the material isn't of high enough academic quality . . ." (Tenopir, 2005, 32).

Tenopir's observations are supported by others. As Friend writes, "We can easily believe that *students* would take to Google like ducks to water. It is easy to use, saves them time in writing essays, and links to a vast amount of information. That students would use Google fits with our prejudice about young people always wanting an easy solution without too much work, and using their familiarity with the new technology to achieve that result" (Friend, 2006). This is all the more the case with Google Scholar, which combines Google's "existing advantages" with a "specialist approach" by retrieving scholarly content.

FACING THE CHALLENGE

The overriding virtues of Google Scholar are unassailable. "As a research tool," it empowers the user by facilitating the quick identification of "useful and significant work," making it, at the very least, "an excellent 'first source' for student and academic researchers" (Kent, 2005, 38). Unfortunately, for many, it proves to be the only source. Wary of this reality, librarians are grappling with the prospect of having to wean students away from over-reliance on Google and Google Scholar as the principal and sometimes sole vehicle for their research.

To be sure, the temptation to rely on Google Scholar is hard to resist. Its sheer ease of use is perhaps the most notable reason researchers gravitate toward it, but its interdisciplinary reach is also one of its most enticing features. "Because Google Scholar is not a discipline specific search engine," it "returns search results for articles from any field that has written about the subject searched for. Because many fields never look at research outside of their own discipline, using Google Scholar can lead to better, more thorough research" (Kent, 2005, 38). Contrast this with the tedium and difficulty of searching subject-specific databases which yield compartmentalized results.

Despite a tendency to idealize Google Scholar, it is far from perfect. Working with and deciphering its search results can be challenging. Results are homogenized and there are content limitations. Some have questioned the value of its eclecticism, especially since the content providers are not clearly identified "and the rationale or methodology for inclusion has not been publicly documented," a point librarians have been quick to seize upon (Cohen, 2005, 12). As Jasco points out, "stunning gaps give a false impression of the scholarly coverage of topics and lead to the omission of highly relevant articles by those who need more than just a few pertinent research documents. The rather enigmatic presentation of the results befuddles many users and the lack of any sort options frustrates the savvy searchers" (Jasco, 2005, 208). Finally, there are abiding concerns over Google's definition of "scholarly," its inclusion criteria, and the currency of its content (Friend, 2006).

To some, however, in light of Google Scholar's overwhelming pop-ularity, its deficiencies are beside the point. An empirical study of the depth and breadth of Google Scholar by Niehaus, Niehaus, and Wrede exposed a variety of weaknesses, but the authors concede that, even cognizant of its inadequacies, it will continue to "attract scholars who are discouraged by the complexity and diversity of the many databases at their disposal" (Niehaus, 2006, 127). Similarly, in his content analysis of Google Scholar, O'Leary concludes that "it's excellent for casual research." Although "it cannot be compared to the far more sophisticated and powerful search capabilities" offered by proprietary databases, "a basic-level search performs superbly for bringing highly relevant citations to the top of the list."

Tapping into library resources "is more complicated than using Google Scholar" inasmuch as it requires "entering passwords, selecting databases, and using more complicated search protocols . . . Google Scholar requires none of this and, within its limits, works quite well" (O'Leary, 2005, 39). Norris stresses Google's inherent simplicity as its major virtue. "One does not have to develop or devise an elaborate search strategy. One does not have to understand the principles of Boolean logic for these are implicit in the search strategy and one can always find something" (Norris, 2006, 11).

Both the general contours and specific aspects of the ongoing debate on Google Scholar have been nicely framed by, among others, Kesselman and Watstein (2005). Not surprisingly, there is a disparity of views. On the one hand, like Google before it, Google Scholar has been heralded as an auspicious breakthrough, ushering in a promising new era for research. On the other, it has been denounced as a "bastardization"of the research process by those who decry its use "as a search tool particularly by students before they search the aggregated subscription databases" (Norris, 2006, 11).

Whether they are prepared to acknowledge it or not, information professionals appear threatened by Google Scholar's capacity to upset the traditional model of library service predicated on their intermediation in the information-gathering process. "Unless trained in the 'rules' of the Library the patron is essentially a supplicant seeking the help of the authoritative librarian." By demystifying and simplifying the scholarly research process, Google Scholar undermines this highly structured power relationship, characterized by "the dependency of the uninformed and incapable patron on the highly skilled librarian" (Norris, 2006, 9-10). The result is the empowerment of the end user and the consequent diminution of the librarian's role.

Some, like Norris, downplay the significance of this development, declaring "Google poses no real threat to the manner in which traditional library service is delivered. The librarian will continue to function as mediator and facilitator between the patron and the information being sought and Google will take its place in the information repertoire available for use within the library" (Norris, 2006, 10-11). This view, however, seems somewhat simplistic, if not naive. When the quest for self-sufficiency in information-seeking behavior becomes paramount, marginalization of librarians' roles or their relegation to the sidelines is a logical consequence. The advent of Google Scholar has clearly changed the playing field.

THE IMPACT ON INSTRUCTION

In contrast with the plethora of articles on Google Scholar generally, there is a surprising paucity of literature explicitly focused on its effect on library instruction. Discussion has, for the most part, been in the broader framework of Google Scholar's overall effects on information literacy (Cathcart & Roberts, 2005). Pomerantz, for example, downplays the negative consequences of search engines like Google Scholar, suggesting that, on balance, their effects are salutary. Inasmuch as the ultimate goal of instruction is fostering student self-sufficiency, because research tools such as Google Scholar enable users to meet their basic information needs, librarians can now focus on teaching higher-order information literacy skills. Because, he argues, they are only discovery tools incapable of answering complex questions, ultimately their utility is limited and likely to remain so for the foreseeable future. Rather than being feared or dismissed, they should be embraced. Their integration into the research process complements rather than detracts from our educational efforts and can play to our advantage (Pomerantz, 2006, 53).

A posting by the author to the instructional librarian listserv, ILI-L, soliciting comments on the proposition that Google Scholar has a debilitative effect on library instruction and, thus, undermines efforts to promote information literacy provoked a spirited discussion. The subject remains contentious and opinion continues to be divided. Responses seemed to track Kesselman's observations that instructional librarians have adopted three basic approaches toward Google Scholar: ignoring it, luring students away from it, or educating them about it (Kesselman, 2005, 384).

Many, if not most, have adopted a fatalistic approach. Bowing to the inevitable, they expose students to Google Scholar, because they know they will be drawn to it anyway. According to one, "Google is already part of people's information seeking workflow and there's no stopping that now" (Ellen Meltzer, e-mail to ILI-L mailing list, February 13, 2007). As another put it, "Multiple, proprietary databases with a range of interfaces makes research more difficult than it should be. . . . We need to meet students on their turf" (Joan Petit, e-mail to ILI-L mailing list, February 13, 2007). If "Google Scholar makes it easier for students to find good information, . . . then we should embrace its potential" (ibid.). The real issue, in the opinion of one respondent, is "the inability of proprietary library resources to provide expediently rendered, easy to use, simple interfaces" (Peter Tagtmeyer, e-mail to ILI-L mailing list, February 13, 2007). Rather than blame students for "not embracing that which we know and are used to," pressure should be placed on the database producers to emulate Google's example and "provide innovative indexing and easy to use, effective query interfaces" (ibid.).

Teaching Google Scholar along with databases seems to be a common theme. As one person wrote, given students' proclivity to "satisfice" their immediate needs to the detriment of the information literacy skills we know they need," talking about Google Scholar and "what it can and cannot do for students is a way to bridge a gap from something they've used to something we want them to use. . . . [It] can create a teachable moment" (Robert Schroeder, e-mail to ILI-L mailing list, February 13, 2007). Timing can be important. "If I touch on Google Scholar (many times I don't)," indicated one reply, "I usually do so after teaching students about databases with controlled vocabulary and effective search strategies. When they see they can't use controlled vocabulary to get highly relevant results through Google, they can draw their own conclusions about which databases to use based on what they need to do" (Eric Frierson, e-mail to ILI-L mailing list, February 13, 2007).

Respondents agreed that helping students make an "informed decision" on which research tool to use by educating them on their relative strengths, weaknesses, and usefulness is part of the librarian's role. In so doing, several replies spoke to the need to stress how Google Scholar complements existing resources, as Wleklinski has suggested. Librarians should "Show students how to search Google Scholar, alongside standard Google, alongside other database resources, and highlight their own expertise. Demonstrate to the students the difference between searching Google and searching other, more complete databases of information. Give students a sense of what a complete search is and what it is not–and how the results differ" (Wleklinski, 2005, 26).

Noting that faculty at some institutions endorse the use of Google Scholar, some librarians are focusing their instructional efforts on teaching students how to understand and incorporate it into their research. While contrasting search results from Google Scholar with those drawn from other information sources such as subscription databases, they ultimately rely on the discernment of students to "decide for themselves." However, as one veteran instruction librarian cautions: "We are not doing students any favors if we leave them with the assumption that [Google Scholar] is a useful alternative to all those much more complicated databases . . ." (Bill Badke, e-mail to ILI-L mailing list, February 14, 2007).

FUTURE DIRECTIONS

What are instruction librarians to do? There is no gainsaying that Google Scholar rivals traditional library resources and, for better or worse, is setting a new standard. Put starkly, "The challenge for information professionals and for service providers is to use the power of the Internet to enable users to search broadly and reach the full-text of a small selection of relevant content within three of four clicks of the mouse" the same way Google does (Friend, 2006).

Librarians have placed their hopes in federated searching, the ability to search several proprietary databases simultaneously, as a viable alternative to Google Scholar. "Federated search tools offer our best chance to imitate Google search breadth and functionality while still directing folks to the tools that have been explicitly chosen to support their research or scholarly efforts" (Abram, 2005, 46). However, although the technical means are already in place, "no current service has yet been able to meet the easy and comprehensive approach offered by Google" (Friend, 2006). This has been affirmed by others, including Chen, who, after studying various federated search technologies, concluded that "they cannot compete with Google in speed, simplicity, ease of use, and convenience, nor can they be truly one-stop shopping" (Chen, 2006, 413).

Faced by these realities and our patrons' predilection for easily navigable Web resources, our options are, admittedly, limited. It is to be expected that in many cases, expediency will, invariably, triumph. Rather than lament the use of tools like Google Scholar, we need to think of ways of strategically assimilating it. Co-opting it into our instruction seems to be the only reasonable course of action. Resourceful librarians are already doing this, drawing upon its similarities to library databases, while exposing its deficiencies.

Clearly, the role of librarians in the new world of information is changing. As Cathcart and Roberts note, our success or failure will ultimately be measured by our adaptability. "With the advent of Google Scholar and the continuing evolution of the online information environment, the way librarians go about educating students–in both the classroom and at the reference desk–will need to evolve as well" (Cathcart and Roberts, 2005, 168).

REFERENCES

Abram, Stephen. 2005. Google scholar: Thin edge of the web. *Information Outlook* 9(1): 44-46.

Cathcart, Rachael & Amanda Roberts. 2005. Evaluating Google Scholar as a tool for information literacy. In *Libraries and Google,* ed. William Miller & Rita M. Pellen, 167-176. Binghamton: Haworth Press.

Chen, Xiaotian. 2006. MetaLib, WebFeat, and Google: The strengths and weaknesses of federated search engines compared with Google. *Online Information Review* 30(4): 413-427.

Cohen, Laura B. 2005. Finding scholarly content on the web: From Google Scholar to RSS feeds. Special issue, *Choice: Current Reviews for Academic Libraries 42*: 7-17.

Friend, Frederick J. 2006. Google Scholar: Potentially good for users of academic information. *Journal of Electronic Publishing* 9, no. 1, <http://hdl.handle.net/2027/spo.3336451.0009.105> (accessed June 6, 2007).

Gorman, G. E. 2006. Giving way to Google. *Online Information Review 30*(2): 97-99.

Jasco, Peter. 2005. Google Scholar: The pros and the cons. *Online Information Review* 29(2): 208-214.

Kent, Michael L. 2005. Conducting better research: Google Scholar and the future of search technology. *Public Relations Quarterly 50*(4): 35-40.

Kesselman, Martin & Sarah Barbara Watstein. 2005. Google Scholar and libraries: Point/counterpoint. *Reference Services Review 33*(4): 38-387.

O'Leary, Mick. 2005. Google Scholar: What's in it for you? *Information Today,* July/August 2005.

Norris, Benjamin P. 2006. Google: Its impact on the library. *Library Hi Tech News* 9: 9-11.

Tenopir, Carol. 2005. Google in the academic library. *Library Journal 130*(2): 32.

Niehaus, Ellen, Alan Asher Niehaus, & Crint Wrede. 2006. The depth and breadth of Google Scholar: An empirical study. *portal: Libraries and the Academy 6*(2): 127-141.

Pomeranz, Jeffrey. 2006. Google Scholar and the 100 percent availability of information. *Information Technology and Libraries 25*(1): 52-56.

Wleklinski, Joann M. 2005. Studying Google Scholar: Wall to wall coverage. *Online* 29(3): 22-26.

Worth the Price?
Virtual Reference, Global
Knowledge Forums, and the Demise
of Google Answers

Kay Cahill

INTRODUCTION

In November 2006, Google announced that it was closing its Answers service. The announcement was met with considerable interest by the information and business communities; Google is not typically known for giving up on things. Even services that have sparked profound and, in some cases, very valid criticism, such as Google Scholar, have generally continued undeterred. What, then, made Google decide to close Answers down?

THE EVOLUTION OF GOOGLE ANSWERS

Google Answers was one of the products born of Google's 20% time, the corporate philosophy that encourages Google Engineers to spend up to 20% of their time working on projects of personal interest. In the case of Answers, an early version ("Google Questions and Answers") emerged briefly in 2001, but closed almost immediately. This service offered users the chance to e-mail questions to Google staff and pay a flat fee for an answer. Little information exists about why the service lasted such a short time, but general agreement is that the demand was almost certainly overwhelming and unsustainable. Google's interest in providing fee-based answers continued, however, and Answers launched in 2002.

Google Answers is credited as being the brainchild of Larry Page, developed in just four months by a four-person group of Google software engineers (Fikes & Bauer, 2006). Rather than attempting to answer questions in-house, Google employed independent contractors (Google Answers Researchers, or GARS) to carry out the research. The service enabled users to post questions, and list a fee they were willing to pay for the answer. A Google Answers Researcher would then carry out the required research and provide the information needed to answer the question, with 25% of the fee going to Google and 75% going to the researcher. Prices for questions initially ranged from $4 to $50, and later expanded to $2.50 to $200. A non-refundable $0.50 listing fee was also included.

An interesting feature of Answers was that although the first researcher to get to a question could close it to other researchers for a fixed time period, giving themselves a window to provide an answer: other users could provide comments on questions. This enabled people to provide additional information, or offer parts of the answer they felt might be useful even if they weren't being paid to provide a full answer to the question. All questions, answers, and additional comments were owned by Google, and made freely available to other users in an online database. At the time of writing, these answers are still available, and Google has given no indication that it plans to withdraw them.

At the height of Google Answers, approximately 800 researchers were participating in the project (Fikes & Bauer, 2006), although not all of these would have been active at a given time. These researchers were selected by Google, which initially put out a call for participants and then selected people to work on the service by requesting that they fill out sample questions to test their research skills. Librarian Jessamyn West, who worked briefly as a Google Answers Researcher, commented that these questions were "clearly designed to separate the people who could use Google from the people who could process and synthesize information" (West, 2002). Google had obviously learned from the experience of the failed Questions and Answers service about its ability to provide a scalable fee-based research service in-house, and also clearly wanted to ensure that if it did turn to outside contractors, the answers provided would be of sufficient quality to justify payment. As part of its quality assurance process, Google also enabled question askers to rate both the official answer and comments, thus encouraging researchers to keep their ratings up (or risk being dropped) and encouraging non-researchers to comment in the hopes of developing a high enough rating to support their own application to be a researcher.

With the appeal of being able to work from home and decide exactly how much of their time they wanted to spend working on the service, Google had no difficulty in recruiting interested research professionals–and keen amateurs–to serve as Google Answers Researchers. For much of the four years the service was open, enquiries about how to work for Google Answers were met with a screen advising interested parties that new applications were no longer being accepted. Existing researchers were required to sign a non-disclosure agreement that meant much of the researcher experience is difficult to explore, with the most widely distributed and best known commentary tending to come from disgruntled researchers who were willing to ignore the NDA.

Between 2002 and 2006, Google Answers ticked steadily along, accumulating over 100,000 posted questions along the way (Google Answers, 2007), until a sudden slump in the number of users occurred in the fall of '06 (Crane, 2006). At the end of November, Google announced that Answers was closing down. Google itself provided little in the way of explanation, referring only to a need to focus on "features rather than products" (Amit, 2006) and that it was "reconsidering our goals for [the] project"

(Fikes & Baugher, 2006). Google Answers Researchers, devastated and homeless, immediately set about finding new places to work. In some cases they gravitated to existing sites such as Assist Me Online <http://www.assistmeonline.com/>; in other cases, they banded together to start their own Google Answers clones <http://www.uclue.com>. Groups for ex-Google Answers Researchers have sprung up all over the Web, a testament to how much they valued being part of the service and their opinion that the closure was unjustified. However, little information is available publicly from ex-GARs, as they are still bound by Google's NDA.

In spite of some of the issues with the Google Answers model, which this article will go on to explore as it examines the reasons for the closure, there's no question that Google Answers was a place where it was possible to get excellent research at a relatively low price. One former Google Answers Researcher, David Sarokin, points out in his 2005 article about Answers:

> *For the most part . . . ratings are high, rejections are rare, and our clients seem quite satisfied. Well they should be. Some of the work provided at Google Answers would easily cost thousands of dollars if it came from a professional marketing research firm, web site customization service, computer programmer or private investigator. Take a look, for instance, at this customized research on the thermoplastics market done under a tight deadline at a bargain-basement price: <http://answers.google.com/answers/threadview?id=519557>.* (Sarokin, 2005)

OUT OF ANSWERS

So why did Google abandon its Answers service if it succeeded so admirably in delivering quality research at a very low cost? The reasons can be broken into two distinct parts: internal reasons, to do with the model Google developed, and external reasons, to do with competing forces in the information marketplace.

THE INTERNAL REASONS FOR GOOGLE ANSWERS' CLOSURE

One of the most easily identifiable problems with the Google Answers service is that it set out to be all things to all people, and as a result did not satisfy anyone effectively. It tried to sell itself as a professional research service staffed with qualified people, and its rigorous selection process and emphasis on rankings showed its commitment to this side of the service. However, at the same time it promoted itself to questioners as a source of cheap information. Many of its processes and mechanisms actively encouraged the service's evolution as a place where questioners could expect to receive quality research at an extremely low price. Great for people asking questions, as Sarokin notes, but perhaps not so great for researchers looking for reasonable compensation for their time. The inherent paradox between quality and cost seems to have caused some resentment, and even attrition, among those researchers who felt that their efforts were being seriously undervalued.

By promoting a competitive atmosphere among researchers as Answers evolved, with GARs racing to be the first to lock a question, Google effectively encouraged researchers to take questions which failed to compensate them adequately for the time required to provide a reasonable answer. For example, how long did bobbie7-ga put into researching thermoplastics in the example quoted by Sarokin, and how much would they have been paid had he or she been working for a professional research service rather than freelancing for Google Answers? Certainly, well over the $200 paid for this very detailed and thorough research.

Jessamyn West felt that the extremely competitive environment was a result of Google failing to address scalability issues as the pool of researchers expanded, and commented on how she felt it had affected the quality of answers:

> When I first began my tenure at Google Answers, there were a plethora of questions and not too many researchers. You could examine questions at your leisure and select the ones that fell in your area of expertise . . . As the pool of researchers got larger and the pool of questions did not grow as quickly, questions became harder and harder to obtain and lock. Researchers no longer searched as hard for questions in their field of expertise; they would just lock a question first, then see if it was one they could answer. (West, 2002)

The increasingly competitive environment at Answers, and its impact on the service, wasn't limited to a scarcity of questions and the resulting competition for compensation. In addition, because of the risk of losing the question to another researcher when the lock expired, researchers often felt unable to take advantage of the option to ask for clarification of questions that were vague or unclear, and simply tried to answer them as best they could.

The problems that developed as a result of these issues were compounded by Google's decision to allow questioners to claim a refund within 30 days of a question being posted if they were not fully satisfied with the answer. This appears to have created huge problems for researchers, who could spend many hours researching a question and providing an answer only to find that the client had demanded a refund and as a result they would not be paid. Former Google Answers Researcher "Silicon Samurai" broke his NDA to go public about how poorly he felt the competitive model reflected researchers' worth.

> *You have no recourse if the client decides not to pay. For any question which pays enough to bother with, you are forced to compete with other researchers to lock in the question within seconds of the time it's posted. You often do a lot of work which you'll never get paid for . . . For Google and questioners it's a win-win situation. But for the researchers, the people who must be highly motivated professionals in order for this whole project to really work, there are a dozen ways to lose even if you do everything exactly by the rules.* (Silicon Samurai, 2002)

This encouraged participation by those researchers who weren't reliant on Google Answers as a source of income, or who were more interested in answering questions than the financial rewards, and discouraged those who were looking for reasonable compensation in return for high quality, professional research. In itself this did not necessarily devalue the quality of questions–it's quite possible for an amateur to be an expert in a field, with a great store of knowledge and experience to draw on–but it certainly seems to have resulted in frustration for those researchers who were professionals hoping to be adequately compensated for their work. Google's commitment to making all past questions and answers freely available also meant that they had no opportunity to exploit additional revenue generation from the resale or reuse of answers, which could have been leveraged to provide additional compensation for both the company and the researchers.

This brings us to the second major internal problem, aside from failures to address issues in the basic model. Essentially, Google Answers was outside of Google's control in a way that none of its other services were or are. Because most of the products and features that Google offers, even those like AdSense that incorporate financial transactions, are either fully or almost fully automated, they are very cost-effective, and do not require extensive oversight or hand-holding at a human resource management level. Quality control is in the hands of software engineers employed directly by Google, and the quality of the code and solutions they develop.

Google Answers was a different beast. By staffing the service with contract researchers, beyond the initial selection process quality control was left very much in the hands of the researchers and users of the service. The model itself, while making several nods to quality control, also incorporated several mechanisms that, as already discussed, actively encouraged researchers to focus on speed and quantity rather than quality. Users were able to rate answers, but the problem with leaving a rating system in the hands of users is that it inevitably ends up being somewhat arbitrary. There was also a real fear among researchers that answers were being rejected, or poor ratings given, simply so that the questioners could claim a refund and avoid having to pay for research that had already been carried out and delivered to them.

Additionally, researchers began to avoid taking certain questions that were known to be a high risk factor for low ratings: for example, questions that weren't clear, or called for more of a personal opinion than an answer, or questions coming in from users who were known to give harsh ratings. This explains the relatively high percentage of questions (approximately a third of all questions posted) that remained unanswered in spite of the fact that competition for questions was generally so intense. While the researchers' tendency to avoid these questions is understandable, the unanswered questions may well have been a factor in the service's failure to attract a greater number of users, since posting a question would incur the 50-cent listing charge even if it remained unanswered forever.

The engineers behind Google Answers found themselves dealing with questions of policy, procedure, and human resource management that simply weren't part of most of Google's services. Tech support questions, scoring of new researcher tests, moderation of questions, answers and comments, allegations of unscrupulous researchers locking multiple questions so that other researchers had no opportunity to answer them, former researchers such as West and Silicon Samurai publishing unauthorized articles about the service–all of these things took time to process. Considering the relatively small percentage of Google traffic that was handled by Answers–just 1%–and the relatively low level of income it brought in for the company–just over $1 million annually–there is no question that it was extremely labor intensive, and not even close to the cost effectiveness level of Google's traditional automated services.

Google also found itself in an atypical arena with the Answers service when it came to public relations, marketing, and publicity. Most Google products have thrived and grown purely through word of mouth and the strength of the Google brand. By putting all the answered questions into a publicly accessible database, Google hoped that potential users would be able to browse the information and gain the reassurances they needed about the quality of answers the service was able to provide. The consistently low traffic levels experienced by Answers suggest this approach did not work as effectively as it had for other Google products. Answers was simply too different: it employed contractors rather than Google staff, and it charged for its services. It's one thing to accept a word-of-mouth verdict on a free service; you have nothing to lose if you try it and it doesn't work out. When you're paying for a service, there's more at stake. Google Answers would almost certainly have benefited hugely from some more traditional marketing and publicity, but this was atypical compared to other Google products and hence not part of its promotional plan.

In retrospect, the NDA also created problems. It created an air of secrecy around Answers, in spite of all the information about the model and the process that existed on the official website. It became a very big deal when people like Silicon Samurai broke the NDA; for example, Jessamyn West's "Information for Sale" article is far better known and more frequently cited than David Sarokin's "An Insider's View of Google Answers." The majority of the GARs were a tight-knit community, deeply committed to Google Answers, its users, and the provision of quality information. Yet the wrangles and resentments caused by flaws in the service model have received far more publicity. NDAs are standard practice from a security and business point of view, but in this case it does seem to have generated some bad publicity–and effectively stifled potentially good publicity.

THE EXTERNAL REASONS FOR GOOGLE ANSWERS' CLOSURE

When anyone begins investigating the external factors that influenced Google's decision to close down Answers, the issue that comes up time and time again is the market dominance of Yahoo! Answers. There's no question that the figures are very impressive. At the time of the Google Answers closure, Yahoo! Answers could claim more than 60 million active users worldwide and over 160 million answers to questions even though it was barely a year old. This is in comparison to the relatively modest figures generated by Google Answers: approximately 120,000 questions asked, and 70,000 answers provided, during the four years the service was running (Google Answers, 2007).

So did Yahoo! Answers kill Google Answers? Certainly Yahoo! would like us to believe so, and numerous articles have been published both online and off arguing that this is the case. But in fact, the two services are very different. Google Answers offered professional, quality assured answers at a price. Yahoo! Answers offers free, community-driven questions and answers: no guarantee, but also no fee. "It's all about community and the intelligence of a mob. Yahoo! Answers is like Google Answers mashed up with Wikipedia" (Hill, 2005). The one similarity is in the fact that askers can rate answers, but this has far fewer repercussions for Yahoo! Answers users than in Google's pay-by-the-answer model. Poor ratings don't bring any risk of being dropped from the team, or excluded from providing answers to questions.

Community driven question and answer forums are not new. A roll call of current and former community-based general information forums shows a consistent appetite for this kind of free information exchange, although not all have survived. WHquestion, an excellent model that is still mourned by its users six years on, existed for barely a year before the company running it pulled the plug in 2001. KnowPost, the brainchild of entrepreneur Clay Johnson and probably the most consistently high quality community-driven general information forum, folded later the same year. Wondir, one of the more sophisticated question and answer forums in terms of technology but notable for the poor quality of many of its questions and answers, not only survived but was bought out by Revolution Health in 2006. Cerescape, a site maintained and run by UK software engineer John Goss, has been quietly thriving for almost six years with 70,000 questions and almost 500,000 answers accumulated. Yahoo! was certainly not doing anything new when it launched its Answers service; what it was doing was tapping into an area of the market where there was proven demand, but doing so with the power and recognition of the Yahoo! brand behind the service.

It does not take a hugely sophisticated user to realize that in terms of quality and consistency, these free question and answer sites–including Yahoo! Answers-and Google Answers are a world apart. It's quite possible to find a detailed and very informative answer on Yahoo! Answers, but because there's no limit on the questions and answers that can be posted, and no financial incentive to provide complete, sourced or accurate information, the good answers can often be buried in a sea of conversation, uninformative one-line answers, and in some cases complete irrelevancies.

However, the sheer number of posted questions and answers suggests that Yahoo! Answers has something that Google Answers lacked. Google Answers promoted competition; Yahoo! Answers promotes collaboration. Maybe your question will receive numerous brief, incomplete answers; but perhaps together, those one-line answers will build into the complete piece of information you need. Google Answers promoted an elite environment, where only those willing to pay were able to ask questions and only a select few were able to join the ranks of the Google Answers Researchers and provide official answers. Yahoo! Answers promotes inclusion, where anyone and everyone can ask a question on any topic, and provide their thoughts, opinions, and experiences in response to the questions posted by others.

Google Answers, essentially, looked backward. It was a traditional information marketplace model: provide your fee, a researcher will take your question, and you'll be provided with an answer. Yahoo! Answers looks forward. It's driven by the principles of Web 2.0, the model of increased collaboration and participation. The sheer number of questions and answers on the site is testament to just how powerful this community-driven model is.

Yahoo! Answers does not offer a comparable service to Google Answers. It is a site where it's perfectly possible to obtain high quality, accurate information, but what it lacks when compared directly to Answers is the consistency and quality assurance. Google's model may have led to some devaluing of answer quality, as already discussed, but it certainly offered a level of consistency that a community-driven, free Q&A forum cannot replicate. Nonetheless, the figures tell their own story when it comes to Yahoo!'s hand in Google Answers' downfall. Even though the services are not directly comparable in terms of the end product, Google Answers closed down within a year of the launch of Yahoo! Answers.

I would argue that this was not necessarily because Yahoo! Answers took away business that would otherwise have found its way to Google Answers, but because the speed at which Yahoo! Answers expanded was a clear message that this free information-trading model has far more appeal to users than a traditional information-purchasing model. The end product was ultimately far too different for Yahoo! Answers to be a direct competitor to Google Answers, at least for the higher end of its business; while users who were willing to pay for information might have tried out Yahoo! Answers first, it's unlikely that it would have met the needs of anyone seeking in-depth information or research. Had Google chosen to continue the Answers service, it would probably have found that the lower end questions–the $2 opinion-driven questions, for example, or the people who were willing to pay $5 to have someone tell them a joke they hadn't heard before–would have dried up as they found a more natural home in the free model, and the service focus would have moved toward the higher-end, in-depth research question.

There is also another external factor that rarely achieves the same kind of prominence as Yahoo! Answers when discussing the fate of Google Answers, but is nonetheless very much worth considering as an influencing factor–especially from the point of view of the information profession. This other factor is Virtual Reference.

Virtual Reference–also known as Live Reference or Chat Reference– is a relatively new but increasingly popular service delivered primarily by public and academic libraries. In the Virtual Reference model, library users connect to librarians through specialized software that allows them to chat live online, and also enables the librarian to push Web pages to the person's computer and even guide him or her through searches and authentication processes using the cobrowse function, where both librarian and user can see what the other is doing as they navigate the Internet. Virtual Reference is another area where collaboration has proved to be a powerful tool, and many of the VR services offered by North American libraries are available on a statewide or provincewide basis. In some cases, libraries in different countries have even formed collaboratives, leveraging the time zones to offer VR services on a 24/7 basis without having to have a single librarian work outside of his or her regular hours.

Virtual Reference offers a whole new take on the information marketplace. VR services offered through public libraries are free of charge, although many do require you to be a resident of the state offering the service. VR offers the user the guidance of a professional searcher who will not only deliver the information sources people need, but will actually guide them step-by-step through the search process in real time, enabling them to absorb and assimilate the search skills displayed. Academic VR services offer the additional assurance that the student is getting help from someone who understands the academic environment and its demands.

So here's a service that gives the user an even greater level of quality assurance than Google Answers, plus the advantage of real-time help available, in many cases, around the clock. Because the service is real-time, librarians can ask as many questions as needed to in order to be sure they have understood the user's information need, and in return the user can request clarification and ask follow-up questions before the session ends–and all free of charge.

There's definitely a value-added element to Virtual Reference that neither Yahoo! Answers nor Google Answers can compete with. The question is whether or not the dramatic growth of VR services played a part in the closure of Google Answers. One way to establish this is to take a look at the statistics for some of the larger VR services. In 2006, AskColorado answered almost 53,000 questions. In the same period, Q&ANJ answered 55,000 questions. Oregon's L-Net service answered close to 17,000 questions in 2005-2006, and Ask?Away Illinois answered over 23,000 questions. The newest collaborative VR service, British Columbia's AskAway, set itself a target of 15,000 questions in its first year, but exceeded that number before it had even reached its four-month anniversary.

Certainly, VR services would be competing with Google Answers more than Yahoo! Answers in terms of both professionalism and quality assurance, and the numbers would indicate that VR services are processing a large number of information seekers who might well have potentially used Google Answers had they not had recourse to the library services. VR services also have the added draw of offering professional assistance at no cost. Given the huge rise in VR services over the past five years, and the continued increase in the number of questions they are answering, it is clear that they have played a significant part in altering the landscape of the information marketplace. A more extensive study would be needed to examine fully the role they played in the Google Answers closure, but it is more than reasonable to conclude that they were a contributing factor.

CONCLUSION

As with any business failure, numerous elements played a part in the closure of Google Answers. It was a step too far removed from Google's typical product portfolio, and took it into uncharted territory where it ultimately had to choose between continuing to make a substantial time investment in something that was clearly neither a strong revenue driver nor something that struck a particularly strong chord with the public, or letting it go. Other developments in the information marketplace highlighted the weaknesses of the Google Answers information model, meaning that even if it had survived it would have required substantial investment and development to evolve into a scalable and sustainable service. The Google Answers model was quite a typical, traditional way of purchasing information, albeit in an electronic environment; as the Web 2.0 ethos of collaboration and community became the primary driver for the net, the new collaborative information models such as Wikipedia and Yahoo! Answers simply proved to be more appealing to the information-seeking audience.

Ultimately, Google Answers was simply not the success that Google had hoped it would be, nor did it achieve the popularity levels it had come to expect from its other products. It lacked the innovative elements that Google works so hard to incorporate into its other core businesses, and it also broke with Google's tradition of providing free access to information for the end user. For all of the different factors that played a role in highlighting Answers' weaknesses, in the end its closure may have come down to the fact that for Google, it simply didn't quite fit.

REFERENCES

Agarwal, Amit. 2006. *Microsoft gets breathing room as Google puts full stop to new products.* <http://labnol.blogspot.com/2006/10/microsoft-gets-breathing-room-as.html> (accessed May 20, 2007).

Crane, Jeremy. 2006. Google Loses a Battle ... But it May Be the Beginning of the End for the War <http://blog.compete.com/2006/12/05/google-answers-Yahoo!-answers/> (accessed May 20, 2007).

Fikes, Andrew and Bauer, Lexi. 2006. *Adieu to Google Answers.* <http://googleblog.blogspot.com/2006/11/adieu-to-google-answers.html> (accessed May 20, 2007).

Google Answers. 2007. <http://answers.google.com/answers/> (accessed May 20, 2007).

Hill, Brad. 2005. Yahoo!! Answers: Smart (or Dumb) Mobs Go to Work. <http://google.weblogsinc.com/2005/12/09/Yahoo!-answers-smart-or-dumb-mobs-go-to-work/> (accessed May 20, 2007).

Sarokin, David. *An Insider's View of Google Answers.* <http://www.freepint.com/issues/300605.htm#tips> (accessed May 20, 2007).

Silicon Samurai. 2002. *Questions About Google Answers.* <http://www.geek.com/features/silicon/071702.htm> (accessed May 20, 2007).

West, Jessamyn. 2002. Information For Sale: My Experience With Google Answers. <http://www.infotoday.com/searcher/oct02/west.htm> (accessed May 20, 2007).

Virtual Reference Statistics:

Oregon: <http://www.oregonlibraries.net/files/lnet-2005-06-final-executive-summary.pdf> (accessed June 10, 2007).

Colorado: <http://www.aclin.org/reference/stats/AC_Usage_2006.pdf> (accessed June 10, 2007).
New Jersey: <http://www.qandanj.org/description/> (accessed June 10, 2007).
Illinois: <http://www.askawayillinois.info/AAAWEEK.doc> (accessed June 10, 2007).
British Columbia: AskAway Monthly Statistical Report. Vancouver Public Library, 2007.

Google and Collaboration

Carrie Newsom
Kathryn Kennedy

INTRODUCTION

Working in a library requires collaboration with many colleagues, including not only those who are local within one's own workplace but also those outside with whom one works on committees, professional organizations, and other projects. Traditionally, such collaboration has required exchange of documents and ideas through mail, fax, phone, and more recently email. Currently, many web companies are developing online services that can greatly enhance collaboration. These new tools allow asynchronous and synchronous collaboration via document editing, chat, discussion boards, and collective calendar management.

Google has developed a suite of applications to help users manage their own documents and those from group projects. The applications include most features found in traditional office applications along with a host of new features to aid in collaborative work (e.g., revision history). Librarians can greatly simplify their email inboxes by taking advantage of these new online tools. This paper discusses four of the new Google services (Docs & Spreadsheets, Calendar, Groups, and Chat) and describes their potential use as collaboration tools.

GOOGLE DOCS AND SPREADSHEETS

Description

Google Docs & Spreadsheets (GDS) is a personalized document center. The Documents part of GDS is set up like Microsoft Word. It has all of the editing capabilities (undo/redo, cut/copy/paste) and style aspects (font/margins/alignment/bullets/highlighting) of a typical word processor. In the "File" menu, saving options include RTF, HTML, PDF, and OFFICE formats.

There are three tabs next to the File drop-down menu–"Edit," "Insert," and "Revisions." Clicking on the "Edit" tab allows users to edit the document. By selecting the "Insert" tab a user is able to insert images, links, comments, tables, bookmarks, page breaks, horizontal lines, and special characters. Previous drafts can be restored by clicking on "Revisions." These revisions note the person who edited each draft and the date and time the document was edited. These drafts also illustrate what changes have been made from one draft to the next so the user can see the history of the document. When the document is ready to be collaborated on, the users can choose who they would like to have as a collaborator and who they would like as a viewer by clicking on "Collaborate." The collaborators will be able to view and edit the document, while the viewers will only be able to view the document. In this area, the user will have to add the Collaborator and Viewer's email addresses. The email addresses must be Gmail accounts for the collaboration tool to work.

All collaborators/viewers whose email addresses are added will be able to view the document in their Google account under the GDS link. By clicking on "Publish," the user can post the document to a web address or to a blog for others to view only.

The Spreadsheets component of GDS is set up like Microsoft Excel. The toolbar has editing and style capabilities similar to Microsoft's version, such as undo/redo, cut/paste/copy, alignment, margins, font, highlighting, etc., as does the documents section.

Under the "File" drop-down menu, the user can choose to start a new spreadsheet, import or open an existing spreadsheet, copy the current spreadsheet, print, upload a new version to the web, rename, or close. The user also has the option to export in the following formats: csv, .html, .ods, .pdf, and .xls. There are four tabs available to use, including "Edit," "Sort," "Formulas," and "Revisions." "Edit" is where the user can work on inputting the data into the spreadsheet. "Sort" allows the user to sort the data alphabetically. The "Formulas" tab allows the user to write an original formula or use an existing one to manipulate the data. The "Revisions" tab is where users can look and see what changes have been made to the spreadsheet in the past and where they can choose to revert back to an older draft. The "Format" drop-down menu gives users the ability to format cells however they want.

One issue the authors found is that GDS limits the number of rows the spreadsheet can have, so GDS is not ideal for large spreadsheets. Also, editing can be slow at times due to the continuous saving mechanism, and the lack of a chart option lessens the functionality.

Uses for Collaboration

GDS is extremely helpful in the collaborative activities required of academic librarians, especially when preparing articles for publication in journals and creating presentations for conferences. In the past, collaborating with others was difficult because communication was based on faxing, scanning, mailing, phone calling, e-mails, and huge attachments, and sometimes involved traveling cross-country to make sure everyone was on the same page. Today, with all of the social networking software and other technology capabilities, collaboration has become easier and convenient. With GDS, a user can start a new article/project, or upload an existing one, and invite all of the collaborators to input/revise ideas in one place. When away from the office, network folders are not easily accessible. GDS is accessible from anywhere.

These revision and collaboration features were advantageous when creating this chapter, all of which took place in GDS. The authors made separate documents for the four services covered in the chapter. Each of the two authors took two services to work on individually. Then, they revised each other's work virtually to make sure the chapter's style and contents were streamlined and cohesive.

In addition to working on the chapter using Google services, the authors are participating in a few projects using GDS as their project management space. This has been convenient for all involved. No matter where collaborators are, they can access the latest version of group documents and spreadsheets without having to have personal storage devices, such as USB drives, or emailing the documents around to each other. And no one has to worry about clogging up everyone else's valuable email storage space when sending newer versions around by email.

There is no need to worry if there is a newer version of the document, since the newest changes are saved in the most recent version of the document when using GDS. The "Revisions" section of GDS is where all the drafts throughout the project are saved. For example, if one author wrote a particular part of this chapter differently in the past and wanted to revert back to it, the authors could do so in the "Revisions" section of GDS, which keeps any and all revisions. This function is especially helpful when the document originator is working with a group of people on the same document. If changes are made, those changes are logged and saved as a whole new draft, and the most recent changes become the most recent document. This makes reverting back to older drafts very easy.

Another time-saving aspect of GDS is its auto-saving mechanism. If something happens to the user's computer and he/she hasn't saved in awhile, the work is not lost. GDS saves continuously so that users do not have to worry about losing anything if technical errors happen with their computer. Google is online rather than on a server or a network, so if the user's computer, server, or network crashes, and the user loses all documents on the hard drive or in a network folder, the user will not have lost any documents prepared with GDS. Everything will still be there.

When the authors first started using GDS, they found themselves saving documents in Word and then uploading them when they were ready, but now that they have come to know and trust GDS, they are able to leave the office knowing that they can access their documents without having to carry them around. And to them and the rest of their collaborators, that feeling is comforting.

GOOGLE CALENDAR

Description

Google Calendar is Google's answer to programs like Microsoft Office Outlook and Lotus Notes Calendar & Scheduling. Like all Google services, it is available online with a Google account. So far, Google Calendar is available in 17 languages. Google Calendar is unique because of the Web 2.0 features Google has incorporated, such as sharing calendars and discussing events.

With Google Calendar, users can create multiple calendars. To do this, the user simply clicks the + icon in the "My Calendars" section on the calendar page. This section also allows users to specify which calendars they would like to view and provides a search box to search for public (i.e., shared) calendars. Users will find public calendars with events organized around a theme (e.g., US Holidays, Music Events, etc.). If the user specifies his or her own calendar as a public calendar, it will be available through this search. This is a great way to share library events with users. In addition to sharing their public calendar through the Google public calendar search, users can also share calendars with others by providing links. HTML, XML and ICAL links are available. HTML links will point users to a web version of the calendar. XML links can be used by people to add calendars to their RSS feed reader. ICAL links allow users to subscribe to calendars using one of several calendar management programs (e.g., Outlook, iCal, Lotus Notes). Instead of sharing calendars with everyone (i.e., making it a public calendar) users can choose to share their calendar with only select individuals. This is helpful for managing classrooms or conference rooms, or scheduling team project deadlines and meetings. All sharing options are available under the Settings section of the web site.

Like most calendar applications, the primary use of Google Calendar is to create events. Users can set recurring and all-day events and specify a location or description just as in other calendar applications. If the user enters an address in the location field, Google Calendar will automatically insert a link to a map of the location. Users can import event information from calendars in other applications (e.g., Outlook, iCal, etc.) by exporting event information from their other calendar in .ical or .csv format.

Users can also invite others to events. To invite others to an event, users simply enter their e-mail address into the "Guest" section when creating an event. The invited guests will then receive an email which allows them to reply to the invitation and to let the users know if they can come to the event. It is not necessary for invited guests to have a Google or gmail account–invites can be sent to anyone with an e-mail address.

There are a variety of ways to set Google Calendar to notify users of events. Google Calendar can send event reminders, event invitations, changed or canceled invitations, invitation replies, and daily agendas to gmail accounts. Notifications can also be sent via text message (SMS) to cell phones.

One unique function of Google Calendar is the ability for invited guests to discuss events. Embedded in the additional information for each event is a comment module that allows users to post comments about the event. The limitation of this function is that users are not notified when new comments are posted and thus might miss the discussion if they do not look at the extended information for the event.

Uses for Collaboration

Within a library, Google Calendar can be very useful for managing staff calendars. Each staff member can maintain his or her own personal schedule using Google Calendar and then share only their free/busy information (i.e., not detailed event information) with everyone or only co-workers. Other venues for shared calendars within a library include staff development and managing conference rooms. For example, the library's staff development office could set up a shared calendar with details of all staff development events and holidays for staff members. To manage conference rooms using Google Calendar, users create a new calendar for the room and then direct Google Calendar to automatically add events that do not conflict with others on the calendar. Users can share the room calendar with their colleagues, and when anyone needs to schedule an event in the conference room, they simply add the room calendar to the event's Guest list.

In cases where group members do not work at the same library and thus cannot "see" each other's calendars, Google Calendar can be extremely useful. For example, when working on a national committee project with other librarians Google Calendar can be used to set up online group meetings and set project deadlines. With a Google Calendar, all members of the group will have access to the calendar, unlike many other calendar management programs which are limited to staff members at a specific library.

The sharing capabilities of Google Calendar make it an excellent vehicle for marketing library events to library users. One can use Google Calendar to make a master calendar of events and then display the calendar on the library web page. In addition, users can display individual event reminders for others to save on their own Google Calendar on the events information page using a Google Calendar event reminder button. As mentioned before, users can also provide XML and ICAL links to allow others to subscribe to calendars from their application of choice.

GOOGLE GROUPS

Description

Google Groups is a cross between an email list-serve and an online discussion board. Anyone can start a group and doing so creates an online space (group home page) and a group email address members can use to start or continue discussions. In addition, group web pages and group document storage are provided.

There are three categories of membership allowed in Google Groups. The person who starts a Google Group is considered the group owner and has complete control over all group settings and member management. The owner can control access to each part of the Google Groups site using the Group Settings tab and manage group memberships via the Management Tasks tab. Functions related to group membership include: adding members, changing membership type (e.g., from Regular Member to Manager or Owner), approving members, un-subscribing, and banning members.

A second, less powerful type of membership is the Manager. Managers are similar to owners in that they can approve posts, invite new members, create managers, control access to the group, and manage the group's membership settings. However, a manager cannot create a co-owner, transfer ownership of the group to another member, or remove the group. Only an owner can perform these functions. The third and least powerful type of membership is regular member. These group members can only perform functions as defined by the group owner in the Group Settings Access tab. At a minimum, they can view group content, and on the most liberal settings, they have almost the same privileges as managers.

There are two ways to interact with the Google Groups discussion board: e-mail and the group home page. All e-mail traffic to the group e-mail address is automatically posted on the discussion board. Discussions with the same e-mail subject line are posted under the same topic on the discussion board. In their profile, members can choose to disable e-mail delivery of messages and only use the group home page to begin and respond to discussions. Additionally, an RSS feed is provided so group members can use their RSS reader to monitor group discussions. However, RSS does not enable members to contribute to discussions, so members must use e-mail or the group home page to post messages.

Pages are web pages that group members create for the group. They are edited using a simple editor or HTML tags. The editor includes the ability to apply basic formatting to text and to include images and links on the page. Viewing and editing the pages can be restricted to Members only or Managers only. Members can create a discussion message each time a page is updated to notify members of changes to the page. In addition, Google Groups keeps track of edits to a page so group members can view previous versions of pages and revert to prior versions if necessary.

The Files section of Google Groups provides 100 MB of document storage for the group. That is approximately 3,400 2-page Microsoft Word documents. However, any type of file may be uploaded to the group File space.

Full control of the group including appearance, e-mail delivery options, and access are available under the Group Settings tab. The most important secondary tabs are the General tab and the Access tab. Under the General secondary tab, users can edit the group's name, description, associated public website (if available), and group e-mail address. This tab also shows the URL for the group home page. The Access tab is where users specify if the group page is listed in the Google Groups directory, who can view group content, who can join, and which type of member (manager only or any member) can post messages, upload files, and create and edit pages. There is also the option of holding all messages for moderation before they are posted to the discussion board and distributed to the e-mail list.

Uses for Collaboration

The rich access and member management features make Google Groups an ideal place for collaboration on projects which require lots of discussion and transfer of large files such as learning modules and instructional games. Typically such collaborations are based on a barrage of emails, and their associated attachments, that are difficult to collect and manage. Google Groups collects and automatically organizes these messages, providing a record of group activity, which is especially useful should the group decide to write a paper about their project at a later date.

Google Groups is also ideal for interlibrary committee collaborations because posting can be restricted to members only, but the group site can be made available for anyone to view, which is a requirement for many state institutions. It is a great place to house a committee website if institutional support is not available to create a highly collaborative space.

For national committees the ability to invite anyone, including those from other institutions, makes collaboration across institutions seamless. If activities are in a planning stage, and it is not desirable to announce them to a wider community, the group owner can easily restrict access to committee members only.

GOOGLE TALK

Description

Google Talk (GT) graduated from Google Labs and hit the ground running. This service is an instant messaging (IM) software, joining the ranks of America On-Line's (AOL's) AOL Instant Messenger commonly known as AIM, and Yahoo!'s Messenger, where users can have real-time text conversations through their computer's internet connection. What is unique about Google Talk is that it also offers a Voice over Internet Protocol, commonly known as VoIP, service, similar to Skype, an earlier VoIP system. This VoIP service allows users to call people through their Internet connection by way of speakers and microphones. Users have commented that using GT's VoIP system is just like using the telephone, especially if the users have headsets. There are two options for users in regard to having access to their Google Talk account.

The first option is for those who want to be connected to their Google contacts as much as possible. For this option, users can download a version of Google Talk to their active desktop. This software will display users as logged in and available to chat whenever they are using their computers.

The second option is for those who only want to be connected to their Google contacts when signed into their Gmail account. Gmail is Google's e-mail service. When logged into Gmail, users are shown as available to chat unless they change their status setting. Status settings tell users if a contact is available to chat. When a person is not logged in, users can see their status as "Offline" which means that person is not available to chat.

If users would rather not add GT to their desktops, they can opt for the GT service through their Gmail account. Once the users sign into their Gmail accounts, they can see their list of contacts and who is online and available to chat. By clicking on the person's name with whom the user would like to chat, the user will see a box pop up where he/she can start chatting. Again, this only shows the user as online and available to chat if and only if he/she is signed into his/her Gmail account.

Uses for Collaboration

GT is especially helpful when collaborators need to quickly touch base with other project members. On the other hand, GT is not as helpful when users need to have an online meeting where multiple people are chatting at once in the same chat space. That option is not available through GT.

A great aspect of GT is that users can save chat sessions in their Gmail account. When working on a project, users can revert back to these chat discussions, using them as an archival system for their project's progress. With the VoIP part of GT, users can call people and talk over the internet, which is helpful when collaborators are not located near each other. When using the VoIP mechanism, users have to ensure that the other collaborators have microphones and speakers on their end. This aspect is wonderful for long distance collaboration. When new collaborators are added, users can add them to their list of contacts. One drawback of GT is the limitations it has when it comes to VoIP and operating systems other than Microsoft. The Desktop version of GT does not work in Unix or MacOSX.

CONCLUSIONS

In this paper we have discussed four specific Google applications librarians can use for collaboration. There are many more Google applications available to explore, but the applications discussed here are the ones to use when working on group projects. Combined, they provide powerful tools for coordinating, communicating, and managing to meet important deadlines.

As evident from the discussion in this paper technology is constantly making collaboration easier. Though there are many companies creating online applications, Google is currently at the top of the technology tree, having established itself very well in the virtual world of the Web. The variety of applications offered and the availability of a single access point for all products make the Google applications a logical choice when searching for free collaboration tools.

Scheduling Smorgasbord:
Google Calendar and Key Contenders

Sara Davidson

INTRODUCTION

Have you ever had this experience of venturing out for a smorgas-bord meal at the local Chinese restaurant and gravitating towards your favorite standard dishes? Despite the abundant selections, you are neither inclined to experiment nor even aware of other choices. Exploring new web calendaring applications may feel the same way. The menu of calendaring applications and the features in those applications are constantly changing. Although well known products like those provided by Google possess excellent functionality, are highly visible, and receive much press, there may be other applications better suited for your calendaring needs and preferences.

The popularity of mash-ups, social bookmarking applications such as MySpace and Facebook, and customized toolbars all support the idea that people want and demand applications which offer a high level of integration with their daily activities. Online calendars are no exception. While users are heavily influenced by usability issues, aesthetics, and familiarity, this review will focus on exploring the capabilities of various calendaring applications to add and extend events; share information with others; provide customizable reminders; sync with other applications; and manipulate event data for embedding in other web environments. The main calendar contenders under discussion are Google Calendar, Yahoo! Calendar, Windows Live, and 30 Boxes.

Google Calendar launched in April 2006 moving the "kitchen calendar" to the computer.[1] Many are adopting this application; HitWise reported in January 2007 that Google Calendar use is steadily increasing while Yahoo and Microsoft products are losing their market share. In fact, during "the six months from June 2006 to December 2006,the market share of visits to Google Calendar increased by 333%, at the expense of its main competitors."[2] Though Google Calendar reaped .0043% of all internet visits, Yahoo! was still at .0051% in December 2006[3] and has been "the most popular tool of its kind since 1998."[4] Microsoft's Hotmail calendar has been available for years as well, but MSN has released Windows Live Calendar (Beta), an AJAX calendaring application, as part of Microsoft's Windows Live initiative announced in November 2005.

While calendaring products have been available from Yahoo! and Microsoft longer, Google currently seems to have the most momentum. However, numerous other calendars are available including 30 Boxes developed by 83°[5], a California based company, whose team also started Webshots.[6] 30 Boxes functions as a social and personal organizer with obvious Web 2.0 capabilities and, in contrast to the other calendars under discussion, resembles Google Calendar most closely in some of its features. While these calendaring applications have a number of features in common, there are also vast differences among them in some areas. Investigating how these applications support event additions, sharing with others, notifying, and syncing with other applications will reveal not only their similarities and differences, but also their overall success at integration.

ADDING EVENTS AND EXTENDING INVITES

The basic functionality of any calendar application supports adding events and extending those events into invitations or meeting requests, but calendars are distinguished by making this process intuitive and flexible. Google Calendar provides two basic ways in which to add events. One of these is a "Quick Add" function which accepts event information in natural language. Simply enter event information in the quick add box on the main calendar display or hit "q" and start typing. Information provided such as time and location will be interpreted and placed in the appropriate event fields.

Quick adds can even be used to create recurring events, specify a time zone, or invite a guest.[7] For example, this quick add string "planning meeting at 2 pm at 5200 N. Lake Road, Merced CA sdavidson2@ucmerced.edu" will generate an event on the user's calendar, send an email to a guest, and generate a link to a Google map. The second method of adding events is initiated by clicking on the event's day to prompt an event bubble for basic information. By clicking on "edit event details," the user can view and edit the complete event profile form. For repeating events, various options are provided such as repeating weekly, or every Tuesday/Thursday, etc. Overall, it is easy to add and edit event information via either method.

Events can also be used as invitations even if the user has not shared the full calendar agenda with others. On the event form, a calendar owner may add guests via an email address and give permissions to view the guest list or to invite others. After saving the event, the user will be prompted to email the guests. When guests receive the invite, they can indicate their attendance with "yes," "no," or "maybe." At this point, if permitted, the responding guests can invite others. Additional features include a link to a Google map of the event location if an address is included. The mail invite also provides an iCalendar file attachment (.ics) which a guest can use to save the event to Microsoft Office Outlook.

Yahoo! Calendar also provides a quick add option for events, but it does not rely as heavily on natural language as does Google's quick add feature. In Yahoo!, the date and time are submitted through drop down menus. On the full event submission page, an event type can be selected such a "performance" or "vacation." Yahoo! does offer extensive repeating options that are far more flexible and extensive than those presented in Google Calendar. For example in Yahoo!, one can add an event to the "3rd Tuesday of every month" or "every 4th Monday, Thursday, Friday." Google, on the other hand, does not offer as many options in this area.

Like Google Calendar, events can turn into invitations once guests are added to the event information. If friends have shared their Yahoo! Calendar, the user can look at his or her unavailable and free times before selecting an event time. To invite friends, one can type in e-mail addresses or insert them from a Yahoo! Address Book. Yahoo! gives the option of requesting an RSVP while invitations from Google Calendar default to request a response. Invited guests with Yahoo IDs will have the option of adding the event to their own Yahoo! Calendar.

In contrast to Google and Yahoo!, Windows Live does not offer a quick add option for events. In fact, the interface operates much more closely to that of Microsoft Office Outlook–no surprise there. Users must select "New" and then choose an appointment or meeting request from a drop down menu. Initially, this may be confusing since the appointment form and meeting request form are almost identical. The meeting room form merely has the addition of a box for inviting attendees.

Interestingly, the terminology used by Windows Live is more business related than that found in Google or Yahoo!. For instance, "meeting request" or "appointment" is used instead of "event" and "attendees" rather than "guests." Recurrence possibilities are very slim in Windows Live as there are only four available choices: daily, monthly, weekly, or yearly. Attendees can be selected from the address book or added manually. Those invited receive an e-mail and will be asked to respond via a hyperlink to an online acceptance form. Like Google, an iCalendar (.ics) file is attached to the e-mail so the event can be easily placed on a calendar such as Outlook. However, the e-mail is somewhat confusing since it tells users to 'Respond by clicking "Accept," "Tentative," or "Decline" at the top of the e-mail, yet these options are not visible until opening the attachment.

30 Boxes has a "One Box" entry which is similar to the quick add feature in Google Calendar. Natural language can be used though 30 Boxes recommends the following format for best results: event, date, time, and notes. Statements typed into this box will be turned into a calendar event. Like Google Calendar, it is possible to invite others and to link to a Google map. The syntax is slightly different since 30 Boxes requires a plus sign in front of the e-mail address, i.e., +sambox@gmail.com and physical addresses to be placed in square brackets. Other shortcuts are possible in "One Box" entries. Placing an exclamation mark at the end of the email will categorize the invite as urgent or adding an asterisk before the event will prioritize the event with a star icon.

Though 30 Boxes offers some interesting shortcut options for adding events, like Windows Live, its repeating options are minimal with only daily, weekly, monthly, and yearly offered. As in the other calendar applications, one can by-pass the "One Box" and add events via the detailed entry link. When friends, called "buddies" in 30 Boxes, are invited, the e-mail will inform them that the event can be added to Outlook or Apple iCal. 30 Boxes makes this option obvious while Google Calendar seems to expect invitees to notice the iCalendar (.ics) attachment and to understand what it does. While the language in 30 Boxes is closer to Google and Yahoo! than to Windows Live, it tends to be the most informal. For example when I received an invite from a friend in 30 Boxes and selected "Not sure–show me details" rather than "accept," I received this popup message: "You are hedging on Kelly's invitation on Apr 2, 2007. It will remain on your calendar until you delete it or you get off the fence."

STRONGEST CONTENDER

Google serves up the best functionality in adding and extending events with the "Quick Add" box and related shortcuts. The invitation process is also flexible and intuitive. Though 30 Boxes was a close second in this category with additional shortcut features, Google does not, for the most part, require special syntax to generate an email invite or produce a hyperlinked location. The invitation process in Google is also straight forward and effective though 30 Boxes does a better job of clearly indicating that the event can be added to Apple iCal or Outlook. Yahoo! provides the best flexibility for adding reoccurring events, but does not provide a natural language entry. Windows Live was the most problematic by requiring users to go to a drop down menu to add an event and then providing two forms with similar functionality.

SHARING

As with any online web calendaring solution, sharing capabilities are expected and they must be customizable. Though extending events into invitations is one form of sharing, sharing also refers to the ability to show a calendar and its events to others, with control over the display of those events, and to benefit from other public calendars. Most applications also allow calendar owners to add generic calendars, such as holidays, to their own calendar instances. Google Calendar has particular strengths in allowing users to share calendars with other Google Calendar users. Within a single account, one can create multiple calendars and sharing options can be specified for each calendar instance. Two major sharing categories are available, sharing with everyone or sharing with specific people. If a calendar is shared with everyone, event details are searchable in Google Calendar, and the public may view that calendar by accessing the calendar's web address or adding the calendar to their own Google Calendar displays. However, calendar owners also have the option of limiting public calendar information to free/busy information which will prevent events from displaying in a Google Calendar search. The third option is to keep the calendar completely private unless shared with specific people. This is the default when a new calendar is created. Even without sharing a calendar, one can benefit from the shared calendars of others by searching for public events by name, category, location, and time. This searching can even be limited to specific locations and times.

The second major category moves from sharing with everyone to sharing with specific people. One can choose to add individuals with varying levels of calendar permissions, and this sharing is not limited to individuals with Google Calendars. In addition, a calendar owner can limit those permissions for each person to one of four options: see all event details; see free/busy times; makes changes to events; or make changes and manage sharing. This variety of sharing options allows for much flexibility. Events added to calendars are given the default mode defined in the settings, but one can override the default for "private" or "public" display when creating or editing a single event. In addition, if Google Calendars are shared and accepted, they are easy to differentiate from each other since the events originating from a single calendar are assigned one color. The names and representative colors of the shared calendars are listed on the left side of the screen. Sharing is easy to initiate, and undesirable shared calendars can be easily hidden or deleted.

Sharing functions allow Google Calendar owners to easily communicate events with each other and to intertwine their separate calendar instances. Other forms of integration are available since Google has made information from various calendars (such as the phases of the moon, and holidays of various countries) available to all calendar owners. For instance, localized weather and holiday information can be integrated into the calendar, and will be represented by small icons which Google Calendar documentation refers to as "eye candy."[8] Instead of manually entering Independence Day, the calendar owner can simply choose to add the US holidays calendar and this holiday will be automatically added to July 4th. The calendar can also be populated by single events by searching public events, i.e., for San Francisco Museums, from within the calendar application. Once finding and selecting an event, one can click a time and copy to a calendar. Overall, Google Calendar offers numerous options for sharing events with others and taking advantage of event information available on public calendars.

Yahoo! Calendar has a number of sharing capabilities ranging from keeping a calendar hidden to making it viewable by anyone. In addition, one can allow friends to view events or to view and modify them. In the sharing module, the default for sharing events is set as private. "Show as busy," like Google's free/busy option, only reveals the event duration while the public setting displays all event details. For a greater degree of flexibility in managing event information, the calendar owner can specify any of these three options when adding new events in order to override the default.

Those who are given permission to modify events must be added to a friends list and require a Yahoo! ID. Friends who do not have a Yahoo! ID can see the calendar if provided with the calendar's URL. Friends are added by typing in the Yahoo ID of the individual. No option is available for easily populating the friends listing with a search of Yahoo!'s Address Book. However, birthday and anniversary dates listed in contacts can be easily added as events to one's calendar from the address book. These events will display with the individual's name and an icon, i.e., birthday cake. While some sharing between the calendar and address book is available, more functionality in this area would benefit the end user. Unlike Google, Yahoo! does not have a search available for other public calendars. Calendar owners are limited to searching for shared calendars via a known Yahoo! ID.

Friends' calendars can be incorporated into one's own calendar display through "My Time Guides." These guides also include financial, sporting, group, and holiday events. If selected, these guides will appear as events on one's own calendar in either a merged or column view and are assigned a specific color. For instance, adding the Vancouver Canucks Schedule to a calendar will overlay the display with time and location information and hyperlinks to Yahoo! Sports details. Other options include adding weather forecasts which appear in day and week views, and horoscopes which display in the left hand menu of the calendar display. While Yahoo! has more sharing capabilities between the contacts found in the address book and its calendar and allows users to integrate "Time Guides," it does not capitalize on making these public calendars searchable.

Windows Live Calendar, available to those with Hotmail and MSN IDs, has sharing capabilities with privacy options similar to those found in Yahoo! Calendar. Yet those options are not visible until a friend with whom to share a calendar is selected. The calendar owner will be asked to choose whether all appointments will be displayed or only free and busy times.

Just as Yahoo! Calendar can only be shared with friends who have Yahoo! IDs, Windows Live Calendar owners are limited to those with a Microsoft Passport (i.e., a @hotmail.com or @msn.com e-mail address) unless one publishes the calendar to the web. Calendar owners will also be prompted to e-mail a personal invitation to each friend which explains the benefits of a shared calendar. Friends will have the option to integrate shared calendar appointments into their own calendar or to view the calendar via a URL. Unfortunately, there is no clear indication of the URL at which the shared calendar resides.

Though the events from shared calendars are color coded, it is very subtle so they are not easy to distinguish from each other. While all event details can be completely exposed or only displayed as free/busy times, one can still specify single events as private so that they will not display even when the calendar is shared. In addition, one can specify who is allowed to view the shared calendar and to what extent.

In the area of permissions, Windows Live provides similar options to those offered by Google and Yahoo! with one limitation. While friends can view calendars, no option is provided to give friends the ability to view and manage. Overall Windows Live has a clean interface which makes it easy to share calendars and to see who has shared calendars. However, it comes up lacking when one wants to add calendars beyond those of friends. If offers a minimal number of holiday calendars as overlays but delivers little in the ways of incorporating other shared calendars.

The sharing capabilities it provides are simple to instigate, but the calendar lacks much of the functionality offered by Google and Yahoo!.

30 Boxes is very much a social web application and sharing between buddies is encouraged. Similar features found in Google, Yahoo! and Windows Live are offered in 30 Boxes. Using 30 Boxes, one can choose to hide calendar information or share it with buddies. Various permission levels can be set from displaying all events, except those marked as private, to displaying events marked with specific tags, i.e., entertainment or work. This tagging feature allows one to generate a default setting for multiple events with the same tag rather than individually setting the permission level on each individual event. This is a particularly useful feature, and may appeal to those who use tagging in applications such as Flickr and del.icio.us.

As with the other calendaring options mentioned, the viewing privileges of each buddy can be specified individually rather than as a group. If buddies share their own 30 Boxes calendar, calendar owners can choose whether or not to have that information display on their own calendar instance. Buddies can be added individually or imported from a contact list and upgraded to buddy status. Email addresses and associated information can be easily imported via Plaxo from Yahoo!, Gmail, Outlook, or Hotmail. One can invite buddies to start and share their own 30 Boxes calendar by sending an email message from within 30 Boxes via Supermail. 30 Boxes offers the ability to incorporate not only the personal calendars of Buddies but also additional web calendars in webcal:// format. Examples of such calendars are found at iCalShare <http://www.icalshare.com/> and range from calendars of Moon Phases to American Politics and Government. All shared calendars can be color coded for easier viewing on the calendar display, similar to the way in which shared calendars are displayed in Google Calendar.

STRONGEST CONTENDER

This one goes to Google for allowing customization of sharing options and permission levels including the ability to initiate sharing with those not using Gmail addresses. It offers unique features such as the possibility of searching events of other public calendars from within Google Calendar and adding those events to one's own calendar instances. Events from different calendars are color coded for easy viewing, and Google offers multiple ways to add other calendars to one's own. Yahoo! offers similar functionality without quite as much flexibility while Windows Live has basic usable features but lacks the comprehensiveness of either Google or Yahoo!. 30 Boxes allows users to set permissions according to tags, but requires users to find calendars in webcal:// format rather than offering a few default options.

NOTIFYING

Notifying is probably one area where there is the least distinction between calendaring options. While some differences exist, notification is a standard service offered by calendaring solutions as a means reminding users of up and coming events and integrating event awareness into one's daily work flow.

Google Calendar owners can specify if they wish to receive reminders. The earliest reminders can arrive a week before the event or, at the latest, up to 5 minutes before the event begins. One can also choose to turn a reminder on or off at the individual event level. Event reminders can be delivered in three formats: email, short messaging service (SMS), better known as text messaging, and pop-ups.

In contrast to events, invitations do not have the same range of formats. For invitations, email and SMS are still available but pop-up notification is not supported. In addition, daily agenda reminders are available via an email reminder. While one can be *sent* text message reminders for events and invitations, it is possible to *initiate* a request for calendar information by texting a message to GVENT. In this sense, the notification is pulled from Google Calendar rather than pushed directly to the calendar owner. For instance, by text messaging "next," one will receive notification via a text message of the next event listed on one's calendar. "Day" will generate a list of all events for the current day and "nday" for the next day.[9] Setting up text notification is very simple.

Yahoo! Calendar also provides reminder options, and the calendar owner can personalize the default settings for how and when to receive those notifications. Without any personalization, Yahoo! will automatically send a reminder for an event to one's Yahoo! Mail account 15 minutes before the event. Calendar owners can opt to receive event reminders via Yahoo! Messenger, Yahoo! Mail, or a mobile device. It is possible to default to no reminders or to select all or any of the delivery options.

Not only can one choose the delivery method for reminders but also the time these reminders will be sent. Reminders can be sent two weeks prior to the event and up until five minutes before. While Google offers eight pre-determined interval options for reminders in the last hour before an event (1 hour, 45 minutes, 30, 25, 20, 15, 10, and 5), Yahoo! only offers four (1 hour, 30 minutes, 15, and 5). However, Yahoo! permits a user to add two reminders to each event.

For instance, one could choose to be reminded two hours before an event *and* to receive an additional reminder 30 minutes prior. All reminder delivery options follow the same schedule so text messages and email messages will be received at the same time. These cannot operate separately for a single event. Though defaults are set, one can change reminders for each event one creates. Like Google, Yahoo! offers a reminder which is a daily calendar view. The only delivery option for this view is an email sent to Yahoo! Mail. Both Google and Yahoo! offer a relatively simple process for initiating text messaging reminders though Yahoo! does ask for specific phone model information.

In Windows Live Calendar, notification of upcoming events is available in a variety of ways. Under the overarching heading of "Reminders," Windows refers to both email reminders and alerts. E-mail reminders are flexible since they can be sent to an e-mail address of one's choosing, not limited to a Microsoft Passport. Those reminders can be sent a week early or up until 10 minutes before the event. The intervals provided in the last hour are 1 hour, 45 minutes, 30, 20, 15, and 10–more options than Yahoo! but slightly less than Google.

Beyond the e-mail reminders, there are additional notifications referred to as "Alerts." All alerts will be sent out at the same time, but the delivery schedule can differ from that of the email reminder. In this way, Windows Live offers a service similar to the two reminder options available through Yahoo! Calendar. Three primary alert options are available: IM (Messenger); e-mail (Hotmail or MSN account); and text messaging to a mobile device. Of these three options, Messenger is the default method for alerts and cannot be changed. This means that if one has selected notification through MSN alerts and is signed into Messenger, notification of future events will arrive through IM. If one is not signed into Messenger, alerts reminders will be sent to the e-mail and/or mobile device as requested. Setting up a MSN Mobile account is a simple process. One has the option of overriding default notification methods for events when created or edited. The defaults are clearly visible for each event, and even the e-mail address to which the reminder will be sent can be changed on the event page.

In 30 Boxes, notification of upcoming events is available by either e-mail or text messaging though the default for events is always set to "no notification." The default cannot be changed except at the individual event level. By choosing a reminder option for an event, one will only receive the reminder through e-mail or SMS as it cannot be sent via multiple methods. Reminders can be sent 4 weeks early, up to 5 minutes before the event takes place. 30 Boxes provides intervals similar to those found in Yahoo!. In the last hour, reminders can be selected in the following intervals: 1 hour, 30 minutes, 15, or 5. E-mail reminders are not limited to a specific e-mail provider and will be sent to the primary email address listed in account information.

Initiating reminders by text messaging is intuitive and does not require phone model information or inserting a confirmation code before future reminders will be sent. 30 Boxes provides a simple test option to ensure that a connection to one's mobile device is working. Those expecting a separate section for selecting reminder options may be surprised to find these options integrated with basic account information. Though notification is limited to e-mail or text messaging, the other tools available in 30 Boxes allow for other methods of keeping track of events, i.e., posting information to blogs, creating an RSS feed, etc., which for some users may reduce the need for other forms of notification.

STRONGEST CONTENDER

Most of these calendaring options offer similar services so defending a solid winner in this area is difficult. Google does offer some text messaging options not available in Yahoo!, Windows Live, or 30 Boxes. I prefer Google Calendar for its flexibility such as more reminder intervals as one approaches an event. While throwing my vote in with Google, I must admit to liking Windows Live's generic e-mail reminder with additional alerts. Yahoo! is also strong and is capable of providing two reminders per event. Though 30 Boxes is simple to use, I wish that the "no reminder" default could be changed. Since viewing permissions can be set by tagging, I expect that reminders can be controlled by tagging too. Though it is a close race, Google wins.

IMPORTING, EXPORTING AND SYNCING

The ability to synchronize events on different calendars is desirable for many users. One-way synchronization is the ability to import and export events and perhaps should not even be referred to as synchronization. True synchronization happens both ways, so if changes are made to either calendar they can be transferred and will appear in both locations. Bi-directional synchronization can often be difficult to implement effectively but is the most useful.

Within Google Calendar, events can be imported from iCal or CSV (comma separated value) files. For instance, it is possible to transfer Google Calendar data in iCal format to other applications[10] or to export a CSV file from Outlook into Google Calendar. Google includes instructions for migrating events from Outlook, Apple iCal and Yahoo! Calendar into Google Calendar.[11] Although a single import or export is relatively simple to achieve, syncing these calendars without duplicating events is another matter. In addition, exporting recurring events to an application, such as Outlook, is problematic and can result in incomplete data transferred to another calendar. Potential solutions to the problem of synchronizing calendars to additional calendars or PDAs are available though not always simple nor reliable.

If looking for an online calendar application with multiple syncing possibilities, Google currently seems to be a viable option–not because Google has provided syncing software but because other developers have produced various programs and add-ons to work with Google Calendar.

To test and illustrate how Google Calendar might synchronize with my work calendar, Outlook, I tried two add-ons, Remote Calendars VSTO (5.81 release)[12] and SyncMyCal (lite edition).[13] Both add-ons to Outlook required additional installations before I could download them, and I had varying levels of success with them. Once downloaded, Remote Calendars allows one to subscribe to a remote iCalendar from within Outlook via its toolbar. Google Calendar provides a private iCal address that can be pasted into Remote Calendar. In the setup one can select, "It's my Google Calendar and I want to sync both ways." This will prompt one to submit a Gmail username and password for authentication.

Though events downloaded from Google Calendar into Microsoft Outlook using Remote Calendar, I found that the automatic update, which I had set to run each time Outlook was opened, actually reloaded *all* the events from Google Calendar into Outlook, resulting in unacceptable duplication. It provided a one way import which was not true synchronization. I was unsuccessful in syncing both ways. This problem coupled with a cumbersome initial set-up may discourage users from using this product.

I also tried SyncMyCal by Nagarro Inc. which supports bi-directional syncing between Google and Outlook and the ability to deal effectively with recurring events. Though the download was relatively simple, it took some coaxing to make the SyncMyCal toolbar appear in Outlook.[14]

The lite version, versus pro version, only allows downloading of events within a seven day window, three days before and after the current date. Google or Outlook can be chosen as the calendar "with precedence" in the bi-directional syncing process, or settings can be restricted to only upload or download events from one calendar to another.

SyncMyCal did not result in uncontrollable spawning of events and successfully transferred events from Outlook to the Google Calendar I specified and vice versa. To successfully remove events, users must be aware that the event has to be deleted from the calendar where it was created; otherwise calendar inconsistencies will result. Though Nagarro Inc. notes that SyncMyCal is in Beta and may act unpredictably at times, the application seems to operate as advertised. Nagarro Inc. is also promising a product to synchronize events with PDAs. Though SyncMyCal seemed much more reliable, it still has its limitations in terms of usability and limited features in the lite version.

Though syncing options are available, often one has to find a product to use with Google Calendar and it may not offer adequate service. More options will likely surface, and they may offer simple yet effective solutions for those who want to sync their calendars. Currently, many solutions seem unpredictable and difficult to implement.

In addition to the add-ons in Outlook, I downloaded Calgoo 0.36, a Java-based desktop calendar application, to aggregate and sync my calendars.[15] Calgoo by Timesearch, Inc. made its first appearance in 2006. It is capable of linking to Google (via URL or browsing), Outlook, and iCal calendars (iCal/webcal) and synchronizing the data between Calgoo and each calendar. Calgoo was first known for its integration with Google Calendar, and this association continues. As stated at "Under the Radar Recap," "If you like Google calendar, you'll love Calgoo."[16] Changes made in Calgoo while offline are synced to the appropriate calendar when an online connection is made. For example, in my own experiences with Calgoo, I found that I could make changes in Calgoo that were then replicated in Google Calendar, and deletions made in Google Calendars could be updated in Calgoo through syncing. This even worked when the event was originally created in Calgoo.

Though this initial transfer of data worked quite seamlessly between Calgoo and Google Calendars, I did occasionally have difficulties maintaining subsequent synchronizations between Calgoo and Outlook though the initial import from Outlook into Calgoo was successful. The release notes from version 0.36 indicate full synchronization is possible.[17] One can choose to synchronize automatically, i.e., every

10 minutes, or to synchronize on demand. Though it may appear as though Calgoo can sync both Outlook Calendar and Google Calendar, this is not currently supported. This important point was addressed on Calgoo's Forum. A lead from the Calgoo team wrote in December 2006 that while Outlook Calendar and Google Calendar can both be imported into Calgoo, there is no functionality to support having all the information sync to both Google and Outlook via Calgoo.[18] However, there are benefits in being able to add events via Calgoo while offline and then transferring changes when online.

In summary, I found that data transferred between Google and Calgoo to be reliable but had greater difficulties with transfers between Calgoo and Outlook. Calgoo plans to offer support for synchronization with mobile devices and will likely continue to improve its synchronization services. For those who want their Google Calendars offline, this is a viable solution.

Yahoo! Calendar will import CSV files and generate files for export. Though I was able to import CSV files, I found that Yahoo! did not generate a readable CSV file of my own Yahoo! Calendar events that could be imported into other applications. In terms of bi-directional syncing, Yahoo! offers Intellisync to transfer information in Yahoo! products to PDAs, Outlook, and other devices/software.[19] The software download is accessible from Yahoo! Calendar. The download warns that no other syncing software should be on one's computer. Though I was able to download Intellisync for Yahoo!, I was never able to complete the set-up since I received repeated error messages. Though it's quite possible that others have used the export features and Intellisync without difficulty, I ran into a number of obstacles.

Unfortunately, there is no evidence of importing, exporting, or true syncing compatibilities in Window Live Calendar. Even online forums have little to say on this topic.

In 30 Boxes one can generate a CSV file or ICS file of one's events for import into another calendar. I found that 30 Boxes generated usable CSV files. It also offers an experimental importing tool to bring in event data from Apple iCal, Microsoft Outlook, and Yahoo! Calendar. Though this tool works as an import, the functionality is limited. As the 30 Boxes documentation states, "This is not true synchronization. If you re-import your data, we will add new events, update existing ones, but NOT delete removed events."[20] 30 Boxes plans to release its application programming interface (API) to encourage developers to build applications such as bi-directional sync applications to work with Microsoft Outlook, Apple iCalendar, and Palm Desktop to make its integration functionality even more robust than it currently exists.[21] Applications like Remote Calendars and Calgoo will bring in events from 30 Boxes since they only require an iCal subscription which 30 Boxes creates.

STRONGEST CONTENDER

While these calendar applications tend to support importing and exporting files, true bi-directional syncing is another story. Google has my vote for syncing not because Google Calendar is providing its own syncing software but because other companies and developers are more likely to offer syncing solutions with Google Calendar than other calendar applications. 30 Boxes is starting to offer more functionality in this area and works with some other syncing applications. I found Yahoo! to be problematic while Windows Live did not offer syncing options.

EMBEDDING

Google Calendar has a number of options available which allow calendar owners to make event information available in other locations or in other formats. A complete view of one's Google Calendar can be embedded on a web page if the calendar is set to public view. The embeddable calendar helper allows for some simple customization of the calendar's appearance and automatically generates the code that can be copied onto a web page. Any changes made in the calendar are immediately visible in the embedded calendar instance. Those viewing the embedded calendar can also click on the events to view event details and will be linked to Google maps if the physical address is included in event details. The calendar also includes a "subscribe" option in the lower right. If visitors select this option, they will be asked if they want to add this calendar to their own Google Calendars.

The same option is available via a Google Calendar button. Visitors can simply view the complete calendar via a hyperlink or even be informed of calendar events by subscribing to an RSS feed via an application such as Bloglines, My Yahoo!, or Google Reader. For all of these options, Google creates the code. Those who frequently use the personalized Google home page will appreciate the mini-view of

Google calendar which can be placed on the home page. Events can be added directly from the mini view and a complete day agenda can be listed. Google offers some useful options to make the calendar information easily available in other web spaces.

Yahoo! Calendar does not offer the ability to embed its calendar into other web environments. Yet, it does clearly provide the URL for the calendar that can be shared with others or linked to from another website.

Windows Live also lacks options which would allow calendar information to be embedded elsewhere. It does provide a link to a shared calendar, but this URL is not as easy to find as the one in Yahoo! Calendar.

30 Boxes has the functionality to aggregate other web applications and encourages the calendar owner to make 30 Boxes a place to integrate feeds and personal account information from other web services such as Flickr, Skype, or WebShots. RSS feeds can also be added to 30 Boxes and appear in the calendar display. After bringing this additional information into 30 Boxes, it can then be included on blogs, web pages, and social networking sites such as MySpace and Facebook.

For instance, by copying code provided by 30 Boxes for a MySpace Flash Badge and copying it into MySpace, anyone viewing the user's profile in MySpace will be able to see a list of the current day's calendar information in a read-only box. The content will include information such as events and RSS feed information displayed on the user's calendar. This can be modified since the 30 Boxes user has the flexibility of displaying all events tagged in a specific way. For each of these options, different HTML code is generated to provide various levels of privacy. Changes made in 30 Boxes will be reflected on the MySpace Flash Badge. Buddies, or total strangers for that matter, can view one's daily events via the MySpace Flash Badge. Variations on this theme are available.

In addition to code for the flash badge, code is also available for a Javascript/HTML Badge which can be pasted into a web page. Though this code builds a window similar to the flash badge, it has greater interactivity. It includes links which will take an individual to the calendar owner's complete event list and the full 30 Boxes calendar view. For those calendar owners with additional web savvy, the HTML code can be edited to modify the style of the badge and the number of events to be displayed.

With 30 Boxes' calendar widget, a version of the calendar can be embedded on a web page rather than simply linking to the calendar. 30

Boxes also provides a miniature version of the calendar to be embedded in blogs, a Google home page, or almost any web location. This calendar application is providing avenues to integrate its presence in other web locations.

STRONGEST CONTENDER

Google and 30 Boxes are definitely the strongest contenders in the area of embedding calendar context elsewhere on the Web. Yahoo! and Windows Live are almost completely lacking in this area. Though I tend to find Google's embedding feature most useful for my purposes, some of the 30 Boxes options are intriguing. For this area Google and 30 Boxes are tied since they both allow calendar information to be displayed in numerous ways by generating HTML code for the calendar owner.

In my analysis, Google Calendar took four of the categories and tied in the fifth with 30 Boxes. Perhaps this is no surprise as evidenced by its increasing market share. Google Calendar is a strong contender with its "Quick Add" box which recognizes natural language, extensive sharing capabilities, many notifying choices, and useful tools which allow customizing the calendar for other purposes. Though it could offer its own syncing solutions, at least there are some choices for synchronizing Google with other calendars. This is one area that could use the most improvement.

Yet, the pervasiveness of the Google name coupled with a feature-filled, intuitive application will likely continue to capture users. While 30 Boxes offers many features similar to Google, perhaps its unfamiliarity is its biggest hurdle. Yet, it is a powerful calendar solution and offers many other features for those wanting to participate fully in the social aspect of Web 2.0. Yahoo! Calendar offers many excellent features too, but may need to adapt to recoup its losing market share. Additional calendar features found in Yahoo! Mail Beta may be indicative of future changes. Windows Live Calendar, though easy to use and visually appealing, lacks the functionality to make it a key player. While all calendaring products have basic functionality, some offer more features that may be of importance to some calendar users. Individual calendaring needs and preferences will determine the best fit for each user. Perhaps this review will provide one measuring stick for evaluating online calendaring solutions.

NOTES

1. Google, "Google Milestones," Google Corporate Information, <http://www. google.com/corporate/history.html> (accessed March 28, 2007).

2. LeeAnn Prescott, comment on "Google Calendar Up Threefold Since June," Hitwise Intelligence Analyst Weblogs, posted January 3, 2007. <http://weblogs. hitwise.com/leeann-prescott/2007/01/google_calendar_up_threefold_s_1.html> (accessed March 28, 2007).

3. Bogdan Popa, "Google Calendar Challenges Yahoo," Softpedia, <http://news. softpedia.com/news/Google-Calendar-Challenges-Yahoo-46541.shtml> (accessed March 28, 2007).

4. Elsa Wenzel, "Calendars: Yahoo vs. Google," CNET, <http://www.cnet.com.au/ software/internet/0,239029524,240063400,00.htm> (accessed March 28, 2007).

5. Julie Davidson, Narendra Rocherolle and Nick Wilder, "About 83°," 83°, <http://www.83degrees.com/#> (accessed March 24, 2007).

6. Nik Cubrilovic, comment on "30 Boxes Ready to Take Out Online Calendar Space," TechCrunch, posted March 11, 2006 <http://www.techcrunch.com/2006/03/ 11/30-boxes-ready-to-take-out-online-calendar-space/> (accessed March 28, 2007).

7. Google, "What's the Quick Add Feature?," Google Help Center, <http://www. google.com/support/calenar/bin/answer.py?answer=36604&query=quick+add&topic= &type=> (accessed March 26, 2007).

8. ——, "What's New with Google Calendar?," About Google Calendar, <http:// www.google.com/googlecalendar/new.html> (accessed March 15, 2007).

9. ——, "Can I Check my Calendar Information via SMS?," Google Help Center, <http://www.google.com/support/calendar/bin/answer.py?answer=37228> (accessed March 15, 2007).

10. ——, "How Do I Export my Google Calendar Data?," Google Help Center, <http://www.google.com/support/calendar/bin/answer.py?answer=37111&ctx=sibling> (acessed March 21, 2007).

11. ——, "Switching to Google Calendar," Google Help Center, <http://www. google.com/support/calendar/bin/topic.py?topic=8559> (accessed March 15, 2007).

12. SourceForge.net, "Remote Calendars," SourceForge Download, <http:// sourceforge.net/projects/remotecalendars/> (accessed March 18, 2007).

13. Nagarro, Inc., "SyncMyCal–Help," SyncMyCal: Outlook Google Calendar Sync Tool, <http://www.syncmycal.com/calendar_sync_software_Help.htm#A9_6> (accessed March 28, 2007).

14. Nagarro, Inc., "I am using Microsoft ActiveSync but certain times, my SyncMyCal toolbar disappears," SyncMyCal Support Center, comment posted March 6, 2007, <http://syncmycal.helpserve.com/index.php?_m=knowledgebase&_a=viewarticle& kbarticleid=23> (accessed March 25, 2007).

15. Time Search Inc., "Calgoo Calendar–Find, Use & Share," Calgoo, <http:// www.calgoo.com/> (accessed March 20, 2007).

16. Under the Radar, "Under the Radar Recap: Office 2.0 Desktop Tools and Team Work," Under the Radar Blog, comment posted March 25, 2007, <http://www. undertheradarblog.com/wp_blog.html> (accessed March 28, 2007).

17. Time Search Inc., "Calgoo Beta Release Notes," Calgoo, <http://calgoo.com/ release_notes.html> (accessed March 20, 2007).

18. Time Search Inc., "Outlook Sync with Google Cal," comment on Calgoo Forum, posted December 13, 2006, <http://www.calgoo.com:8080/JForum-2.1.6/posts/list/142.page> (accessed March 21, 2007).

19. Yahoo! Inc., "Working With Intellisync for Yahoo!," Yahoo! Address Book Tutorials, <http://help.yahoo.com/us/tutorials/mail/ab/ab_intellisync1.html> (accessed March 22, 2007).

20. 83°, "Import Your Events to 30 Boxes!," 30 Boxes, <http://30boxes.com/import.php> (accessed March 20, 2007).

21. Julie Davidson, comment on "Third Party Developer API," 30 Boxes News/Blog, comment posted January 1, 2006, <http://30boxes.com/blog/index.php/developers/> (accessed March 20, 2007).

Blogger:
Your Thoughts Here

Tricia Juettemeyer

INTRODUCTION

Online diaries have existed since the burgeoning of the Internet in the mid-1990s, but the proliferation of blogging tools exponentially increased the number of blogs on the web. In early 1999, there existed relatively few weblogs or "blogs," as we call them today.[1] Some of the earliest blogs date back to 1994-97; these bloggers created their own content management systems with hand-coded HTML (hypertext markup language)–technical knowledge was required to create a true blog.[2] This changed in August 1999, when Pyra Labs, a small company out of San Francisco, released the first version of Blogger.[3] Blogger was one of the first programs to provide the web-publishing interface that now defines blog software; this eliminated the requirement that bloggers have advanced technical knowledge to publish to the web. Moreover, it was free. Tech magazines and early bloggers quickly commented on Blogger's release.[4] These writings informed potential bloggers about the new program, and just one year later, there were tens of thousands of bloggers publishing online.[5]

HISTORY

Throughout its first year of release, Blogger required users to have their own web space to publish to, via Blogger's web form;[6] in spite of this constraint, Blogger use grew dramatically in its fledgling years. On September 3, 2000, Pyra released <http://www.blogspot.com>. Users could continue to host blogs on their own server or use Pyra's server, at no cost, and as a result, users created over 10,000 blogs there by November.[7] By 2001, Pyra was providing potential bloggers with options for their blogging needs, such as "Free Blogger," an advertisement-free, no-cost blog, or the for-fee products No-Branding Blogger, Enterprise Blogger, and Custom Blogger. Blogger Pro was in development at this time.[8] Released by early 2002,[9] it provided upgraded features for self-hosted blogs, including spellchecking, title fields, image posting, date-time adjustments, drafts of posts, and more to bloggers who wanted to pay a small fee. A part of Pyra Lab's start-up approach was to allow Blogger users to send a personal check to pay for the pro service.[10]

Following up on Blogger Pro, in August 2002, Pyra announced a service called BlogSpot Plus, a for-fee service used to upgrade blogs hosted on the blogspot.com server. By this time, free BlogSpot blogs were subject to ads,[11] but bloggers could pay a yearly fee for an ad-free BlogSpot account or upgrade to BlogSpot Plus or Plus 100 accounts for a monthly fee. By late 2002, Blogger had hundreds of thousands of registered users. Evan Williams, co-founder of Pyra Labs, calculated that during July 2002, 1.5 Blogger blogs were created per minute.[12] Williams hoped Blogger would "reach as many people as possible . . .

while I may be able to cover small costs by charging users, I think that would ultimately be severely limiting on Blogger's potential."[13]

Because it offered its products at low or no cost, Pyra struggled financially. It was able to create a few partnerships[14]–these kept the company functioning through the early 2000s, but it needed a partnership that would not alienate those who were already using Blogger.[15] Google, whose unofficial motto is, "Don't be evil." acquired Pyra Labs in February 2003. Evan Williams blogged after the acquisition, "It wasn't a case of needing to sell, we were doing well and getting better. It was actually a difficult decision . . . I was only convinced after brainstorming with our people and their people about why and how we could do much cooler things for our users and the [W]eb at an incredibly large scale by being part of Google."[16] This development helped to propel both blogging and the blogosphere to the masses.[17] Bloggers hoped the server issues that Pyra dealt with would be quickly resolved under Google's leadership, and that the service would move forward quickly with new features. This, however, did not happen with the swiftness expected by those already in the blogosphere;[18] Google did not release the first major update of Blogger until early May, 2004.[19]

Blogger has regularly released updates with new features since 2004, but nothing that other blog providers did not already offer. However, while Blogger was (and continues to be) free, these providers had associated fees or required download and self-supplied server space to run a blog. In May 2005, Google released Mobile Blogger, which allowed people to moblog, or blog via their cell phones. This, however, was not innovative, as Moblog, a site for uploaded photos from cell phones already existed, and Flickr, the online photo sharing service allowed for mobile photo uploading by this time.[20]

In late 2006, Google released a beta version of Blogger, called New Blogger; Blogger removed the "beta" in early 2007. The new version of Blogger addressed many issues with Blogger's software but it received mixed reviews. "The new version of Blogger embraces its place as the entry-level blogging software, staying incredibly user-friendly at all costs."[21] *InformationWeek* noted that none of Blogger's new features are innovative; Six Apart's platforms already contain all the newly released features.[22] According to Ziff Davis, "the improvements may not make Blogger the best weblog publishing software out there, but they do go far to re-establish the service as a contender."[23]

THE BLOGOSPHERE

As Blogger continues to release updated software, the blogosphere grows.[24] As of April 11, 2007, Technorati.com, the blog-tracking website, was tracking seventy-five million blogs.[25] David Sifry claims, "we're seeing about 120,000 new weblogs being created worldwide each day . . . about 1.4 blogs created every second of every day . . . 1.5 million posts per day . . . about 17 posts per second."[26] On April 11, 2007, Blogpulse (a newer blog search, statistics, and trends tracking site) identified 43.6 million blogs, indicated that 72,033 blogs were created in the prior twenty-four hours, and indexed 791,771 unique posts in the prior twenty-four hours.[27] While some of these new blogs are "splogs" or spam blogs,[28] Technorati reports much more vigilance to filtering and removing these blogs from its indexes, and applauds efforts by blog providers to address the spam blog problem.

According to a Pew Internet Study, almost two in three bloggers had not published to the web before beginning to blog.[29] Given these numbers, it makes sense that free, hosted, blog software programs that provide a platform for publishing without extensive technical knowledge are popular. While Blogger is a popular, free, blog provider, it is not the only free blogging tool available and not necessarily the best, depending on individual needs. A variety of blogging software is available online: open-source and proprietary, web-hosted and self-hosted, free and for-fee.

This chapter compares Blogger with two programs that most closely approximate Google's intent–to provide free, easy-to-use, hosted software to anyone who wants to start a blog.

BLOGGER, VOX, AND WordPress.com

The two hosted-blog providers chosen for comparison with Blogger are Vox, by Six Apart, Ltd., and WordPress.com, by Automattic, Inc.

Six Apart is well known for its blog software MovableType and TypePad. However, these programs are fee-based and directed at professional and business bloggers in addition to first-time bloggers. Although MovableType offers a personal license for one person and one blog, it must be self-hosted. TypePad is a hosted platform, but its most basic package costs $4.95 per month.[30] Vox is Six Apart's newest blog software release. Supported by ads, it is hosted and entirely free to users. Released in October 26, 2006, and still in beta,[31] Vox appears to be a response to Web 2.0 and other free, hosted blog publishing platforms like Blogger.

Automattic, Inc. runs WordPress.com, and includes members who have worked on WordPress 2.0–the free, open-source, highly customizable blog software which must be installed on a hard drive and be server-supported. WordPress.com grew out of the original WordPress creators' desire to offer a hosted platform for blogs. The hosted version of the open-source software, released in 2005, is another recent addition to blog software choices.

Free blog providers sometimes do not offer as many options as fee-based providers. In 2007, all blogs provide a basic "what you see is what you get" (WYSIWYG) interface, but from there, features among providers vary. Table 1 (in the Appendix) provides a brief overview of blog software features of Blogger, Vox, and WordPress.com; it addresses whether or not the reviewed programs provide each feature. Beyond basic features, there are differences between blog software providers in innovation, presentation, dynamism, and interactivity with Web 2.0 programs and other software programs. Table 2 (in the Appendix) looks at the reviewed blog software's Web 2.0 integration.

The next section highlights some of the differences amongst the features provided by these free, hosted, blog software providers.

SIGN-UP PROCESS

Blogger, Vox, and WordPress.com each have a relatively easy sign-up process. Google has transitioned Blogger from a separate accounts system to one tied to Google Accounts. If an account has already been set up, users log in to Blogger with their Google Accounts username and password (the same as for Gmail, Google Page Creator, Google Reader, etc.). Blogger creates a blog once a person accepts the terms of service (TOS) and chooses a blog name, address, and template. Vox asks for the name, blog address, email, date of birth, gender, country, postal code, TOS acceptance, and requires e-mail confirmation before it will create a blog. WordPress.com asks for a username, e-mail address, and TOS acceptance. The next screen shows the new blog's address, asks if the blog should be publicly searchable, and asks a user to select the language they will primarily use. The site sends an e-mail confirmation to the submitted address, which provides a username and password, and the blog is immediately available.

DASHBOARD

Each blog provider uses a kind of dashboard as a jumping off point into a user's blog management options. Vox calls this page "home," while Blogger and WordPress.com use the term "dashboard." In Blogger, the dashboard functions as a portal into the blog's management area. From the dashboard, users can click to manage their Account, Posts, Settings, or Layout. They can also create a new blog, read the Blogger Buzz blog, or view Blogger blogs of note. If a user has multiple blogs on Blogger, links into all of them will appear on the dashboard. Once in the blog management area, options–Posting, Settings, Template–display in tabs. Vox's design is not as simple to navigate as Blogger's, because most options hide in drop-down menus. In April 2007, Vox released a navigation bar to all blogs which lives above the drop-down menus list and provides one-click access to what Vox sees as important links: Compose, Messages, Invite a Friend, and Help. This bar also includes a color picker, which allows a user to change the background color of the banner behind the menus with the click of a button.

Both Blogger and WordPress.com provide tabbed blog management options but overall, WordPress.com provides the most selections from its dashboard. The dashboard tab shows links to get started with blogging, the blog's updates from the last week, and a "What's Hot" section that lists news, top blogs, and top posts from WordPress. com. WordPress.com's tabbed display sets it apart from Blogger and Vox. Because the dashboard is but one clickable tab, other tabs are Write, Manage, Comments, Blogroll, Presentation, Users, Options, and Upgrades. When clicked, these tabs display a sub-set of tabs that link to blog management features. WordPress.com's consistently visible, understandable tabs help to simplify blog management.

TEMPLATES

Templates allow a user to customize the look of a blog. The current trend is toward offering completely modifiable templates. With its template customization options and total external widget integration,[32] Blogger provides the most options for a highly individualized blog. Blogger allows a user to integrate any HTML or JavaScript widget into the blog's sidebar–the area to the left and/or right of a blog's posts. It provides pre-selected sidebar options, such as the Linklist, what Blogger calls a Blogrolla–list of links, often to other blogs. Blogger has the most visual and usable way of customizing a template, allowing users to drag and drop page elements–sidebar and layout items–anywhere inside the template design. It also allows the advanced user to work with CSS (Cascading Style Sheets) and HTML to customize the template further. Additionally, Blogger provides a complete color palette with which a user can control the color on all areas of the page, including the text, links, background, and headings. This function also uses drag and drop, making it more accessible. It would appeal to a blogger who does not have any HTML or CSS knowledge, but wants to create a unique looking template.

Vox's template options are quite limited, as there are only four layout options and few template colors from which to choose. Users can select their own banner image to go behind a blog; this is the most a user can do to change the look of the template. Vox's FAQ (frequently asked questions) states that it is working on more template options. Vox offers pre-selected sidebar options and does not allow any external widget integration.

WordPress.com's template choices are not expansive, but they have noted in the FAQ that they are working to develop more templates. Slightly different customizations are available depending on the template chosen, including sidebar widgets and customized banners. Word Press.com offers a fee-based CSS upgrade, if users want to make their template more customized. WordPress.com also offers pre-selected sidebar options. It does allow HTML widget code but not JavaScript integration–this limits how much a user can customize the blog.

POST EDITOR

Each blog provider has a WYSIWYG interface. In addition, Blogger and WordPress.com provide tabs to click into an HTML editor; Vox does not support this feature. For those bloggers who embed code in their posts, it is useful to have the HTML editor available. Blogger has a settings selection to show only the WYSIWYG interface, a good option for entry-level users. If a Vox blogger types in HTML, a box will pop up to ask if it should translate the code to a WYSIWYG view. Besides its WYSIWYG and HTML interfaces, WordPress.com has the only customizable post page layout; users can click and drag post page elements, such as the post timestamp editor and the categories and tags editor, in a hierarchal way to suit their needs. Because of this, WordPress.com offers the most flexible post editor options.

PRIVACY CONTROLS

Privacy controls have become more important to bloggers as more information is exposed online. Accordingly, "6.5 to 10 million blogs [already] exist behind firewalls or passwords," and these blogs are not searchable in the blogosphere.[33] In response to increasing privacy concerns, free blog providers now offer more access controls–each of the three reviewed providers allow a user to decide whether a blog is searchable via engines.

Blogger offers the fewest privacy controls of the three providers. Blogger allows a user to invite selected readers via email to a private blog, but these readers do not have to register with Blogger. Blogger does not offer per-post privacy–selecting who can see any individual post–but it allows a user to decide if comments will or will not be allowed on the post. In the settings, a user can customize the privacy settings Blogger offers to apply to all posts.

Vox offers the most privacy control of the reviewed blog software; however, it can be limiting. Vox users have the option to decide who sees what on their blog, from profile information to posts or comments. Only registered Vox users can comment on other Vox blogs, a feature Blogger and WordPress.com offer, but do not require. This is likely an attempt to build a community, but it is limiting for the writers and readers of these blogs. While outsiders may be able to read a blog entry, they cannot offer their commentary unless they become a member of the Vox community. Additionally, a user's selected readers list can only include Vox members. This requires people to join Vox to be a part of any blog there, alienating some potential users.

Vox and WordPress.com both provide privacy controls for individual posts; each time a user creates a new post, he or she can choose who (i.e., the general public, community members, blog members) can view it and comment on it. Additionally, WordPress.com offers the option of password protecting a post. WordPress.com allows a user to make a blog viewable only by WordPress.com's users (up to thirty-five people) and unlike Vox, anyone can come to WordPress.com and get a username and password for this purpose without having to sign-up for a blog.

TAGS

Tags are a way to catalog information on the Web, by labeling posts, images, or media with a word or series of words. Tags are searchable in many Web 2.0 sites, such as Flickr, the photo-sharing site, and Technorati, the blog-tracking site, but also within some blogging communities. For the first time, Technorati's April 2007 "State of the Live Web" included a section on the State of Tags. This data indicates that in February 2007, 35% of all posts tracked used tags.[34]

Blogger offers labels, not tags, for its posts. These labels provide a way to organize posts within individual Blogger blogs but do not function as tags do. If users want to add tags to a Blogger blog, they must use a third-party sidebar widget, like Technorati's Blog Top Tag widget.

Vox and WordPress.com offer a system of tags for each post. In Vox, users can tag posts, or their interests (e.g., music, photography, reading). Tags display on individual posts, and also within a "tag cloud," which displays tags as a group in a blog's sidebar. More frequently used tags display in a larger font, which helps readers identify a blogger's most-used tags.[35] Tags lend themselves to a feature unique to Vox, called Groups. Vox Groups are a way for users to interact with each other; they aggregate related individual blog posts into a group blog. WordPress.com has a function similar to Vox's groups, called "tag surfer." Searching for a tag using this feature will return a list of blog posts tagged with that word, in effect creating a group for that tag.

COMMENTS

Enabling comments can create a spam problem on blogs. Spammers send out automated comments with links leading to spam sites. All blog providers reviewed provide an option for disenabling comments on posts. To prevent spam, Blogger offers a word verification option, CAPTCHA.[36] This setting requires anyone who wants to leave a comment to look at a word on a screen that a computer cannot parse, and type it into a box before posting the comment, which prevents automated comments from posting to a blog. Blogger also allows a user to set comments to anyone, only registered Blogger users, or only blog members, in addition to the option of disenabling them altogether or by specific posts. Additionally, Blogger offers comment moderation, which sends new comments to a queue and allows a user to approve them before they appear on the blog.

Vox allows only registered users to post comments to its blogs automatically; but this can be further limited to a user's neighborhood, friends, and/or family. Alternately, users can moderate all comments before they publish to the blog, and can decide whether to allow comments on specific posts.

In addition to a per-post, allow comments option, WordPress.com has extensive options for preventing spam from reaching blogs. These include optional comment moderation and a comment blacklist, which allow users to enter into a box any word they do not want to show on their comments–comments containing these words are automatically marked as spam. WordPress.com integrates with Automattic's Akismet blog spam-catching software. This program automatically scans comments for spam and routes them to an Askimet spam area within the blog, which can be reviewed for incorrectly marked comments. Automattic provides this feature to WordPress.com blogs; it is free to download and use on personal blogs from other providers, with a WordPress.com API key. WordPress.com also has a unique feature called "My Comments," which keeps track of comments a user leaves on other WordPress.com blogs; this helps to keep track of what posts a user has commented on, and what comments followed theirs.

STATISTICS

Blogger does not have internally provided statistics but offers integration with Google Analytics or other third party statistics providers. Vox does not yet provide a blog counter or blog statistics, while WordPress.com offers an extensive blog statistics section, including statistics on total blog views, total posts, comments, tags, top posts by view, clicked links, referred links, and search engine terms (if the blog is searchable in engines). There are additional statistics for feeds. WordPress.com also makes public its entire site statistics. User growth at WordPress.com was up 78% between December 2006 and March 2007.[37]

WEB 2.0 INTEGRATION

It is arguable that blogs marked the beginnings of Web 2.0; to this end, some providers have integrated considerable Web 2.0 functionality into their software. Blogger supports no two-way functionality with Web 2.0 sites; it integrates externally via third-party providers, but provides no internal support.[38] In its Help pages, Blogger provides instructions for setting up an account at Flickr to post photos directly to its blogs. Internally, images are uploadable to Blogger and are stored via Picasa Web Albums (Google product). Blogger does not offer support for uploading audio or video files. In Help, Blogger does not provide information about embedding video into posts, so unless a user searches the forums, or already knows to go to an external site, find the embed code, and paste it into Blogger's HTML post editor, he or she might not realize this is an option.

Vox, the most recently released blog software, does the best job of working together with Web 2.0 applications. Seamless integration is actually part of the software's intent, "[to play] well with other software providers."[39] With Vox, users can easily incorporate their photos, audio files, video files, book covers, and collections–a folder-like grouping of thematically similar links, videos, audio, photos, books, posts, or comments–into each blog post. Vox allows users to upload media directly to the blog and store it there, though Vox imposes a monthly two-gigabyte upload limit and individual file size limits. Vox is able to interact directly with Flickr and Photobucket.[40] With a few clicks, users can give Vox permission to access these accounts through the Web and have seamless access to media housed at those sites. Vox collaborates with Amazon to provide a search for book and CD covers from within a Vox blog. Users can post these images, which have links to Amazon's content to their blog. Additionally, by clicking the video link from the post editor, a user can search and import videos directly from YouTube. Vox also has a very usable embed feature which allows a user to paste in and embed code for media–such as videos from Google Video or Revver–with the click of a button.

WordPress.com does not have two-way functionality with any Web 2.0 programs, but like Blogger, gives directions for posting images to WordPress.com via Flickr. However, WordPress.com goes a step further by also providing instructions in the post editor for embedding media. However, this requires a modicum of technical ability. Users cannot simply cut and paste external video links from YouTube, Google Video, or DailyMotion into the post editor; they have to create a bit of new code and enter it in. This might be too difficult or confusing for new bloggers, or bloggers with no web knowledge. WordPress.com also makes available directions within the post editor for integrating RockYou and Slide.com, web-based slideshow creators, and SplashCast, a web-based media channel creator. WordPress.com offers a small amount (fifty megabytes) of free space for uploading image files; users can pay for a space upgrade, which allows them to upload and store not only image files but also video and audio files.

Having access to instant messenger (IM) is an integral part of online interconnectedness. Blogger can support any instant messenger widget, including MeeboMe or Plugoo.[41] WordPress.com offers integration with the MeeboMe widget. Although it is Web 2.0 oriented, Vox is not yet able to support instant messaging. Vox can display instant messenger names for AOL, Yahoo, MSN, Skype, and Google Talk, but clicking these links will launch an attempt to open an IM application from the hard drive and if the application does not exist there, the link will not function. This is fixable simply by adding Meebo or Plugoo integration.

IMPORT/EXPORT FUNCTION

Importing and exporting options for posts make it easier to switch blog providers, or to host multiple blogs. Blogger does not have a feature for importing posts from other blogs, nor does it have an official export feature. However, a user can create a backup file of all posts, though this requires enough knowledge to be able to edit the template (in the code) and alter numerous settings. Vox is able to import posts from any blog that contains an Atom feed; it cannot export posts, but it does provide a cross-posting option with Six Apart blog software Live Journal and TypePad, to simultaneously post to users' other blogs. WordPress.com allows bloggers to import their posts from other blog providers, including Blogger, MovableType, TypePad, and other WordPress. com blogs. Wordpress.com also allows for export of blog posts. A user can create an xml file of all blog data to import to any other blog provider that supports it.

FEEDS

Feeds are a way to syndicate blogs using XML-based Really Simple Syndication (RSS 2.0) or Atom 1.0. A user clicks on an icon from within a blog, which sends the feed to a feed reader like Google Reader or Bloglines. These readers automatically check the blogs for updates and aggregate the content in one place. All three blog providers allow users to syndicate their blog. Blogger does not allow a user to specify the text that appears in a feed reader, but does give a short option, which shows the first paragraph or the first 255 characters of a post in a reader.

Vox has no feed reader display options. WordPress.com has a function within the post page called "optional excerpt," where a user can type in a short amount of text to show up in lieu of having the entire text of a post sent to feed readers.

ADVERTISEMENTS

Each blog software provider has a different system of ads that show on blogs. Blogger provides the most options for customizing advertising on a blog. A blogger can: choose an ad-free blog, apply for Google's AdSense program, which places ads relevant to content on a blog and pays the blog owner when someone clicks on an ad, or display paid advertising from third-party providers on their blog. Ads support Vox so that it remains free, it is not an option to remove these ads from a blog, and a user does not have control over placement of ads or ad content. Vox users are not able to integrate third-party advertisements. WordPress.com's very limited VIP blogs, which are fee-based, high-traffic blogs (500,000 page views per month) allow ad incorporation, but most WordPress.com blogs are free of advertisements, and users are not allowed to integrate third-party advertising programs like AdSense or Amazon Associates. However, WordPress.com has begun to place AdSense ads on limited numbers of blogs, which helps WordPress.com to stay free; users do not have control over these ads.

SUPPORT

Blogger has a somewhat limited Help section. Contacting Blogger Support from Help entails clicking one of a few radio buttons and submitting a query–from complaints on the help forums and blogs, it appears that Blogger employees do not always answer these queries.[42] The Blogger Help Group allows users to post questions and answers and Blogger employees do respond to some of these forum questions. However, basic questions and answers are not easily located within the site's documentation. Some outdated information still appears in Blogger Help, which may be because the Blogger team has been focusing on the rollout of the new Blogger. However, it would be very helpful to have more easily searchable documentation for their software.

Vox's help function is its searchable help pages and a knowledge base, which a user can browse, though both appear to include the same information. Alternately, users can search other Vox blogs for answers to software questions–perhaps there is a way to mine this data, or tag it, in order to help direct users to information on the software's capabilities and limitations. WordPress.com has an extensive FAQ and forum, to which users are always adding questions and answers. Additionally, WordPress.com provides human support via email for questions that are not answerable by browsing either the FAQ or forums.

ASSESSMENT

Blogger, Vox, and WordPress.com each have a unique set of strengths and weaknesses, and none of the three stands out as the clear choice among free blog software providers. Blogger seems most appealing to the blogger who is interested in customizations; its most attractive features are the ability to change the template completely to specifications, and to integrate any external widget from the web. The scope of Blogger appears to be different from that of WordPress.com or Vox. Without groups or tags, it does not provide the same sense of community these other blog providers do–Blogger searches with Google's Blog Search, hosts images with Picasa, and provides statistics though Analytics. It does not seek cross-functionality with products Google does not own; Google uses its other applications and programs to support Blogger and provide some of the functions that Vox and WordPress.com choose to provide as a part of a blogging community. If it is going to continue to integrate its various applications, Google might consider creating a Google Talk help desk for Blogger and other programs so that users who need help could communicate with a person; this could go a long way towards retaining users.

Vox is fresh, forward thinking, and future-oriented, and it would be most appealing to a media and web savvy user. With its focus on media and web application integration, Six Apart's Vox is clearly in tune with the social web and its possibilities. Because it is new and focused on innovation, it will likely evolve considerably over the next year. If Vox continues to do more work to improve basic options and open access to its blogs, the software will likely draw some displeased users away from less Web 2.0-friendly blog software.

WordPress.com is a good choice for the blogger who already has a small amount of technical knowledge. The open-source model that WordPress.com was born out of increases its appeal. WordPress will continue to grow and change as open-source software, and these improvements may eventually make their way to the hosted software. In addition to its usable layout, options like "tag surfer" and "my comments" set the software apart from Blogger and Vox, and make it an appealing free blog software choice.

GOOGLE, BLOGGER, AND THE FUTURE

As Web 2.0 continues to grow and develop, and the number of people starting blogs finally crests, blogs may begin an evolution into another web-based medium altogether. Technorati's user testing in the first quarter of 2007 indicates that Internet users are not differentiating as much between traditional online news sites (MSM or mainstream media) and blogs; "these are [all] sites for news, information, entertainment, gossip, etc."[43] Blogger could focus on making sweeping changes to address this potential future of the web, but it will likely choose not to do so. It remains comfortably steadfast in the blogosphere, consistently offering a solid product that is not the most innovative or flashy, but is free, simple, and accessible.

Blogger has not grown extensively since its acquisition by Google, often making features available after more forward-thinking blog providers release them. Nevertheless, it has name recognition, remains free, appeals to the masses, and is a simple entry-level blogging tool. Blogger fits into Google's mission[44] to organize the world's information and make it universally accessible and useful. Like Google's "Search," Blogger does one thing really well; it provides an interface for bloggers to blog. Google may simply want to offer a product that meets the needs of the blogger majority: to have a free place to write and publish online. Google sees the need to make information (and blogging) globally available, which trumps the desire to be trendy and cool. While Blogger may be lagging on developing Web 2.0 integrations, it continues to provide a solid publishing platform free-of-charge. By offering free software worldwide, which requires only an Internet-connected computer, Blogger is doing a service for many people all over the world who hope to have their voice heard.[45]

Simplicity may reign; regardless of Blogger's slow development and reluctance to embrace cross-functionality with Web 2.0 programs, it continues to be popular on the Internet and a media darling. In 2006, *Time* listed Blogger as one of the twenty-five sites it cannot live without,[46] touted because of its ease of use and its lack of cost.

In some ways, Blogger has lasting value because it remains very much the same. In the end, a blogging tool that is trendy and cool may not be what is most important, but consistency and longevity just may be.

NOTES

1. Morris states that there were fewer than fifty weblogs in 1999, but after much research on the Internet and in the Internet Archive, this number is a very low estimate; it does not account for the thousands of web diaries and on-line journals that functioned as precursors to the blog. Holly Morris, "Blogging Burgeons as Form of Web Expression," *U.S. News and World Report,* Jan 15 2001, <http://www.lexis-nexis.com/>.

2. Stone, *Who Let the Blogs Out?* 37.

3. Evan Williams, Pyra Labs co-founder, blogged about the release of Blogger on 8/23/1999, <http://evhead.com/1999/08/we-just-launched-cool-new-tool-at-pyra.asp>.

4. Doughtery, Dale. "Vortigo (Pyra's Blogger service for creating Weblog)," *Web Techniques* 5, no. 2 (2000): 88. <http://find.galegroup.com/itx/infomark.do?&contentSet= IAC-Documents&type=retrieve&tabID=T003&prodId=ITOF&docId=A59426029& source=gale&userGroupName=lom_oaklandu&version=1.0/>. See also: Bill Humphries' blog entry from 1999, <http://www.whump.com/more LikeThis/link/01312>, or Ben Williams's blog entry, <http://plasticboy.com/archives/1999/08/>.

5. Pyra employee Matt Haughey (Mathowie) posted on the Blogger main page newsblog that Blogger had over 60,000 users by 11/10/2000: <http://web.archive.org/ web/20001119075200/www.blogger.com>.

6. Pyra Lab's website from 3/3/2000 is viewable through the Internet Archive: <http://web.archive.org/web/20000302203930/www.pyra.com/blogger.asp>.

7. Evan Williams, Blogger blog post, 11/8/2000: <http://web.archive.org/web/ 20001119075200/www.blogger.com>.

8. Early list of Pyra Lab's Blogger products, <http://web.archive.org/web/ 20010124082200/www.blogger.com/products>.

9. There is a gap in the Internet Archive for the <http://pro.blogger.com> website; the earliest link that exists in the Internet Archive is 2/10/02. Prior to that, there is a link to the Blogger index page from 9/30/01. <http://web.archive.org/web/*/http://pro. blogger.com/>. The first available version of <http://pro.blogger.com> is <http:// web.archive.org/web/20020210153252/http://pro.blogger.com>.

10. Blogger Pro information, <http://web.archive.org/web/20020210153252/http://pro. blogger.com>.

11. Blogger.com Micro Ads, <http://web.archive.org/web/20021001115455/www. blogger.com/spons/micro_ads.pyra>.

12. Evan Williams, Blogger blog post, 8/6/2002, <http://web.archive.org/web/ 20020810071100/www.blogger.com>.

13. Stone, *Who Let the Blogs Out?* Interview with Evan Williams, 23.

14. Pyra received funding from Trellix, created a partnership with Brazil-based Globo, and received some income from the previously mentioned Blogger Pro and BlogSpot Plus; these deals helped to keep Pyra Labs afloat, financially. Stone, *Who Let the Blogs Out?* 24-25.

15. Stone, *Who Let the Blogs Out?* 26.

16. Evan Williams, "Bloogleplications," Evhead blog, <http://web.archive.org/web/20030401103450/www.evhead.com/archives/2003_02_01_archive_default.asp #104545291840524070>.

17. Perhaps not entirely coincidentally, *The Oxford English Dictionary* added entries for "blog," "blogging," and "blogger," in March 2003. According to one entry, "blog" derives from "weblog" (origin 1997–Jorn Barger) and the term dates back to Peter Merholz's 5/28/99 blog post, <http://web.archive.org/web/20001031113210/peterme.com/browsed/browsed0599.html>.

18. Ziff Davis, "Blogger," *PC Magazine Online*, January 10, 2007, <http://find.galegroup.com/itx/infomark.do?&contentSet=IAC-Documents&type=retrieve&tabID=T003&prodId=ITOF&docId=A157253388&source=gale&userGroupName=lom_oaklandu&version=1.0>.

19. Catherine Moore. "Google Unveils New Version of Blogger," *InfoWorld.com*, May 10, 2004, <http://find.galegroup.com/itx/infomark.do?&contentSet=IAC-Documents&type=retrieve&tabID=T003&prodId=ITOF&docId=A116430645&source=gale&userGroupName=lom_oaklandu&version=1.0>.

20. "Google Introduces Mobile Blogging," *PC Magazine Online*, May 6, 2005, <http://find.galegroup.com/itx/infomark.do?&contentSet=IAC-Documents&type=retrieve&tabID=T003&prodId=ITOF&docId=A133019157&source=gale&userGroupName=lom_oaklandu&version=1.0>.

21. Ziff Davis, "Blogger."

22. "Google Takes Blogger out of Beta," *InformationWeek*, December 21, 2006, <http://find.galegroup.com/itx/infomark.do?&contentSet=IAC-Documents&type=retrieve&tabID=T003&prodId=ITOF&docId=A156236565&source=gale&userGroupName=lom_oaklandu&version=1.0>.

23. Ziff Davis, "Blogger."

24. Brad Graham coined the term blogosphere in 1999, <http://www.bradlands.com/weblog/1999-09.shtml#September%2010,%201999>.

25. Technorati's current blog tracking numbers, <http://www.technorati.com/about/>.

26. David Sifry, "The State of the Live Web, April 2007," Sifry's Alerts, <http://www.sifry.com/alerts/archives/000493.html>.

27. BlogPulse statistics updated daily, <http://www.blogpulse.com/index.html>.

28. Blogger Help, "About Spam Blogs", Spam blogs or "splogs" "can be recognized by their irrelevant, repetitive, or nonsensical text, along with a large number of links, usually all pointing to a single site." <http://help.blogger.com/bin/answer.py?answer=42577>. Sifry's "State of the Live Web, 2007" notes there are between 3,000 and 7,000 new spam blogs created each day.

29. Amanda Lenhart, and Susannah Fox, "Bloggers: A Portrait of the Internet's New Storytellers."

30. For more information on SixApart's blog software and pricing, <http://www.sixapart.com>.

31. Vox terms of service, <http://www.sixapart.com/vox/us/tos/>.

32. A sidebar widget is a bit of HTML, JavaScript, or flash code that a user inserts into a box in the sidebar. Widgets increase the functionality of a blog. The *Oxford English Dictionary* added a draft addition, March 2004, for widget: A visual symbol on a computer screen; a graphical device in a graphical user interface; the software and data involved when the operations represented by such a device are invoked, esp. regarded as jointly constituting a tool.

33. Anne Eisenberg, "So, Who Says that a Blog has to Blare?," *New York Times,* February 18, 2007, <http://www.nytimes.com>.

34. David Sifry, "State of the Live Web, April 2007."

35. "Introduction to the Published Blog" Vox Help, <http://help.vox.com>.

36. CAPTCHA (Completely Automated Public Turing Test to Tell Computers and Humans Apart) Project, <http://www.captcha.net>.

37. WordPress Blog, "March Wrap-up," April 4, 2007, <http://wordpress.com/blog/2007/04/05/march-wrap-up/>.

38. Blogger's help page for Third-Party Applications, <http://help.blogger.com/bin/answer.py?answer=42347&query=third-party&topic=&type=f>.

39. "What is Vox?" FAQ answer, <http://www.vox.com>.

40. Flickr, <http://www.flickr.com>, and Photobucket, <http://photobucket.com>, are photo and media storage websites. Each site offers a limited amount of storage free, and paid upgrades for more storage.

41. Meebo, <http://www.meebo.com>, is a web-based instant messenger aggregator, and supports all major IM platforms, AOL, Yahoo, MSN, ICQ, Google Talk, and Jabber. Plugoo, <http://www.plugoo.com>, is a flash-based plug-in widget, which allows a user to place an IM window on their website.

42. A blogger called Chuck posts insightfully about Blogger's silence at <http://bloggerstatusforreal.blogspot.com/>.

43. David Sifry, "State of the Live Web, April 2007."

44. Google Company Overview, <http://www.google.com/corporate>.

45. Statistically, the top five blog posts by language are Japanese, English, Chinese, Italian and Spanish. David Sifry, "State of the Live Web, April 2007."

46. Maryanne Murray Buechner, "25 Sites We Can't Live Without," *Time,* August 3, 2006, <http://www.time.com/time/business/article/0,8599,1222769,00.html>.

REFERENCES

Battelle, John. *The Search: How Google and its Rivals Rewrote the Rules of Business and Transformed our Culture.* New York: Portfolio, 2005.

Castro, Elizabeth. *Publishing a Blog with Blogger.* Visual Quickproject Guide. Berkeley, CA: Peachpit Press, 2005.

Jenkins, Henry. *Fans, Bloggers, and Gamers: Exploring Participatory Culture.* New York: New York University Press, 2006.

Kline, David, Daniel Burstein, Arne J. De Keijzer, & Paul Berger. *Blog!: How the Newest Media Revolution is Changing Politics, Business, and Culture.* New York: CDS Books, 2006.

Lee, Wei Meng. *The Rational Guide to Google Blogger.* Rollinsfold, NH: Rational Press, 2006.

Lenhart, Amanda, & Fox, Susannah. "Bloggers: A Portrait of the Internet's New Storytellers." *Pew / Internet* (July 19, 2006), Pew Internet & American Life Project, <http://www.pewinternet.org/>.

Rolls, Albert. *New Media.* The Reference Shelf, v. 78, no. 2. Bronx, NY: H.W. Wilson, 2006.

Sifry, David. "State of the Blogosphere" and "State of the Live Web" reports. <http://www.sifry.com/stateoftheliveweb/>, October 2004–current.

Stone, Biz. *Who Let the Blogs Out?: A Hyperconnected Peek at the World of Weblogs.* New York: St. Martin's Griffin, 2004.

Vise, David A., & Mark Malseed. *The Google Story.* New York: Delacorte Press, 2005.

APPENDIX

TABLE 1. Features

	Blogger	Vox	WordPress.com
Labels/tags	Labels	Tags	Tags
Media uploads	Images	Images, video, audio	Images
Preview posts	Yes	No	Yes
Privacy options	Yes	Yes	Yes
Wysiwyg editor	Yes	Yes	Yes
HTML editor	Yes	No	Yes
Template customization	Extensive	Minimal	Some
Trackbacks/ backlinks	Backlinks	No	Trackbacks
Comments	Yes	Yes	Yes
Blog statistics	Third-party	No	Yes
Support/ documentation	Yes	Yes	Yes
Ads on blogs	If relevant	Yes	No
Upload Limits (free)	via Picasa	2G per month	50MB total
Advertising that pays the blogger	Yes, AdSense and third-party	No	No
Blogroll/Linklist	Yes	Five links	Yes
Multiple authors	Yes	No	Yes
Redirect blog to different url	Yes	No	Yes
Host blog on external server	Yes	No	No

APPENDIX (continued)

TABLE 2. Web 2.0 Integration

	Blogger	Vox	WordPress.com
Photoblogging	Yes	Yes	Yes
Videoblogging	Yes	Yes	Yes
Audioblogging	Third-party	Upload audio	Upload audio with upgrade
Music player	Yes, widgets	No	Yes, widgets
Moblogging	Yes	Yes	Yes
Blog from email	Yes	Yes	No
Instant messaging	Meebo widget Plugoo widget	No	Meebo widget
Private messaging	No	Yes (with other Vox users)	No
RSS/Atom Feeds	Yes	Yes	Yes
Widget integration	Extensive	No	Limited
Import blog posts from other blogs	No	Yes	Yes
Export blog posts	XML back-up	No	Yes
Cross-blogging	No	Yes, with Six Apart blogs	No

Blogger, WordPress.com, and Their Pseudoblog Alternatives: A Comparison of Focus, Features, and Feel

Robert J. Lackie
John W. LeMasney

INTRODUCTION: FOCUS AND INTENT

In many, many Web sites, articles, postings, and workshops, Web 2.0 and its impact on collaborative library communication is being explored and discussed. Classic examples of the Web 2.0 phenomenon are blogs and RSS (they are so integrated now it is hard to separate them–and don't worry if the technical language is unfamiliar as a glossary of terms is supplied after this introduction). Yet, it seems that many library administrators, librarians, and other library staff members are still not sure how best to get started with this social, participatory Web. Certainly, there is a lot of interest and excitement–not to mention concern–about blogs (or Web logs, which are chronological publishing of thought and comments on the Web), but as mentioned in *MultiMedia & Internet@ Schools* magazine's Web 2.0 article (Lackie, 2006, 12), in libraries, we "need to look at [blogs and other Web 2.0 applications] as a new opportunity, a possible way to better communicate, interact, share, create, and publish information online–to connect with those we are already serving and to those we wish to serve in the near future."

Many in the library field are reading about this exciting new attitude and the new or improved tools and techniques that are constantly emerging. The software platforms for blogs have certainly improved over the past year, and many people are now using blogs, with blog search engine Technorati placing the "number of active blogs at around 56 million this past October [2006]. By January 2007 that number had grown to 63.2 million, with 175,000 new blogs begun each day" (Dalton, 2007, 17). Now in April 2007, "Technorati is now tracking over 70 million Weblogs . . . [with] about 120,000 new Weblogs being created worldwide each day. That's about 1.4 blogs created every second of every day" (Sifry, 2007).

Blogs seem to be replacing "mailing lists, which tend to clog inboxes, handicapping productive use of e-mail. Moving low-priority messages to a blog with an RSS feed–and encouraging use of feed readers–can increase productivity inexpensively" (Windley, 2007, 26).

Yes, there is a lot of hype–some good, some not–surrounding blogging, but fortunately, for all of us, librarians and administrators everywhere are now responsibly using blogs in practical and worthwhile ways. For example, a library might want to have a blog of audio clips of poetry for an upcoming featured festival or invited speaker. A university might want to have a voice-of-the-students blog to give a more natural accompaniment to the student newspaper. A director or dean of libraries might want to create a blog, especially when traditional face-to-face interaction with library employees is not viable or frequent enough. Blogging can allow for more personal, informal interaction and dialogue between administrators and library users where he or she can share thoughts about the current and future plans or ideas the library is considering, and to welcome comments and ideas. By the way, if you want to review and explore many different types of library blogs before jumping into the mix, take a look at the Blogging Libraries Wiki, created by Amanda Etches-Johnson, Reference and User Experience Librarian (and now a 2007 *Library Journal* Mover & Shaker) at McMaster University. Her wiki includes academic, public, school, and special libraries' blogs, as well as blog examples for internal library communication, library associations, library directors, and more (see LISWiki on her wiki).

Still a bit apprehensive or unclear about where or how to get started blogging? That's OK. Stephen Abram, SirsiDynix Vice President of Innovation and President-Elect of the Special Libraries Association, encourages us in "library land" to not worry if all of "this seems like common knowledge" to some because there are more "folks heading up these learning curves every day. Those who've trod the path before need to share the tricks and tips" (2006).

There has been a lot of dialogue recently about implementing blogs within libraries, and Google has certainly made blogging ubiquitous with Blogger, its freely available and very popular blogging tool. Blogger is good, but it might not be right for you, and other free and practical blogging solutions do exist for librarians and staff. It helps to understand that "the core things that make a blog a blog [and not just an interactive Web site] are how it interacts with other blogs and how it promotes itself to search engines, blog aggregators and other sites" (Rapoza, 2006). You realize this to be true, and after reviewing several library blogs, you are now planning to start one for yourself and/or your library. Maybe you are thinking of just creating an internal blog for librarian and staff communication or possibly team-blogging with librarians or administrators from other libraries around your state in order to foster communication and complement professional expertise, as Library Garden does within New Jersey.

This article will compare blogging solutions for the average library administrator, librarian, or library staff member. The solutions that this article concentrates on are free, hosted solutions, meaning that no money is given for either the software, the hosting, or the domain. The choices for blogging solutions that are no-cost, freely-hosted, relatively popular, of good quality, and usable by most end users results in a very short list: WordPress and Blogger are two solutions that meet these requirements very well. While there are others discussed in this article, including Windows Live Spaces, Bloglines, Flickr, and Yahoo! 360°, we believe that WordPress and Blogger are the best solutions within these constraints that focus squarely on blogging, while the others often go off into technology or media tangents, resulting in what will be referred to here as pseudoblogs or blogalikes. Blogger is only available as an online service, rather than as a stand alone, locally-installed application. WordPress is an open source blogging engine that can be installed locally or used online. Again, in the interest of comparing solutions that are alike, only the remote service, freely-hosted offerings will be compared here.

BLOG FEATURES GLOSSARY

What might be most useful is to start with a glossary of terms, so that some context is given when a feature or group of features is talked about in the discussion of the characteristics or attributes of a given blogging engine, as well as in this article's accompanying appendices (Appendix A. Comparison Matrix on the Functions/Awareness of Blogger, WordPress.com, Bloglines, Google Reader, and Tumblr; Appendix B. Comparison Matrix on the Functions/Awareness of Twitter, Flickr, Picasa Web Albums, del.icio.us, Digg, and Technorati; and Appendix C. Comparison Matrix on the Functions/Awareness of popurls, YouTube, IFILM, Yahoo! 360°, and Windows Live Spaces). This Blog Features Glossary is broken down into the following eight sets of features: Audience Centric, Portability, Administration Centric, Content Creation, Extra-Site Relations, Comment Management, Design, and Media Management. This collection of terms is not comprehensive by any means, but it gives one a conversational understanding of the most common, useful, or popular features that are available in free, hosted blogging engines today.

Audience Centric Features allow the audience to participate in various ways:

- **RSS and Atom Feeds**: These are methods for getting information from a blog, Web site, or online service without actually visiting it. RSS is an acronym that has come to mean Really Simple Syndication, after some lengthy debate, with Rich Site Summary being another contender for the name. Atom is simply an agreed upon name for a standard that was built as a competitor to RSS. Arguably the most useful feature to be born of the blogosphere, these eXtensible-Markup-Language (XML)-based files contain abbreviated, up-to-the-second information filtered from the latest content on a blog. While these feeds can be constructed by hand due to the human readable and open format, scripts most often create these feeds automatically whenever a change occurs in the content on a blog, such as a new post being created or a comment being left. Most often, the RSS feeds of various blogs that one is interested in are subscribed to (for free) using an RSS or Atom Feed Aggregator or Feed Reader, so that the aggregate information from all of the subscribed feeds can be seen as headlines or teaser articles, at a glance, free of distractions like color, ads, or layout.

- **syndication and aggregation**: The ability for the blog to produce (syndicate) and/or collect and display (aggregate) RSS or Atom feeds using the blog itself.
- **podcasting**: A special ability of RSS Version 2.0 to encapsulate files as part of a feed retrieval, so that in addition to textual content, one can receive audio, video, or other content in a podcast-capable aggregator, such as Songbird, Democracy Player, iPodder, Juice, iTunes, or Mozilla Thunderbird.
- **tagging**: The ability for a content author/reader to label a post or other content with a representative word or phrase. This might be a topic, category, subject, or group where the content can be seen in a focused context when a viewer subsequently chooses the tag. This allows for a personalized index of the content on a site or sites, and it is meant to aid in navigating a long history of posts in a diverse blog. This sort of functionality is generally also referred to as folksonomy (a play on the word "taxonomy"), referring to informal socially generated classification (Vander Wal, 2005).
- **search**: This is the ability to find content in a blog by searching for a word, a phrase, or keywords.

Portability Features are those that allow the owner to move content from one platform, engine, or database to another:

- **license**: The contract under which the blogging engine is distributed. The license dictates to what extent you can modify the underlying code in a local installation. In the case of WordPress, the code is freely available under the GNU General Public License (GNU, 2007), which means that it can be modified freely by anyone who agrees to the license, given that their modifications to the code become available to be further modified. The hosted version of WordPress (WordPress.com) does not allow the same level of modification as a locally-installed version, despite the same license. Blogger is used under a proprietary license, meaning the blog doesn't cost anything to use, but the source is not made freely available for local installations. GNU is a recursive acronym, a geeky joke, which means GNU's Not Unix.

- **standards**: The level to which an engine adheres to agreed-upon rules and methods like XML, RSS, PHP, and other protocols, as opposed to proprietary, custom-built protocols which might make it harder to migrate content.
- **proprietary**: Indicates that the company has decided to keep the code, protocols, Application Program Interfaces (APIs), or other information about the workings of its product a secret in order to prevent unintended use. This is the antithesis of the open source model.
- **import/export**: The ability for the content to be extracted and saved to a commonly usable, non-proprietary format, such as ASCII text, like an XML or CSV file, or even just a simple continuous text file.

Administration Centric Features are those that allow blog administrators to do their job better:

- **multiple authors**: The ability for a blog to allow multiple authors to work separately on the same blog and collaborate on posts, as well as how the blog handles identification of multiple authors.
- **user management**: How authors, contributors, editors, and other users are managed in terms of password, abilities, and other information. Also, the ability to temporarily disable or otherwise change a user's status.
- **post moderation and workflow**: The ability for post editing and approval. In the case of a blog with many authors, it's important to have an approval process for continuity, style, and other filters.
- **e-mail notification**: The ability to send out e-mails to notify authors of replies, notify administrators of trouble, notify readers of updates, and other uses.
- **dashboard**: The control center for the blog, where administrators and authors can get to all of the functions in one place.

Content Creation Features are those that allow blog authors to create posts and other content:

- **e-mail entries**: The ability to create new posts and complete other tasks via an e-mail.
- **draft status**: The ability to work on a post over time without making it public.
- **timestamping**: The ability to change the time at which a story appears to have been created. This includes bringing back a story from last week as today's story, as well as having an already written story appear some time in the future.
- **bookmarklets**: These are lines of JavaScript saved as bookmarks in a browser that allow you to do common tasks with a blog, such as adding a site to your blogroll or posting a story about the page you just visited in your browser.
- **media management**: The ability to integrate rich media formats like photos, video, and audio.
- **uploading and support**: The ability to copy local files, such as photos, to the server where the blog is hosted. Often there are restrictions on format and data size to protect the blog from being compromised.

Extra-Site Relations Features are those that allow one blog to be a hub to other blogs, services, and sites:

- **trackback pings**: Pings are "shout outs" to sites you mention in your posts. Many blogs always listen for pings and will let you know who is talking about your blog. A good blog will automatically scan your newly created posts for URLs. If a URL is found, it will attempt to let that URL know that your blog is linking to it. This automatic process sometimes results in new relationships between content providers.
- **links**: The abilities of a blog to recognize and turn URLs into links in posts, or to allow quick and easy updating of links in a sidebar or elsewhere.
- **microformats**: XML-based standard presentations of information, such as hCard to represent contact information, hCalendar to represent calendar events, and XFN to represent relationships. These are used by search engines and other services to

find pertinent supplemental information about the content on your blog.
- **blogrolls**: The ability to show links to other blogs, possibly with other information updated via RSS feeds from those sites.

Comment Management Features are those that allow for audience feedback and interaction, and that deal with the unique problems those abilities create:

- **comments**: The ability for viewers to give feedback on a post, as well as how that ability is defined.
- **per-post comment availability**: The ability to turn comments on or off per post.
- **spam**: The posting of unsolicited, unrelated comments that only serve to advertise for the commenter. These can often appear as legitimate posts with friendly text asking viewers to click on a link to a completely unrelated site to make the site owner money.
- **moderation**: The automatic ability of the blog to take steps to hold or delete illegitimate comments based on their content.
- **threaded discussion**: The ability for the comments to be made as replies to other comments and shown as such (threaded).

Design Features are those that deal with the color, look, feel, and layout of a blog:

- **templates and themes**: The ability to change the color, look, and feel of your blog with pre-designed or original designs.
- **layout**: The ability for you to place reusable blocks of content in different areas on your blog page, change the position of page elements like headers, columns, and pictures, and generally edit the graphic design of your blog.
- **CSS**: Cascading Style Sheets are text files that contain instructions for the browser on how to render the page. CSS is completely open and human readable, much like HTML. The most versatile blogging engines use CSS for templates and theming.
- **plugins**: This is the ability to install optional functions in modular chunks. One might add a plugin to show pictures from Flickr, or to show an RSS feed of the latest movie showings in their area.

BLOGGER AND WORDPRESS.COM:
COMPARISON OF FOCUS, FEATURES, AND FEEL

In this section, Blogger and WordPress will be examined against the criteria laid out in the glossary section. Specifically, each of their reader, portability, administrative, creation, site relation, comment management, design, and media related features will be looked at in turn. Where similarities or differences are key, those will be noted. For a comprehensive, simplified comparison of the focus, features, and feel of Blogger and WordPress.com, see Appendix A. Again, in the interest of comparing solutions that are alike, only the remote service, freely-hosted offerings will be compared here.

While both of the freely-hosted versions of these blogs are up to the task of basic blogging, for a more adventurous librarian or technician who is able to install a Web server like Apache, a database engine like MySQL, and an interpreter like PHP, there are loads of other locally hosted, free, extensible solutions that are far more dynamic in ability than anything that is discussed here. For instance, if you want the ability to install from a list of thousands of plugins, need control over the look and feel of your blog to the finest detail, or crave the ability to do anything outside of what is allowed by the hosted solutions, you should look at WordPress.org, the open source blogging engine that is the basis for WordPress.com. However, many of these require much more in the way of technical knowledge, administration, responsibility and maintenance, or a host that supports these components for you–not to mention, usually, money.

So, again, our choices for true blogging solutions that are no-cost, freely-hosted, relatively popular, of good quality, and usable by most end users are Blogger and WordPress.com. Let's begin by looking at the focus, features, and feel (presentation, "themeability," or layout) of Blogger.

Blogger

Blogger offers viewers Atom feeds, which are updated every time a post is created by an author on the blog. At this point in syndication technology, any current aggregator-reader that can handle RSS is likely to have no problem with Atom. You can choose how much information is sent out in the feed–the entire post, part of each post, or none. In advanced settings, you can choose to create a feed of comments for the entire blog, as well as per post. You can also change the level of content that is sent in each of these feeds. Blogger also offers the ability to add a "feed" page element to the sidebar, which will "Add content from a site feed to your blog" (Blogger, 2007).

Blogger does not support media embedding, podcasting, or other methods of audio or video distribution out of the box. You can make a link to a piece of media that exists on another site, you can embed a video from a Web site that supports embedding (i.e., Google's YouTube), and your site viewer can use some third party tools (i.e., some key Greasemonkey scripts) that allow the playing of linked audio feeds from other sites, but there is no easy way to upload and distribute media just using Blogger without other services being involved. Tagging is now supported in Blogger, but as in other Google products (i.e., Gmail) the idea of folksonomy is represented with the word "labels" instead of "tags." Google being Google, you know that the search features are well integrated, thorough, and useful. At the top of every Blogger page, a search box sits, waiting for searches on the contents of each blog.

Blogger's portability is limited, to say the least. While Google is friendly to the open source movement, as evidenced by its Summer of Code projects, Blogger is licensed under a proprietary license, and so although there is no cost associated with using the blog, you are not free to reverse engineer, re-use, or otherwise touch the source code for Blogger. If you want a major change in the engine or system, you should apply for a job at Google now, as employment in its internal Blogger development group is likely the only way that you can get some assurance that you will have the chance to alter the code. Blogger is good about adhering to lots of standards, such as Atom, but users of Blogger do not have the ability to simply press a button and export a blog's posts from either the entire blog (or posts from a single year, month, week, etc.) to a comma separated values file or any other simple text or XML based file format, except for Atom. This would be very helpful in performing other tasks with that information, such as researching past blog posts for the number of times a certain word appears.

There are some methods for a full "dump" of your Blogger blog, but it involves reformatting your blog template, which may keep many from even attempting it. If you are interested in learning how to back up an entire Blogger blog, detailed instructions exist (Blogger Help: How to 2007). This lack of a simple export limits portability in a finite way, and it is designed to keep you and your blog content from leaving Blogger for greener pastures in a different system. Unfortunately, Blogger is often a gateway blogging system, and when the time comes to move to a more sophisticated system, the move is that much more difficult, by Google's design. Even if you are simply moving from one Blogger blog to another Blogger blog, there is no way to merge filtered or unfiltered content of the old blog into the new blog easily. One workaround would simply be to rename and re-brand the original Blogger blog, but if you have a blog that is cluttered with lots of extraneous content, comments, sidebar elements, and other items you would rather leave behind, while gathering all of the former blog's posts in a fresh new blog, you're likely to have trouble.

If you want to move to another blog system, there is some hope with WordPress, discussed later in this article, as it has a simple way to import Blogger content, as long as the Blogger blog has been updated to the latest version. If you think you might change your mind about where your blog content is housed, know that Blogger may make it difficult for you to move, since it is in its best interest to keep you from moving. However, it is not in your best interest to be forced to stay or else to lose all of the content you created. Without content, a blog is nothing. Blogger also does not have an import function for migrating the content of another blogging system, which causes a different kind of headache (Google Groups: Blogger Help Group, 2007).

Blogger's administrative features are possibly the best part of the system. The original creator of a blog is the default administrator for the blog. The default administrator can add additional "members of the blog"–co-authors and co-administrators. Members must be free Google account holders, and they must sign in using their Google account. Viewers can be anonymous, or administrators can deny all but selected users or blog authors. This is very useful for an internal administrative, classroom, or library blog where the outside world need not enter. Comments can be turned on or off, and administrators can allow commenters to be anonymous or require them to sign in.

Blogger very nicely addresses the issue of "splogging," or spam blogging, in which automated software is used to bombard blogs with ads, via the ability to require CAPTCHA entry for comments. Wikipedia tells us "A CAPTCHA (an acronym for "completely automated public Turing test to tell computers and humans apart") is a type of challenge-response test used in computing to determine whether or not the user is human. The term was coined in 2000 by Luis von Ahn, Manuel Blum, and Nicholas J. Hopper of Carnegie Mellon University, and John Langford of IBM" (CAPTCHA, 2007). This can be a nuisance for a casual commenter to interpret, but the reason for it is to prevent automated spambots (software designed for the singular purpose of advertising for free on your blog at the expense of the focus of your content) from submitting ads for weight loss plans on your library administration blog! If the spambot can't pass the CAPTCHA test, it can't post on your blog, and since it often takes the interpretive and cognitive abilities of a human to interpret the twisted and pattern overlaid phrases in the CAPTCHA test, they are fairly effective at weeding out the spambots.

Posts and comments can be moderated quite easily, and you can require notification by e-mail of any activity, post, comment. You can also require approval of each and every comment, which can alienate an audience that expects immediate publishing of commentary as on social sites such as Digg and YouTube, but this can protect against embarrassing moments for a more structured blog used for best practices, student highlights, or library programs, where social networking's commonly expected "this topic is lame" comment might not be welcome, but screened comments would be.

Blogger's dashboard is clean, streamlined, and easy to navigate. The help database at <http://help.blogger.com> is extensive, clearly written, and answers most questions definitively. It was especially useful for writing this article. When you are looking to find whether or not you can do something, for instance, the answer is usually very clearly stated as yes or no with a well written why or why not, and part of the reason is the controlled format in which the help is written, and the fact that Blogger is the author of the help. WordPress takes a different, but equally effective approach, which will be discussed below.

Blogger's creation features are fairly complete. You can easily set up the ability to mail blog posts by typing in a "secret" word that becomes an e-mail address to which any e-mail becomes a post on your blog. You have the ability to work on a post, and save it to draft so that you can continue to work on it later without having to show your work-in-progress to the world. You can edit the post timestamp to have it appear to have been created at a different time than it was actually created, but there is no way to have the post appear automatically at a given time in the future. This feature would be useful for teams publishing a weekly newsletter. As the feature exists now, you could use this to make a post "sticky." A sticky post will stay at the top of your blog until your timestamp set time arrives, while other new posts without special timestamp settings appear below it in a regular chronological order.

Interestingly, there are also many ways that one can publish to a Blogger blog without actually going to <http://www.blogger.com> and logging in. For instance, there have been plugins built to allow you to use Microsoft Word to publish to Blogger; however, this particular plugin only works with older versions of Blogger while Blogger was in beta (Blogger Help: About Blogger for Word, 2007). There are many stand-alone blogging clients, such as BlogJet, Deepest Sender, and w.bloggar, that allow you to post content to Blogger and other blogs from your desktop or browser itself. There are stand-alone Google products such as Picasa, a desktop-based photo-cataloging client, which allow one-click publishing to Blogger.

Perhaps the easiest way to post is using a bookmarklet. As stated in the glossary, bookmarklets are simple lines of JavaScript code that you can execute by clicking on them in your browser's bookmarks. Blogger has a bookmarklet called "BlogThis!" that you can use to post. Install the bookmarklet by dragging it to your browser's bookmark bar from the Blogger Web site. Then, when you're at a site you'd like to share with others in your blog, click on the "BlogThis!" button and a window pops up allowing you to post information to your blog. If you highlight text on the page you're visiting before you click on the bookmarklet, that text will become part of your post. If you are using your blog for research, sharing, or best practices, the "BlogThis!" bookmarklet can be a very quick way of adding content to your blog.

Blogger's site relation tools have improved dramatically in their latest release. Once you have updated your blog by creating a post, it will automatically ping (notify) <http://www.weblogs.com> to let them know this. Blogger, unlike WordPress, will not ping any blogs whose URLs appear in your post; this can be useful, but it takes more effort on the part of the blogging engine. You can, however, show trackbacks (Google calls these "Backlinks") to show who is talking about your posts on other blogs, which one might regard as a sort of extended comment. These trackbacks provide incoming links for both the original poster and the referring poster, advertise both sites to the viewers on either site, and generally speaking, increase the awareness, social activity, and usefulness of both blogs. This feature relies on the backlinking blog to be indexed in Google's Blog Search, which is a given for referring Blogger blogs, and many other blogs, but not necessarily everyone's blog. Blogger does give you the ability to add links to others' sites, blogs, and resources by way of a simple template plugin block called Links, but Blogger's links do not make use of any microformatting, though, such as XFN (discussed later in the WordPress section); however, you could build your own using the freeform XHTML template plugin block.

Blogger's comment management tools are fairly standard. If you turn on the CAPTCHA test, spam reduces dramatically, since most spammers rely on automated spambots to generate spam. Without the CAPTCHA enabled, you can opt for other restrictions, such as the requirement for a

Blogger account login, though this alone is fairly easy for spambots to get past. There is also the issue of comment graffiti, where anonymous commenters use the comments area in an unsociable way, such as berating other commenters, leaving comments that exist only to start fights about a topic, or just being rude. You can require the approval of each individual comment to counter this, but on a busy blog, this may become difficult to manage. Also, a commenter likes to leave a mark right away, and comment approval slows down that process. Discussions on Blogger are facilitated via the comments function. It might be called a flat discussion method, meaning that it is always the commenter responding to the post, rather than a threaded discussion, with commenters responding directly to each other. There are popular conventions to allow for comment-based discussions, such as preceding the commenter's name with an "at" sign (@), to indicate that the following statement is directed at the commenter, rather than, or in addition to, the post itself. This convention would be unnecessary with a threaded discussion. E-mail notification can be turned on for all comments, whether or not they need to be approved.

Blogger's design features should be enough for most average bloggers, but a style-minded author may find the defaults limiting. There are sixteen basic themes, some of which have up to four variations. These themes can further be modified using the template feature, where you can edit the Cascading Style Sheet (CSS) that defines the look and feel of each theme. CSS is a standardized scripting language that defines the look of a page and is most often paired with XHTML. Since users may not want to learn CSS just for the purposes of changing the look and feel of Blogger, the number of themes present may be important to those who don't already know how to edit CSS. In addition to the ability to edit the template, there is the ability to add functionality through template plugins, which Google calls "Page Elements," such as the inclusion of another site's RSS feed, a small block of XHTML to allow for third party functionality, a list of links or items, or a picture.

Blogger's media features are great in some areas and lacking in others. Specifically, if you want to use Blogger to show photos, or embed video from sites that publish embed snippets, like Google's own YouTube, it's quite easy to do. In the case of adding a photo, you can simply click the "Add Photo" button in the editor for the post, browse for a photo from your local hard drive, and it will be uploaded to the server, where it is stored for free, and included in your post. No coding is necessary to add a picture. If you want to upload, play, or manage MP3s, movies, or other media only using Blogger, you will have a very hard time. In fact, even if you upload an MP3 or a movie to another online storage space, you'll only be able to connect to that file with a simple link, rather than be able to play the media directly in Blogger.

There are simple workarounds to allow for this functionality, such as the scripts provided via the Firefox extension Greasemonkey. Greasemonkey is a free add-on for browsers like Firefox, which lets you run community-created Dynamic HTML scripts to modify the behavior of a page or set of pages; in this case, there is a script for adding a Flash-based audio player to a page wherever a link to an MP3 is found. There is no direct support for this by Blogger. This means that Google expects you to use your Blogger blog for blogging, not for video distribution, audio distribution, or broadcasting. Given that Google has two full-blown operations for video distribution in Google Video and YouTube, it makes sense that Google would rather have you use one of those for video distribution and simply embed the video within your blog.

Uploading files to Blogger is a limited affair. Only image uploads are allowed–other formats won't be permitted. Also, if you wish to upload TIFFs, RAW images, PSDs, or XCF formatted images for your students or users to work with, you're out of luck. At the time of this writing, the image upload dialog says, "We accept jpg, gif, bmp and png images, 8 MB maximum size." If you are just sharing photos with friends, this is no limitation at all. If you're using this blog as an organizational tool for a team that works with images, Office documents, or any other file formats, you may need to look elsewhere. Many bloggers mentioned earlier this year that they were still having problems uploading images with Blogger. According to *Network World* (2007), Blogger was "generating a steady stream of complaints . . . including hours-long outages, feature malfunctions, and data loss. The problems are particularly frustrating to users who migrated to the service's new version." Google says most bugs are isolated incidents and that Blogger's stability will improve as migration to the new platform progresses (5).

While Blogger may or may not be the best bet for librarians and library administrators, *PC World* gave the newest version of Blogger the "Best Buy" pick for blogging software in January 2007, citing that the "recent upgrade has made Blogger an extremely versatile platform, with templates that you can easily modify to include advertisements, RSS feeds, and even third-party HTML applications, such as a slide-show viewer. All of the controls and features are arranged in a simple interface that's easy to work with. The only drawback: Your photo galleries must be hosted externally by a service such as Flickr or Picasa" (Ettenson, 2007, 61).

Now let's take a look at WordPress.com's focus, features, and feel in comparison. Note that unless otherwise specified, when the phrase WordPress is used in this article, it refers to the hosted version, also known as WordPress.com, as opposed to the locally-installed version, also known as WordPress.org.

WordPress.com

WordPress reader features are robust and far-reaching. RSS syndication is available by default on every page for both the whole blog and for every category (categories are collections of posts according to a keyword, and are the WordPress implementation of tagging, which Blogger calls labels), so that people can subscribe to a feed of all of the activity on your blog or just the activity related to a particular category. Let's assume for our examples that our WordPress blog has been installed at <http://matt.wordpress.com>. An RSS feed is always available at <http://matt.wordpress.com/feed> and an Atom feed always exists at <http://matt.wordpress.com/feed/atom>. You can also use the feed and feed/atom keywords at the end of a category (tag) URL like this: <http://matt.wordpress.com/tag/sometagname/feed> to get RSS and Atom feeds for categories. This is useful if you use your blog to post about broad or diverse topics, but you want to be able to advertise some topics to some RSS subscribers, but different ones to others.

In the case of a library blog, you may have a category on "New Acquisitions" and another on "Issues of Library Management" and while some RSS readers may be interested in both of those topics, it's likely that people/users would be most interested in the former, and peer administrators would be most interested in the latter. With WordPress, you can allow each audience to choose to subscribe to just that single category or subscribe to all posts on the blog. Blogger does not have a similar feature right now for using labels to generate Atom feeds, and it does not support RSS feeds at all. WordPress includes a diverse set of plugins (a small subset of the thousands of plugins available to WordPress.org locally hosted blogs) which allow extended functionalities including the ability to show the feed of another blog, as Blogger does.

WordPress allows for podcasting and broadcasting out of the box. WordPress does not allow the uploading of audio files in MP3 format, so you can't store your audio media on its server, but it has a remarkably easy to implement feature that allows the playing of remote digital audio media right on the page, complete with a play button. You can even choose to use this player tool to point to an MP3 that resides on another server somewhere, such as a podcast on someone else's blog. Adding the code [audio:http://some/server.com/youraudiofilename.mp3] to a post will automatically create a play button and timeline for that audio in the post with which anyone with Adobe's familiar Flash Player installed (e.g., most users) will be able to listen to your media right away.

Tagging posts is easy in WordPress. You can add tags to posts as you create the posts, and you can select tags you've created before by clicking checkboxes. These tags are called categories in WordPress, and have the added benefits of per-category feeds as described above. As soon as a post is created, all of its textual content is searchable with your blog's search bar, meaning that any word, anywhere in your post, will be available for matching search terms your blog's viewers type in, immediately after you post.

WordPress portability features are a clear winner in this comparison. WordPress is available under an open source license, meaning that every piece of code that was written to create it is open and available for viewing, modification, and improvement by everyone, with improvements being worked back into the project as a requirement of the license agreement. This has many benefits, including added security since everyone can read the code and look for security flaws, and added portability, since anyone can see exactly how the content is stored, moved, and saved. Since the system has nothing to hide, and the content and its handling are thus transparent, the ability to move your content to and from the WordPress system is a given. Standards such as XML, XHTML, CSS, and others are used everywhere, so that in the event that you need to use your content, look and feel, semantic structure, or any other aspect of your blog in another project that also makes use of standards, the solutions are self evident.

There are some restrictions in the hosted version of the software that are not present in the locally hosted version, such as the ability to install additional plugins, the amount of space available for free hosting, and modification of the CSS in the themes provided with the system. You can opt to pay for additional space, the ability to modify the CSS, or to purchase a domain of your own without the WordPress.com URL. However, since anyone who wishes to can download and install his or her own system free of charge with no such restrictions, payment for these features is more about gathering monetary support for the project than any real restriction of features.

You can import blog content (using built-in WordPress import tools) from a LiveJournal XML export file, a Movable Type or TypePad blog, a new Blogger blog, or a WordPress export file. You can export your content to a "WordPress eXtended RSS" or WXR file, which contains posts, comments, custom fields, and categories, in human readable XML format, which can then be imported into another WordPress blog, as stated above, or modified to be imported into another blogging system, if that blog provides an import tool.

WordPress administrative features let you manage blogs for teams or individuals effectively. You can have multiple WordPress members and each member can have one of four different levels of administrative rights: reader, contributor, editor, or administrator, each with increasing abilities. WordPress does not have a CAPTCHA tool, but spam is managed using other tools, one of which is a plugin called Akismet that automatically and effectively catches spam-based comments, and hides them, but holds on to them for optional review. Another tool allows you to create a list of words that will either trigger a hold on a comment, or delete it outright. If you want a profanity-laced-comment-free blog, you can require each word submitted as part of a comment that includes a word on your list to be approved by you manually before the comment appears, or you can set any comment with a profane word to be deleted immediately.

You can also set it so that one member's post must be approved by another member before publishing. Post moderation like this is essential in a blog where a team must work according to a workflow similar to a traditional writer/editor model. E-mail notifications can be sent whenever certain activities occur, such as when comments or posts are created, so that certain members are acutely aware of any activity on the blog. The dashboard for WordPress is much more cluttered than Blogger's dashboard with functionality and settings, but for an administrator who is willing to get to know the system, it can be a more powerful and rewarding way to administer a blog. <http://codex.wordpress.org> provides a community-driven support site that anyone can add to or edit, thanks to the community-editable wiki that drives it. This makes for a comprehensive site that can be at once overwhelming, inconsistent, and incorrect at times, but can also have an answer for the most minute and particular question–just the answer you were looking for–whereas a more controlled support site, like Blogger's, might not get to the heart of your particular issue in the same way or to the same degree.

WordPress creation features give you many options for updating your blogs. You can allow WordPress to publish, as a blog entry, any e-mail in a particular POP-based e-mail account. You could set up a Gmail account, for example, which allows POP-based access, and use it solely as an address to which you e-mail blog entries. Anyone who sends an e-mail to this account will have the e-mail published as a post, so you will want to keep the e-mail address a secret, unless you intend for a team to use this method for publishing. Posts can be worked on and saved as drafts, or published immediately. You can also set a post to be automatically published at a particular time in the future, long after you or your team has finalized an important draft. You can alter the timestamp of a post, so that a post you first published last week appears to have first been published today, or a week from now.

WordPress has an open publishing interface, so many stand-alone blogging clients can send posts to it, but one of the easiest ways to publish is using the "PressIt" bookmarklet advertised at the bottom of the posting page in the Dashboard. For more information on blogging clients that work with WordPress, see <http://codex.wordpress.org/Weblog_Client>. One thing that you can do with WordPress that you just can't do with Blogger is create a static set of pages outside of the blog stream. If you want to present a set of pages that do not move down with chronologically added content, you can use WordPress' "Pages" feature. This is particularly useful for adding program information, an About page, a gallery, or something else that you want to appear alongside your blog.

WordPress site relation tools are well integrated and seamless. When you create a post, any URLs that appear in your post are pinged to let those sites know that you are referring to them. If the remote site recognizes pings, it can treat the ping as an invite to link back to your blog as though it were a sort of comment. Again, as mentioned previously in the Blogger section, this is sometimes referred to as a trackback and is very useful for both blogs. You can add links to any site, and WordPress even has a "LinkThis!" bookmarklet to make it that much easier to bookmark a site on your blog. Unlike Blogger, WordPress, through its "Create Link" dialog, makes use of the XHTML Friends Network (XFN, 2007) microformat, which can tell an interested search engine not only that you are linking to another site but also what your relationship is with a person associated with that site. For more information about microformats, please visit <http://microformats.org>.

WordPress comment management might be considered flawed by some. It focuses on dealing with spam after it is created, rather than on preventing it with a CAPTCHA, or something like it. The Akismet plugin is very good at catching and hiding spam, but we have to think that preventing spam before a filter would need to be applied would be much more effective. Given that WordPress' parent company makes the Akismet plugin, we are not surprised that they don't want to make it obsolete, but this seems like a bad reason to continue with it, instead of finding a new method for dealing with the issue, if for no other reason than to save the bandwidth used up by the bots and the processor cycles used up for the filtering. Since lots of spam must be reviewed from time to time to check for false positives, or legitimate messages mistakenly put in the junk pile, one redeeming quality is that WordPress' moderation tools are easy to use and very efficient. WordPress comments also do not thread, but rather use a flat leave-a-reply style discussion system. A reply-to-this-comment style discussion system would be much preferred, and at least in the locally-installed WordPress.org version, this can be achieved via plugins.

WordPress design features make other template systems blush with envy. With over 50 themes to choose from, WordPress makes the choices for look and feel from Blogger seem very limited. The designs are professional, interesting, dynamic, and sometimes funny or even funky. Many of them allow very specific tweaks, such as the ability to replace headers with your own images, which means that even with the constraints of a set number of themes, you can have seemingly limitless possibilities. Layouts can often be modified in wildly varying ways, with some themes in a two-column configuration, and others in three or four, with individual blocks of content able to be moved throughout. While CSS editing can be allowed unfettered for a fee, many themes allow for the editing of at least some of their CSS for free. If you want the ability to make the look of your blog very distinct and individualized, WordPress can efficiently and effectively meet the need. More often, the problem is one of clutter, where too many options are enabled, simply because they can be. Bloggers who spend time getting to know WordPress learn to use layouts and blocks to streamline their communication, rather than to knock their viewer down with content, though both approaches are possible.

WordPress media features allow you to create a blog that makes use of almost any media you could throw at it, though not always without some help from another site or service. WordPress.com says, "Currently you can upload the following: jpg, jpeg, png, gif, pdf, doc, ppt. With the space upgrade you can also upload: mp3, avi, ogg, m4a, mp4, mpg, mov, wav, and wmv" (WordPress FAQ: What filetypes, 2007). The space upgrade that the FAQ refers to is an additional purchase of space from WordPress of 1GB, 5GB, or 10GB, which also adds the ability to add the additional file formats. If all you want to do is upload JPG pictures or PowerPoint presentations, you can do that right away in WordPress, right inside the Create Post dialog. For a blog that you want to focus on music or spoken poetry, it might be helpful to be able to up-load MP3 files. For a blog where you want to feature screencasts of applications for technology training, you may want to upload MP4 or WMV files.

Without the WordPress space upgrade, you'll have to find another place on the Internet where you can upload these files for free, such as archive.org, or YouTube, so that you can still reference and use those files from WordPress. Using those file formats in your WordPress blog is relatively easy after they exist somewhere else online. In the case of an MP3 file on archive.org for which you have the URL, you can add the following code to your post, complete with brackets: [audio http://archive.org/some/path/mattmullenweg-interview.mp3]. When you put this code in a post, WordPress will show a player in its place that when clicked will begin to stream the MP3. The player itself requires Adobe Flash to be installed on the viewer's computer. Also, any MP3 with a full URL will be treated as an enclosure by the RSS2 feed, in which case a podcast is created. If an MP3 exists somewhere on the Web, you can refer to it in your WordPress blog, even if it is not yours, which may raise issues of ownership, but gives you lots of options, technically speaking. In the case of a video on YouTube, you can use a code like this, again, complete with brackets [youtube=http://www.youtube.com/watch?v=AgEmZ39EtFk], and the video will appear as though it were a part of your own post. Detailed instructions on how to do this are available in the video tab of the upload section of the Create Post dialog.

Now that we have talked in detail about many of the specifics of what these two great blogging engines are currently doing, let's take a look at what some other pseudoblogging sites, or "blogalikes," are doing to provide valuable, related but more specialized services.

PSEUDOBLOGS: SEVEN CATEGORIES OF "BLOGALIKES"

We chose to add pseudoblogs to this article, not to criticize them or accuse them of being "not genuine," but, instead, to highlight some of our favorite and popular free resources on the Web which offer interesting options for bloggers and want-to-be bloggers. Many of these pseudoblogs, somewhat superficially resembling major, free, popular blogging platforms like Blogger and WordPress, are not impostors lacking interactivity or real usefulness to administrators, librarians, or other educators interested in blogging activities. They do possess great value and are related in many ways to true blogs, and thus, we have included this section to highlight some of these pseudoblogs. Again, please note that we have also provided a comparison of the focus, features, and feel of these pseudoblogs within this article's accompanying appendices (Appendix A, Appendix B, and Appendix C).

However, most of these pseudoblogs don't place as much emphasis on blogging, instead, focusing on technology, media, or some other area, and performing blogging-related, but more specialized, tasks. Some have even considered using pseudoblogs as a beginning step into the interactive blogosphere to learn more about it, especially when that participant is unsure whether he or she is ready to venture out in the world of online interactive conversations via blogging. We think you will love learning about and playing with these tools and technologies. With the potential for inviting debate on how the following services have been classified, we have broken these pseudoblogs into seven categories: Social Networks, Zeitgeist, Photoblogs, Metablogs, Videoblogs, Geekblogs, and Filterblogs–we hope you appreciate them as much as we do.

Social Networks: Facebook, MySpace, and Others

It is well established that high school and higher education students are extremely interested in and very active within Web sites that are customizable, controllable, and provide opportunities to connect and contribute. These social networking Web sites provide online spaces for these students to gather and continually, constantly share and exchange opinions, music, and pictures. The particular sites listed here are not as popular right now among librarians and other educators for "professional use" as Blogger and WordPress are and, therefore, did not meet our criteria for what makes a true blog. Again, that does not mean that these pseudoblogging sites are irrelevant–far from it.

For instance, MySpace (2007) and Facebook (2007) have rapidly gained in popularity because of their ability to facilitate the introduction of and communication between people with common interests. As of mid-March, MySpace and Facebook are ranked by Alexa Internet (2007) as the 3rd and 7th most popular sites within the United States, basing their traffic ranking findings on "three months of aggregated historical traffic data from millions of Alexa Toolbar [can be installed just like the Google or Yahoo! toolbars] users and is a combined measure of page views and users (reach)." Only Yahoo! (1st) and Google (2nd) surpassed MySpace in traffic, with MySpace beating out MSN (4th), eBay (5th), and YouTube (6th), and Facebook listed higher than Wikipedia

(8th), Craigslist (9th), and Amazon (11th). Other social networking sites that we have noticed quickly rising in use are Windows Live Spaces and Yahoo! 360° (not surprising due to their owners) and a social networking site aimed at professionals instead of students, LinkedIn–this has very recently become popular for librarians, teachers, and other professionals, probably because of the publicity it has received at some recent national conferences.

All of these social networking sites foster connections and collaborations, and they are attracting more attention and users as they attempt to bring people with common interests together online. Librarians and libraries of all types are beginning to turn their attention to these networks because of the intense interest and participation that they have generated–and librarians are also beginning to understand this community and its current and potential library use. In fact, many individual librarians and administrators have set up personal MySpace and Facebook pages, and libraries and higher education institutions have begun converting their home pages to blogs or incorporating MySpace pages in order to seek better interactions with those whom they serve.

Good examples for these in our area of the Northeast are the West Long Branch Public Library in New Jersey converting its traditional static library page to a blog-based one using Blogger (a nice interview of David Lisa, Director of this library, on the process can be found on the Library Garden blog). Allegheny College in Pennsylvania has a MySpace page (Thoughts and Experiments, 2006), as well as the Brooklyn College Library (2007) in New York and the Bradley Beach Public Library (2007) in New Jersey. Librarians, administrators, staff, and teachers (including us) have MySpace, Facebook, and other social networking accounts, which offer a convenient place to bring people together and interact online. Librarians and other educators should know about this exciting trend. However, these and other social networking sites are not the only examples of pseudoblogs for which we should be aware–zeitgeist/social bookmarking sites are also very useful and popular to librarians and those we serve.

Zeitgeist: del.icio.us, Digg, Reddit

Zeitgeist, a German term generally meaning "the spirit of the time," is being used here to emphasize the power of everyone coming together to accomplish something, and in this case, to make something popular. The services in this category keep to our previously stated mantra of free and hosted productive tools for blogging, or tools that require nothing more than a familiar Web browser to enable users to access and edit materials. del.icio.us, for instance, is a social bookmarking site that primarily allows you to access and add your favorite sites from any computer with Internet access. You can easily share your own bookmarks and find the bookmarks of others. Additionally, you and other del.icio.us users can use tags (descriptive words added to bookmarks) to help you remember what you liked about your favorite sites and organize them in order to quickly retrieve them. Your bookmarks or favorites previously saved on only your personal or work computer's browser become available to only you and/or anyone you want at any time or at any location. It's your collection of favorites on steroids!

The "wisdom of the crowds" philosophy works here, where the more people that link to or tag an item, the more popular it gets, which means you have a better chance of finding other popular or like-minded items or people. del.icio.us is owned by Yahoo! and ranked by Alexa Internet as 65th in the U.S. (2007). Other interesting zeitgeist sites offer librarians and other educators interesting ways to discover, share, and contribute, such as Digg (2007) and reddit (2007). Alexa Internet ranks Digg as the 20th most popular site in the U.S., and while reddit does not fall into the U.S. top 100 sites, it received a lot of publicity here this past winter (2007). Digg, reddit, and other social networking/community-based popularity sites are valuable to us because they can introduce or expose us to news content or sites that we would not otherwise read. For instance, the Digg and the reddit.com communities (all users of Digg or reddit) vote on story submissions and comment on them, with the most popular stories getting discovered quickly and easily. del.icio.us, Digg, reddit, and other social zeitgeist sites, even with all of their imperfections, have presented and continue to present great opportunities for librarians, students, administrators, and teachers to access, share, discover, promote (or bury), and contribute to new and valuable information and materials online.

Photoblogs: Flickr, Picasa Web Albums

Not just an online photo album, and more than simply a blog with pictures, photoblogs combine features of both, allowing bloggers and viewers to place more emphasis on images instead of text, but also to create a community around images, with comments, groupings, and ratings. The images might be from an amateur photographer, photos of objects, or a collection of family snapshots published with a narrative, or, as some libraries have done, pictures of the latest events they have hosted. The content can go beyond photos to include images from sources other than a camera, like illustrations, designs, fine arts, diagrams, schematics, mindmaps, and any other visually communicated media.

Combining the structural abilities of a blog and the social aspects of a centralized service, photoblogs can be quite powerful tools to bring people together in a different way than other kinds of blogs. Digital pictures can be quickly and simply uploaded to the host site and stored there. Usually there is a way to tag the pictures to make sorting and navigation easier. Descriptions vary in allowed length, but are almost universally permitted. As with text-based blogs, viewers can see the entries in chronological order, but with photoblogs, there are typically other sorting methods available as well. Viewers can comment on images, and search for images by user, tag, group or keyword.

Flickr (2007), a Yahoo! company, is undoubtedly one of the most popular photoblogging sites used today, ranked 19th by Alexa Internet in the U.S. (2007). It advertises itself as having two goals: getting photos online and organized in as many ways as possible and sharing those photos in as many ways as possible. Flickr allows users with a Yahoo! username to upload pictures from their camera phone, digital camera, or even e-mail right to their Flickr account. Users can permit or restrict viewers' ability to see those pictures with the click of a button. Restrictive downsides of the free account are the limit set on how many pictures can be uploaded each month and only the 200 most recent images are viewable. The Newark Public Library is an interesting example of a library with a Flickr account (Newark Public Library, 2007).

While Google released Picasa (2007), a desktop client that will store your images, with the intention of making it easier for users to post to Blogger, it launched Picasa Web Albums as a photoblogging resource comparable to Flickr. Picasa Web Albums has over 1GB of free storage space; video uploading; no limit at any time on how many pictures are available to view; easy posting to blogs, social networking sites or e-mail; and an unlimited number of albums to organize the images. Both Flickr and Picasa Web Albums provide solutions for library team members, for instance, who need to share a project's working images with each other, but not the world. In Picasa Web Albums, it is easy to share one picture or whole albums; URLs are provided with each picture and each collection, so you can e-mail a link to an image or a set of images, or post the same to your site or blog. Flickr requires a Pro account in order to get most of these features. Because Picasa Web Albums is a part of the Google domain, it is not separately ranked by Alexa Internet, but the blogosphere has been making a lot of comparisons between Flickr and Picasa Web Albums this past winter, so we wanted to do a quick comparison.

Keeping with the focus of this article on free popular hosted solutions with great quality, value, and service, we suggest using Picasa Web Albums for a free, simple, good Web album. You may opt for the free version of Flickr for a feature-rich but potentially limiting album. If you are willing to pay $2 per month, then a Flickr Pro account is your best choice, with unlimited images and sets, plus all of Flickr's image manipulation tools.

Metablogs: Technorati, popurls

If you are amazed at the variety of all of this blogging and pseudoblogging, metablogs like Technorati (2007) and popurls (2007) are a great place to sample what's out there. Metablogs typically aggregate sites, sometimes grouped around a particular theme, into one place. Technorati (Alexa Internet ranked 57th in the U.S.) allows users to search blogs based on keywords or topics and you can sort the results by authority (how often a blog is cited or mentioned in other blogs). Technorati could just as easily by listed in the Zeitgeist section, but the focus here is not what's popular on the Internet as a whole, but very specifically, what's popular in the blogosphere. Where Alexa can tell you what traditional Internet sites are most visited, Technorati can tell you the top searched words on blogs, the most popular videos, music, movies, games on blogs, and the top tags used on blogs in its database of blogs, which is nearly comprehensive.

If you want your blog to count, you will want to use the "Claim Your Blog" feature on Technorati, like so many others, to begin seeing your rank in the blogosphere, and to learn what people want to see more of on your blog. If you want to know what the people who are blogging are blogging about, and if you want to know the mind of the technorati, you should get to know this site. If you are interested in seeing the zeitgeist aspects of this service in a quick way, visit <http://technorati.com/pop> or <http://technorati.com/search/libraries> to see what the very latest posts on blogs are saying about libraries, as well as a graph of how often your keyword was mentioned per day for the last 30 days. You can even subscribe to an RSS feed for this search on this site, to be kept up-to-the-minute on the topic of libraries as it's bandied about on blogs everywhere. And for an excellent comprehensive report of the world's most visited blog search engine, see the April 2007 posting by the person who knows Technorati best, its founder and CEO, David Sifry (2007b).

popurls is "a single page that encapsulates up-to-the-minute headlines from the most popular sites on the Internet." It has yet to receive widespread notice in the U.S., but we think it is very under-acknowledged! Not limited only to blogs, popurls (short for popular universal resource locators) surveys many of the most popular user-defined sites such as YouTube, Flickr, del.icio.us, and more traditional Web headline newssites like <http://news.yahoo.com>, <http://www.wired.com>, or <http://slashdot.org>–popurls is definitely an interesting "dashboard for the latest Web-buzz." Keeping with our previous idea of zeitgeist pseudoblogs, both Technorati and popurls rank their content based on user-defined popularity.

Search engine Zuula provides a blog-specific search and "if you're looking for all the recent blog postings on a certain subject, there's no better place to do your searching than at Zuula" (Simkovich, 2007). It searches nine different blog search engines including Technorati, Google, and Bloglines, and provides the results in easy tabbed pages. "It's also worth mentioning that, for all included blog search engines, Zuula always displays blog search results. By default, some of the source engines return a mix of blog, news, and other types of search results" (2007).

Videoblogs: YouTube, IFILM, Google Video, Heavy

We've all heard that "the medium is the message." Nowhere is that more evident than online communities whose focus is on video sharing. YouTube (now a Google company) seems to be omnipresent. Viral video (movie clips that spread quickly via viewer sharing) pops up everywhere. Alexa Internet ranks YouTube as the 6th most popular site in the U.S., but it isn't the only major video sharing site; Google Video (not ranked separately from Google itself by Alexa) has handy links on the main page to search comedy clips, sporting events, and music videos, in addition to searching private videos that have been uploaded by users (2007). It also provides a "Blog Buzz" section, so if you heard about a film somewhere in one of those blogs you're beginning to explore, try looking for it here. Although not as popular as YouTube or Google Video, Heavy, and IFILM rank in the top 500 sites in the World (2007). Heavy provides some original programming to round out the media that others provide, while IFILM partners with some standard television broadcast channels like MTV and Comedy Central in addition to providing movie previews and clips.

Geekblogs: Blosxom, MovableType

Geekblogs are–you guessed it–geared towards users with a little more interest in the technical workings of their blog than perhaps the average user. Using a series of predefined templates might not answer the needs of some bloggers; enter Blosxom, a simple, clean-looking, locally installable blog platform that allows users to create and design their blog from almost a blank screen to chock-full of content. Blosxom is different from typical blog platforms; any account holder can blog simply by placing ASCII text files into a particular directory on a server where Blosxom is installed and they are an author or co-author. For example, typing "cd ~; cd blog/posts; echo 'this is my new post' > newpost.txt" will give you a new blog post titled "newpost" with the post content "this is my new post." What this essentially means is that you can create any kind of design or look you want, make it an ASCII file, and then put it into Blosxom and you have a blog. This is a great way to microblog and a fantastic way to create blogging bots, since so many Linux and Unix tools can already output to simple text files, all of which could potentially be fully automated blog posts with RSS feeds or even additional features.

MovableType, a SixApart Company, allows similar creative license with more options than many blog platforms. While it doesn't allow quite as much freedom as Blosxom, users can get very nice looking custom blogs without having to know *very much* programming. It markets its service to private users and small and large business and organizations, even offering educational or non-profit discounts for upgraded service. The upgrade might be useful for larger organizations that will have many users updating the blog since the company will install it and provide support for you. Otherwise, the free version is loaded with the same features, enough for the average user, although we did not find it anywhere near as user-friendly overall as Blogger and WordPress.

Filterblogs: Twitter, Tumbler, Google Reader, Bloglines

Filterblogs are perhaps the ultimate distillation of blogs–not in content, but in purpose. Rather than posting a commentary or narrative, it is used to maintain a blog scrapbook or new and noteworthy notebook for public consumption. Users can quickly post a picture, a link, a thought, or a status update, usually in two clicks or less. A new sort of filterblog has emerged very recently in the form of microblogging, where the whole point is to get an update about what you are doing, looking at, listening to, reading, or watching, right now, as quickly as possible. Microblogging's quickly rising star, Twitter, proclaims that it answers the ultimate question: "What are you doing?" (2007). A mashup of social networking site features like Facebook's "Status Update" and MySpace's text message updates, users can post or receive their latest actions or planned activities on the site using their computer or texting from their mobile phones.

"Twitter probably wouldn't have existed before blogging" and is starting to receive a lot more notice as a quick and easy way to share short (140 characters or less) bursts of information with many people (Waters & Nutall, 2007). In fact, you can even use Twitter (and its text messaging features) or any other service that provides an RSS feed to post entries on a Tumblr blog. Tumblr provides a quick way of jotting down notes on the best things you find when browsing the Web. Tumblr really exemplifies the scrapbook blog mentality; you can place a Tumblr bookmarklet on your toolbar and it will post entries, links, quotes, videos, or photos from most any site to your page for you with minimal fuss–unbelievably easy, actually (2007).

Two more services provide the same kind of bulletin board function, even though their main purpose is that of an RSS feed reader: Google Reader and Bloglines. We found that the Google Reader's "Share" feature and Bloglines' "Clip/Blog" feature were fairly new additions to what are still considered excellent hosted readers. For instance, Google Reader does not allow the posting of original content at all, but does make it very easy to share items from the RSS feeds of other sites. Bloglines, however, does allow you to create a blog and post original content. Both of these filterblogs are missing key functionalities of a true blog, such as comments or trackbacks. Although Google Reader and Bloglines are more than just RSS feed readers, they are not fully functional blogs.

CONCLUSIONS, OUTCOMES, IMPRESSIONS: OVERVIEW OF FOCUS AND AUDIENCE

The Sophisticated Blogger

The best choice for the technologist, system administrator, programmer, experimenter, or experienced blogger is WordPress. There is a complexity and sophistication to the WordPress dashboard that is not present in the Blogger Dashboard, and this sophistication has the potential to delight the initiated and frustrate the novice. If, for instance, HTML confuses you, you will likely do better with other solutions.

The Basic Blogger

The best choice for the minimalist, end user, slow adopter, non-adapter, conservative computer user, or basic blogger is Google's Blogger. There is Zen simplicity to Blogger that allows for an easy initiation to blogging. This simplicity allows the most technophobic user to become a blogger, but it will quickly limit an advanced user who needs to do a particular task in a particular way. Blogger also has the edge in popularity. Google's installed user base is immense, and being a part of that user base has its benefits. If you want a quick, streamlined tool to publish information on a regular basis in a chronological format, without having to know anything more than how to write an e-mail, Blogger is a good solution.

Teaching and Learning

The best choice for blogging for librarians, administrators, teachers, and learners really depends on the application. For a team of technically savvy reference or instruction librarians who want to collaborate and present ideas in a highly controllable way, the team will likely enjoy the technical flexibility of WordPress. For an administrator or instructor who is setting up a blog for a course in which user teams (with varying levels of technical sophistication) will be working together, Blogger is likely the best bet. For individuals who want to blog for academic purposes, your choice is the result of this question: Do you consider yourself technically challenged or do you test the limits of technology? If the former is true, the simplicity of Blogger will be a welcome choice. Advanced technology users, or users who are familiar with various technologies will relish the depth and control that the WordPress dashboard gives. In situations where multiple users are asked to blog independently, but to the same end purpose, such as research on a topic, the results of 10 different blogging engines could be followed via an Outline Processor Markup Language (OPML) list of RSS feeds in a feed reader like Google Reader fairly easily. This way, an administrator could follow the blogging pursuits of the class without restricting students to either of these two blogging solutions, as long as the solutions they use send out standard RSS or Atom feeds.

Social/Personal/Journal

The best choice for a social, personal, or journal blog also depends upon the application. If it is very important to be able to tweak the look and feel of a personal blog, it is important to consider the advanced interface editing features of WordPress. Blogger allows for simple interface changes on a large scale, but not the minute and personal changes that WordPress allows. The fact that Google has so many more resources and users than WordPress is something to keep in mind when considering the social aspects of a blog. For instance, in order to comment on some user-only restricted blogs, you must be logged into that system as a user. Many people already have a Blogger compatible, Google based Gmail account, making it that much easier for those people to participate in Blogger blogs.

From a journaling perspective, there are many tools for posting to blogs, and the tools that you already use may help determine which engine to use for journal blogging. There was a plugin for Microsoft Word to publish to a previous version of Blogger, as an example. Many standalone desktop blogging applications, like those we mentioned here, and even some Firefox extensions, can publish posts to Blogger. If you already use Picasa to manage your photos, you may have noticed that there is a "Publish to Blogger" feature, as well as the ability to upload to Picasa Web Albums. While it is a simple task to publish documents or photos to WordPress, it is not yet as simple as clicking a button from within your word processor or photo organizing applications. This is testament to the power of Google's reach into the desktop space, and its emphasis on ease of use.

If you are using tools that do not already publish in the same way as these applications do to Blogger, it matters much less which tool you use as a blog. For instance, if you are using Audacity, the prevalent open source audio editor, to edit audio for lectures or podcasts, you can export an MP3 of your audio project, and upload the MP3 onto a server somewhere. From there, you can refer to it in a post on either your Blogger or WordPress blog. This modular approach means that you must manage each part of your workflow separately, since there is no "Publish to WordPress" button built into Audacity, but it also means that there is no benefit to using one blogging engine over another for this particular purpose, including the fact that neither Blogger nor WordPress allows the upload of MP3s to its online hosted storage system.

If you either pay for additional space on WordPress.com or install the free WordPress.org version locally, this restriction and many others are lifted. Two benefits in this issue for WordPress.com over Blogger are the built-in MP3 player functionality and the automatic podcasting abilities. In addition, with the open nature of both Audacity and the WordPress APIs, developing a plugin for the purpose of uploading audio to WordPress from Audacity is quite possible for an interested developer.

If you're not sure of your place in the blogosphere, consider starting small: create a Flickr stream of your pet or set up a Facebook page. If you're the kind of person who becomes more comfortable playing with and tweaking things on a small scale at first, turn to Tumblr. Do you think there is bias in the top five headlines from a major news source? Try registering a Digg account to determine what deserves to be news.

Topical/Filter/Collection

The best choice for a topic, filter, or collection blog depends heavily upon the specific application. Since both Blogger and WordPress have various tools that allow posting selected content from within a browser, the reasons for choosing one or another are much more tightly tied to the type of content being collected. For instance, if you want to make a catalog of audio clips or an audio blog that focuses on music or poetry, WordPress has that great simple feature where you simply add a line of code to a post like [audio: http://path.to/audio. mp3] which results in that remote file being cued up in a Flash based player right inside your post. WordPress has had the ability to create podcasts from links to media files in posts for a long while, but this new additional tool makes it very easy to create a blog centered on listening.

Simplicity is the reason that blogging has surpassed static HTML pages as the main form of Web publishing for the average user, so ease-of-use tricks like this one give WordPress an advantage where blogs are used for media publishing. The spike in popularity of services like Tumblr, mentioned earlier in the Pseudoblogs section of this article, is a very good example of the desire of bloggers to increase the speed and simplicity of posting, even at the cost of layers of functionality. In Tumbler Blogs, or tumblelogs, some blogging functions that are essential to WordPress and Blogger just become superfluous and secondary. For more on the phenomenon, see Wikipedia's article (Tumblelog, 2007).

In cases where you are already using Flickr, del.icio.us, YouTube, or other Web 2.0 tools or services, and you want to use that tool to populate your blog, you should determine that capability before considering other factors. Many of these services have code that you can paste into your posts or in your sidebar on either of these blogging engines (and elsewhere) to add new functionality. If the service you plan to use is proprietary or only specifically supports one or another blogging solution, as YouTube did until very recently, it may help you to make a decision about which blog to use. More importantly, you may want to consider looking for a more open format that does not require one type of blog or another in order to work.

Static Presence/Web Page

To create a static presence, there is a clear winner. With the WordPress "pages" feature, you can create static pages that exist outside of the normal chronological flow of a blog. It amounts to having a Content Management System right inside your blog, and with certain themes, like the revered k2 lite, will work very well as a replacement for a 20-30 page traditional Web site. Sites larger than this would have real difficulty migrating to WordPress as a main site, but smaller sites can be managed quite effectively this way. There is no equivalent feature in Blogger for static pages.

Team Blogging/Newspaper/Magazine

For the purposes of team blogging, either solution will provide some team management, but WordPress will provide some additional granularity in the way editors, users, and administrators can use the blog. For instance, if you want some users to be able to change the theme, others to only add new stories, and others to submit stories but not post until approved, you will need to use WordPress. In Blogger, the creator of the blog is the administrator; everyone else is an author who can create new posts, or a reader, who can not. Authors in Blogger can be bumped up to co-administrators. You can choose whether readers can comment anonymously. If you need to share the administration responsibilities with someone else, you may use either system. If you need more robust hierarchical differences and abilities between users, use WordPress.

Final Words

So, with all of the above in mind, simply put, we recommend Blogger for the most simple blogging applications, while we recommend

WordPress.com for anything even remotely out of the ordinary. But whatever blogging platform you decide to use initially, know that setting up a blog can now be done easily, with a few clicks of the mouse and a smile still on your face. We believe that you will find that the social networking capabilities of blogs will offer you and others you work with unprecedented opportunities to contribute, communicate, and collaborate–both inside and outside of your libraries and organizations.

Don't forget, too, about some favorite popular and free resources we highlighted earlier in the pseudoblogs section to this article. They truly do offer interesting options for librarians and other educators actively entering the blogosphere, providing unique interactivity and information for anyone interested in blogging activities, even though they are not full-fledged true blogs. Highlighted Social Networks, Zeitgeist, Photoblogs, Metablogs, Videoblogs, Geekblogs, and Filterblogs, with all of their specialized tasks, do possess great value and are related in many ways to true blogs, which is why we discussed them earlier in the article and included them in this article's accompanying appendices (Appendix A: Comparison Matrix on the Functions/Awareness of Blogger, WordPress.com, Bloglines, Google Reader, and Tumblr; Appendix B: Comparison Matrix on the Functions/Awareness of Twitter, Flickr, Picasa Web Albums, del.icio.us, Digg, and Technorati; and Appendix C: Comparison Matrix on the Functions/Awareness of popurls, YouTube, IFILM, Yahoo! 360°, and Windows Live Spaces). We think you will find these pseudoblogs, along with Blogger and WordPress, to be intriguing, practical, and useful in your professional and personal lives.

The blogging revolution within the library field is currently in full force, with the pervasive use of blogs continuing to grow, so isn't it time for you to be a part of the user-generated Web conversation? Blogs are not just for technologists or journalists–they have become undeniably useful to libraries. Remember, Time's Person of the Year can be you! (Grossman, 2006).

REFERENCES

Abram, Stephen. 2006. Bloglines. Stephen's Lighthouse blog, December 4. <http://stephenslighthouse.sirsidynix.com/archives/2006/12/bloglines.html> (accessed March 15, 2007).

Allegheny College [Richard J. Cook, President]. 2007. <http://www.myspace.com/alleghenycollege> (accessed April 5, 2007).

Alexa Internet. 2007. <http://www.alexa.com> (accessed April 1, 2007).

Blogger. 2007. <http://www.blogger.com> (accessed April 4, 2007).

Blogger Help: How do I create a backup of my entire blog? Blogger. <http://help. blogger.com/bin/answer.py?answer=41447> (accessed April 5, 2007).

Blogger Help: About Blogger for Word. Blogger. <http://help.blogger.com/bin/ answer.py?answer=42497> (accessed April 5, 2007).

Bloglines. 2007. <http://www.bloglines.com> (accessed April 4, 2007).

Blosxom. 2007. <http://www.blosxom.com> (accessed April 1, 2007).

Bradley Beach Public Library [Karen Klapperstuck, Director]. 2007. <http://www. myspace.com/bradleybeachlibrary> (accessed April 5, 2007).

Bromberg, Peter. 2006. Blog-based library Websites: An interview with David Lisa. Library Garden blog, September 24. <http://librarygarden.blogspot.com/2006/09/ blog-based-library-websites-interview.html> (accessed April 1, 2007).

Brooklyn College Library [Barbra Buckner Higginbothan, Chief Librarian & Executive Director]. 2007. <http://www.myspace.com/brooklyncollegelibrary> (accessed April 5, 2007).

CAPTCHA. 2007. Wikipedia. <http://en.wikipedia.org/wiki/CAPTCHA> (accessed April 5, 2007).

Coding Robots. 2007. BlogJet 2.0. <http://www.codingrobots.com/blogjet> (accessed April 5, 2007).

Dalton, Aaron. 2007. All typed out? *PC Magazine*, March 6, 17-18.

Deepest Sender. 2007. <http://deepestsender.mozdev.org> (accessed April 5, 2007).

del.icio.us. 2007. <http://del.icio.us> (accessed April 1, 2007).

Digg. 2007. <http://www.digg.com> (accessed April 1, 2007).

Etches-Johnson, Amanda. 2006. Blogging Libraries wiki, October 9. <http://www. blogwithoutalibrary.net/links/index.php?title=Welcome_to_the_Blogging_Libraries_ Wiki> (accessed March 15, 2007).

Ettenson, Kalpana. 2007. Powerful software for better blogging. *PC World*, March, 61.

Facebook. 2007. <http://www.facebook.com> (accessed April 1, 2007).

Fadden, James. 2007. Allegheny on MySpace. Thoughts and Experiments blog, January 26. <http://webpub.allegheny.edu/employee/j/jfadden/wordpress/?p=367> (accessed April 1, 2007).

Flickr. 2007. <http://www.flickr.com> (accessed April 1, 2007).

Free Software Foundation, Inc. 1991. GNU General Public License. <http://www.gnu. org/licenses/gpl.txt> (accessed April 5, 2007).

GNU Operating System. 2007. <http://www.gnu.org> (accessed April 5, 2007).

Google Groups: Blogger Help Group. 2007. <http://groups.google.com/group/blogger-help/search?hl=en&group=blogger-help&q=%22import+*+blogger% 22&qt_g=Search+this+group> (accessed April 7, 2007).

Google Reader. 2007. <http://www.google.com/reader> (accessed April 4, 2007).

Google Video. 2007. <http://video.google.com> (accessed April 1, 2007).

Grossman, Lev. 2006. Time's person of the year: You. *Time*, December 25, 38-41.

Heater, Brian. 2007. Quick and easy blogging. *PC Magazine*, March 6, 38.

Heavy. 2007. <http://www.heavy.com> (accessed April 1, 2007).

IFILM. 2007. <http://www.ifilm.com> (accessed April 1, 2007).

Lackie, Robert J. 2006. Web 2.0 and its technologies for collaborative library communication. *MultiMedia & Internet@Schools*, November/December, 9-12.

Library Garden blog. 2007. <http://librarygarden.blogspot.com> (accessed April 5, 2007).

LinkedIn. 2007. <http://www.linkedin.com> (accessed April 1, 2007).
MoveableType. 2007. <http://www.moveabletype.org> (accessed April 1, 2007).
MySpace. 2007. <http://www.myspace.com> (accessed April 1, 2007).
Newark Public Library [Wilma J. Grey, Director]. 2007. <http://www.flickr.com/photos/31599291@N00> (accessed April 1, 2007).
Picasa Web Albums. 2007. <http://picasaweb.google.com> (accessed April 1, 2007).
popurls. 2007. <http://www.popurls.com> (accessed April 1, 2007).
Rapoza, Jim. 2006. How to spot fake blogs. *eWeek*, October 9, 45. reddit. 2007. <http://www.reddit.com> (accessed April 1, 2007).
Sifry, David. 2007a. The state of the live Web, April 2007. Sifry's Alerts blog, April 5. <http://www.sifry.com/alerts/archives/000493.html> (accessed April 10, 2007).
Sifry, David. 2007b. The state of the Technorati, April 2007. Sifry's Alerts blog, April 3. <http://www.sifry.com/alerts/archives/000492.html> (accessed April 10, 2007).
Simkovich, Boris. 2007. More blog search options at Zuula. March 28. <http://www.zuulablog.com> (accessed April 6, 2007).
Technorati. 2007. <http://www.techorati.com> (accessed April 1, 2007).
TheGood TheBad TheUgly: Don't get the bloggers mad. 2007. *Network World*, February 12, 5. Tumblelog. 2007. Wikipedia. <http://en.wikipedia.org/wiki/Tumblelog> (accessed April 7, 2007).
Tumblr. 2007. <http://www.tumblr.com> (accessed April 1, 2007).
Twitter. 2007. <http://www.twitter.com> (accessed April 1, 2007).
Vander Wal, Thomas. 2005. Explaining and showing broad and narrow folksonomies. Personal InfoCloud blog, February 21. <http://www.personalinfocloud.com/2005/02/explaining_and_.html> (accessed April 6, 2007).
Waters, Richard and Nutall, Chris. 2007. Mini-blog is the talk of Silicon Valley. *Financial Times*, March 25. <http://www.ft.com/cms/s/d0ccbc46-daf7-11db-ba4d-000b5df10621.html> (accessed April 1, 2007).
West Long Branch Public Library [David Lisa, Director]. 2007. <http://www.wlbpl.org> (accessed April 1, 2007).
Windley, Phillip J. 2007. Capitalize on emerging collaboration options. *InfoWorld*, January 8, 26.
Windows Live Spaces. 2007. <http://spaces.live.com> (accessed April 1, 2007).
WordPress. 2007. <http://wordpress.com> (accessed April 4, 2007).
WordPress FAQ: What filetypes can I upload? 2007. <http://faq.wordpress.com/2006/05/07/what-filetypes-can-i-upload> (accessed April 4, 2007).
w.bloggar. 2007. <http://www.wbloggar.com> (accessed April 5, 2007).
XFN. 2007. <http://www.gmpg.org/xfn> (access April 5, 2007).
Yahoo! 360° 2007. <http://360.yahoo.com/login.html> (accessed April 1, 2007).
YouTube. 2007. <http://www.youtube.com> (accessed April 1, 2007).
Zuula. 2007. <http://www.zuula.com> (accessed April 4, 2007).

APPENDIX A. Comparison Matrix on the Functions/Awareness of Blogger, WordPress.Com, Bloglines, Google Reader, and Tumblr

Functions/awareness	Blogger	WordPress. com	Bloglines	Google Reader	Tumblr
URL	blogger. com	wordpress. com	bloglines. com	google.com/ reader	tumblr.com
Reader interaction					
Reader configurable interface	No	No	No	No	No
Comments	Yes	Yes	No	No	No
Comment moderation	Yes	Yes	N/A	N/A	N/A
Comment notification	Yes	Yes	N/A	N/A	N/A
Search functionality	Yes	Yes	Yes	No	No
Admin					
Administrative interface	Yes	Yes	Yes	Yes	Yes
Tagging	Labels	Categories	No	Yes	No
Ping support	weblogs. com	Configurable	No	Yes	No
Trackback support	No	Yes	Yes	No	No
Blogrolls	Yes	Yes	Yes	Yes	No
Multiple authors, User management	Yes	Yes	No	No	No
Standalone blogging client interface	Yes	Yes	No	No	No
Bookmarklet blogging	Yes	Yes	No	No	Yes
Media handling					
Microblogging (tweets)	No	No	No	No	Yes
Podcasting ability	No	Yes	No	No	No
Photoblog ability	Yes	Yes	No	No	Yes
Image uploads	Yes	Yes	No	No	No
Video uploads	No	No	No	No	No
Image embeds	Yes	Yes	No	No	No
Video Embeds	Yes	Yes	No	No	No
Amount of storage	Uses Picasa Web Albums	50MB	N/A	N/A	N/A
Security					
Visitor registration ability	Yes	Yes	No	No	No

APPENDIX A (continued)

Functions/awareness	Blogger	WordPress. com	Bloglines	Google Reader	Tumblr
URL	blogger.com	wordpress. com	bloglines. com	google. com/ reader	tumblr. com
Post password protection	No, but reader restriction	Yes	N/A	No	No
Statistics reports	No	Yes	No	Yes	No
Logs	No	Yes	No	No	No
Static pages	No	Yes	No	No	No
Spam protection methods	CAPTCHAs	Akismet, keyword filtering	No	No	N/A
Help					
Forums	No	No	Yes	Yes	No
Support	Yes	Yes	Yes	Yes	No
Feeds					
OPML Support	No	Yes	Yes	Yes	No
RSS feed creation	No	Yes	Yes	No	Yes
Atom feed creation	Yes	Yes	No	Yes	No
Feed aggregation	Yes	Yes	Yes	Yes	Yes
Design					
Configurable layout	Limited	Yes	No	No	Yes
Number of provided themes	<20	>50	N/A	N/A	>5

APPENDIX B. Comparison Matrix on the Functions/Awareness of Twitter, Flickr, Picasa Web Albums, del.icio.us, Digg, and Technorati

Functions/awareness	Twitter	Flickr	Picasa Web Albums	del.icio.us	Digg	Technorati
URL	twitter.com	flickr.com	picasaweb. google.com	del.icio.us	digg.com	technorati. com
Reader interaction						
Reader configurable interface	No	No	No	No	No	No
Comments	No	Yes	Yes	No	Yes	No
Comment moderation	N/A	Yes	Yes	N/A	No	N/A
Comment notification	N/A	Yes	Yes	N/A	No	N/A
Search functionality	No	Yes	Yes	Yes	Yes	Yes
Admin						
Administrative interface	No	Yes	Yes	Yes	No	No
Tagging	No	Yes	Yes	Yes	No	Yes
Ping support	Yes	N/A	N/A	No	No	Yes
Trackback support	No	No	N/A	No	No	No
Blogrolls	No	No	No	No	No	Yes
Multiple authors, User management	No	No	No	No	No	No
Standalone blogging client interface	No	Yes	Yes	No	No	No
Bookmarklet blogging	Yes	Yes	No	Yes	Yes	Yes
Media handling						
Microblogging (tweets)	Yes	No	No	Yes	No	No
Podcasting ability	No	No	No	No	No	No
Photoblog ability	No	Yes	Yes	No	No	No
Image uploads	No	Yes	Yes	No	No	No
Video uploads	No	No	No	No	No	No
Image embeds	No	Yes	Yes	No	No	No
Video Embeds	No	No	No	No	No	No
Amount of storage	N/A	100MB trans./mon.	1GB	N/A	N/A	N/A

APPENDIX B (continued)

Functions/awareness	Twitter	Flickr	Picasa Web Albums	del.icio.us	Digg	Technorati
URL	twitter.com	flickr.com	picasaweb. google.com	del.icio.us	digg.com	technorati. com
Security						
Visitor registration ability	No	Yes	Yes	No	No	No
Post password protection	No	Yes	No	Yes	No	No
Statistics reports	No	Yes	No	No	No	Yes
Logs	No	No	No	No	No	No
Static pages	No	No	No	No	No	No
Spam protection methods	N/A	No	No	Yes	No	N/A
Help						
Forums	No	Yes	No	No	No	Yes
Support	No	Yes	Yes	No	No	Yes
Feeds						
OPML Support	No	No	No	No	Yes	Yes
RSS feed creation	Yes	Yes	Yes	Yes	Yes	Yes
Atom feed creation	No	No	No	No	No	No
Feed aggregation	No	No	No	No	No	Yes
Design						
Configurable layout	No	Yes	No	No	No	No
Number of provided themes	N/A	4	N/A	N/A	N/A	N/A

APPENDIX C. Comparison Matrix on the Functions/Awareness of popurls, YouTube, IFILM, Yahoo! 360°, and Windows Live Spaces

Functions/awareness	popurls	YouTube	IFILM	Yahoo! 360°	Windows Live Spaces
URL	popurls.com	youtube.com	ifilm.com	360. yahoo.com	spaces. live.com
Reader interaction					
Reader configurable interface	Yes	No	No	No	No
Comments	No	Yes	Yes	Yes	Yes
Comment moderation	N/A	Yes	No	Yes	Yes
Comment notification	N/A	Yes	No	Yes	Yes
Search functionality	Yes	Yes	Yes	Yes	Yes
Admin					
Administrative interface	No	Yes	No	Yes	Yes
Tagging	No	Yes	Yes	Yes	Yes
Ping support	No	No	No	No	Yes
Trackback support	No	No	No	No	Yes
Blogrolls	No	No	No	Yes	Yes
Multiple authors, User management	No	No	No	No	No
Standalone blogging client interface	No	No	No	No	Yes
Bookmarklet blogging	No	No	No	Yes	No
Media handling					
Microblogging (tweets)	No	No	No	Yes	Yes
Podcasting ability	No	Yes	Yes	No	No
Photoblog ability	No	No	No	Yes	Yes
Image uploads	No	No	No	Yes	Yes
Video uploads	No	Yes	Yes	Yes	Yes
Image embeds	No	No	No	Yes	Yes
Video Embeds	No	No	No	Yes	Yes
Amount of storage	N/A	Unlimited	Unknown	Unknown	500 photos/mon.

APPENDIX C (continued)

Functions/awareness	popurls	YouTube	IFILM	Yahoo! 360°	Windows Live Spaces
URL	popurls.com	youtube.com	ifilm.com	360. yahoo.com	spaces. live.com
Security					
Visitor registration ability	No	Yes	No	No	Yes
Post password protection	No	Yes	No	No	No
Statistics reports	No	Yes	No	Yes	Yes
Logs	No	No	No	No	No
Static pages	No	No	No	No	No
Spam protection methods	No	Yes	No	Yes	Yes
Help					
Forums	No	No	No	Yes	No
Support	No	Yes	Yes	Yes	Yes
Feeds					
OPML Support	No	No	No	No	No
RSS feed creation	No	Yes	No	Yes	Yes
Atom feed creation	No	No	No	No	Yes
Feed aggregation	Yes	Yes	No	Yes	Yes
Design					
Configurable layout	Yes	No	No	Yes	Yes
Number of provided themes	2	<10	N/A	>100	>50

Libraries and Google Co-op

Dawn Bassett
Maha Kumaran

INTRODUCTION

Recently, social bookmarking sites such as *del.icio.us* and other Web phenomena such as blogs, wikis, podcasts, and RSS feeds have emerged in the growing area of online communities. These applications are often collectively referred to as Web 2.0, which some library professionals believe is helping the Internet evolve into a more collaborative and interactive space (Abram, 2005; Barsky, 2006; Boulos & Wheeler, 2007). Web 2.0 applications appear to be very popular with Internet users. According to *The Pew Internet and American Life Project*, 28% of "online Americans" have already used the Internet to tag digital media and information (Rainey, 2007). The *2007 Digital Future Project* found that the use of blogs and the creation and sharing of Web content has doubled in the past three years. These applications are already an important part of the online world, and many libraries are already using blogs and podcasts as part of how they deliver content to their users. It is important to continue to experiment with new technologies as they emerge. By doing so, librarians can continue to provide authoritative content, and position themselves to help those who are new to these tools to use them effectively.

Google users can take full advantage of Web 2.0 through a variety of services. They can create blogs using Blogger, share text documents and spreadsheets via Google Docs and Spreadsheets, share photos with Picasa, share notes with Google Notebook, or create a social network through Google Groups. One of Google's newer features is Google Co-op, a platform that includes *subscribed links*, *custom search engines*, and *topics*. Since it is important for librarians to be aware of the changing landscape of the Internet and trends in searching, it is particularly essential for them to explore custom search engines. This application has a real practical purpose, particularly for small or non-profit special libraries, which can use it to develop tools their users can access from any desktop with an Internet connection. With this in mind, we decided to use ourselves as a case study and experiment with Google Co-op's subscribed links and custom search features, and where applicable, compare them to similar products from other providers. Our objectives were two-fold:

- To provide examples of how librarians can use these tools to develop information literacy skills of their organizations as well as their users;
- To provide examples of how librarians can use these tools to promote their collections.

SUBSCRIBED LINKS

Subscribed Links are also known as vertical searches. In vertical marketing, companies market to a certain population segment or industry to be more successful and cost effective. Similarly, vertical search is a way of searching specialized sites that focus on specific audiences or content. In a vertical search, search results "are drawn from content related to a specific industry segment or profession to maximize the relevancy" (Zillmer & Furlong, 2005). Consequently, this constrained searching results in unambiguous, relevant searches in a more manageable size instead of offering a billion irrelevant hits. Google already uses this and calls it sponsored links. Through Google Co-op's subscribed links feature, Internet search providers can use a similar scheme to offer their own vertical searches or use the small directory of providers already available in Google. A good example of this is <http://www.fightstats.com/go/Home.do>, available from Google Co-op's Subscribed Links Directory.

Creating one's own subscribed links is a bit more complicated than it looks, but Google offers tools that a search provider can follow. There are two kinds of subscribed links in Google Co-op: basic subscribed links and dynamic subscribed links. For more on this follow <google.com/Co-op/docs/subscribedlinks/faq.html#what>.

Librarians and educators can use these subscribed links or create their own custom search engines to help their immediate users. For example, a law librarian or anyone interested in law with no access to expensive law databases could develop a good vertical search by using search engines such as findlaw.com, CanLII, BAILII, or Lawyers.com., etc. Of course not all of the needed information is going to be available from these sites alone, but creating subscribed links is a good start and certainly a much better way of searching than trying on the open Web. Example: using the term "Divorce Lawyer" in Google retrieved over 3 million results but using the same term in my Law Library search engine created with Google Co-op produced 4 hits. On top were two sponsored links such as lawyers.com and Lawyerdiscovery.com. A small law library or a library with no means of accessing legal information otherwise could create this site-specific niche search that includes law portals or gateways, law libraries, and legislative and judicial Web sites that have free content for a quicker and efficient search. This technique could be used by a variety of other libraries. School librarians, for example, could create sub-scribed links and add them to their library Web page. This will ensure that when students do search for information, they have searched the most authentic, trustworthy sites.

Another example is a small library such as that of the Saskatchewan Literacy Network, a provincial organization that survives solely on funding from provincial and federal governments. Not much money can be spent on updated, new resources each year. In this case subscribed links could be composed of literacy networks in Canada and elsewhere, Web sites such as Health Canada, Statistics Canada, and other literacy portals.

CUSTOM SEARCH ENGINES

While Google has been extremely successful in making *searching* for information online easier, *finding* the right information is more daunting than ever. In *The Emerging Opportunity in Vertical Search* (2005), Nicole Zillmer and Bill Furlong report that 41.2% of Internet searchers did not find results directly relevant to their query and 32.5% found that there were too many results returned. Reasons for this in-clude the fact that casual searchers may be unaware of advanced search features or may not know which keywords are best used to return the most valid results. Once they have a results set, searchers may not be aware which, if any of the thousands of Web sites that are returned to them are current, authoritative, or objective. The custom search engine, however, allows the developer to narrow an enormous amount of information into a more manageable and specific results set providing librarians with an-other tool they can employ to share search expertise with their users.

Google's custom search engine feature was launched in October 2006, competing with Rollyo's *searchrolls*, Eurekster's *Swicki,* and Yahoo's *Search Builder.* According to Jennifer Hyman, Product Market-ing Manager for Google, over 100,000 custom search engines have been created since the launch of Google Co-op (2007). Several of these search engines were developed by librarians and information professionals. For example, David Rothman has developed the *Consumer Health and Patient Education Information Search Engine* based on Web sites provided by the National Library of Medicine and the Medical Library Association (2006). There is probably no better place to help consumers with their searching than in the area of consumer health. Rothman's simple search engine allows the searcher to explore Web sites specifically chosen by medical search experts. Similar custom search engines have been designed by the American Library Association, which created the *Librarian's E-Library* (2006), a site that searches 275 sites for information on librarians and librarianship.

To start a custom search engine in Google Co-op, users simply sign up and Google Co-op guides them through a straightforward set up process. The most complicated part of our sample custom search engine on library job hunting was choosing the web sites that would be included. We wanted to include the most consistently updated and authoritative sites so a bit of background search was done on each of the first ten sites before adding them to the custom search <http://www.google.com/coop/cse?ex= 015493651578812821377%Aay4k5r8kdtm>.

Once the basic custom search is saved, the developer can use the "control panel," to add or edit new content, invite collaborators, change the look and feel of the search engine, or preview the search results. For the advanced Web content developer, XML can be used to create a more sophisticated search engine. For example, *Jump Up*, a small business Web portal designed by Intuit, has used a custom search engine to allow visitors to their Web site to search within some top business sites. Not only has *Jump Up* made the Google search engine blend seamlessly into its site, but it has also changed the text colours to match the overall design and style (2007).

Other features that can help users develop their search engine are *Refinements* and *Google Marker*. The Refinements feature helps guide users to a particular set of results within their original search set. For example, Garret Hungerford has *LISZEN*, which searches 600 library blogs (2007). A search in *LISZEN* for "Intellectual Freedom" provides several pages worth of hits; the initial search can then be refined using the links listed at the top of the search results page. In this case, users can refine the search by individual blogs, special libraries, academic libraries, or school libraries. Users can create their own refinements control panel, or select a pre-defined refinement from a list of "search refinement labels" that are used in Topics (the third tool in Google Co-op which we have not covered here). If they choose to use one of these pre-defined labels, searchers who use the search engine will have the added benefit of "seeing relevant sites labeled by others" (Google *Existing Search Refinement Labels,* 2007). Google Marker allows one to add new Web sites to one's custom search while searching, thus making updating a custom search engine easy from any desk top. Once a custom search engine is completed, users can either link to it within Google Co-op or copy or paste the code into their Web page or blog. Finally, the *Statistics* feature can be used to track how many queries the search engine has had.

Clearly, creating a custom search engine is relatively easy, but why spend time doing it? As with other Web 2.0 applications, the collaborative nature of custom search engines allows individuals to develop, create, and share their searches. Thus, solo librarians can request help from other librarians, information professionals, or experts in a particular area to contribute, with minimal reliance on over-stressed information systems departments. Librarians from large library organizations such as the ALA are also participating in this new collaborative atmosphere by sharing information with each other and their users through wikis, blogs, and podcasts (Coombs, 2007).

Both the *LISZEN* and ALA's *E-Library for Librarians* search engines are currently making use of collaborative volunteers this way. Collaboration saves both the large and small library money as it costs nothing but time to create the search engine and time can be shared among multiple collaborators. Of course, there will be an initial investment of time to research the topic prior to starting the search engine, but the potential benefit is much greater than the time spent to create it. For many special libraries, a few simple custom search engines in the top subject areas of the company can help guide the rest of the company when staff is doing a Google search, thus saving time and frustration for the employee and money for the company.

Saving costs inevitably helps the organization, but collaboration and community building can lead to other benefits for both librarians and their users. Studies on social bookmarking indicate that "collaboration, interactivity and flexibility" lead to "greater participation in learning activities" by both teachers and students (Bolous & Wheeler, 2007). Since many librarians are in the position of educating users about technology and search strategies, this is an important potential benefit, particularly for users who are interested in learning about technology and searching, or who are accessing their library remotely. Collaborative technologies, such as social bookmarking, can also lead to a greater understanding of a topic because participants can express different preferences and perspectives (Educause, 2005).

Finally, it is important for librarians to help users develop their information literacy skills, and using new technologies such as Google Co-op is an excellent way to do this. A recent study about digital media and learning for young people suggests that participating in an online social environment is creating the need for "new media literacies: a set of cultural competencies and social skills that young people need in the new media landscape" (Jenkins, 2006). Jenkins states that "schools as institutions have been slow to react to the emergence of this new participatory culture" and that "schools and after school programs, must devote more attention to fostering these skills which are built on the foundation of traditional literacy, research skills, technical skills, and critical analysis skills taught in the classroom." Since many libraries offer or are part of those after school programs they need to be on the forefront of this as well, so that they can help young people develop these crucial information and media literacies. For example, librarians could enhance classes on search strategies by having students participate in a collaborative custom search engine. Custom search engines could also be used to deliver already trusted resources such as subject guides. Thus users can be directed towards a more authoritative and relevant list of results, which would make search experience less daunting.

While there are many benefits to custom search engines, there are also potential drawbacks. Information professionals warn that because technologies such as wikis, blogs, and social bookmarking reflect "the values" of a particular "community of users, there is a risk of presenting a skewed view of the value of any particular topic" (Boulos & Wheeler, 2007). Google Co-op allows the custom search engine creator to decide how to interact with collaborators. This can be limited to only those the user chooses to invite, or can be opened up to the general population as long as they have a g-mail account. Another potential drawback is that results could be too limited, thus leaving out a potentially important piece of information either intentionally or unintentionally. Regardless of this particular drawback, it is important to remember that these applications are additional resources that librarians and information professionals can use to re-package and deliver the same quality of authoritative and balanced content that they normally provide.

CONCLUSION

According to a 2006 report from the *Pew Internet and American Life Project*, as of March of 2006, 42% of all adults in the US had a high speed Internet connection. This is double the amount since 2005 (Horrigan, 2006). This suggests that North American adults are able to do more from their home and work computers, including sharing content and using new applications to get the most out of their Internet experience. As librarians, we know that each individual will have different levels of skill using the Internet regardless of his or her purpose for using it. For those who want to access the Internet to participate socially, we cannot assume that they will know how to use these tools. Thus it is important for us to be aware of the potential uses of these tools, so that we can, as Stephen Abram suggests,

> inform them [the users] about and train them in the newest technologies that can have an impact on their success. For those users that can quickly become comfortable using technologies such as wikis, RSS, instant messaging, news aggregators and blogs, we can help them to leverage these in making a difference in reaching their goals. (2005)

In this paper we have demonstrated a few of the practical ways of using Google's subscribed links and custom search engine features in a library setting, and we have also discussed some reasons why experimenting with new technologies continues to be an important aspect of library service. Using emerging technologies to deliver library content is nothing new. Librarians have been doing this for years. We hope that this paper will inspire librarians and information professionals to continue to participate in this interesting way of searching for information online.

REFERENCES

Abram, Stephen. 2005. "Web 2.0, Library 2.0, and Librarian 2.0: Preparing for the 2.0 World." *SyrsiDynixOnesource*.2, no.1. <http://www.imakenews.com/sirsi/e_article 000505688.cfm> (accessed March 24, 2007).

American Library Association. 2007. *E-Library for Librarians Custom Search Engine.* <http://google.com/Co-op/cse?cx=015271347771663724636%3Acmwvisovdsg> (accessed March 25, 2007).

Coombs, Karen. 2007. "Building a Library Website on the Pillars of Web 2.0." *Computers in Libraries.* (January): 16-19.

Barsky, Eugene, & Michelle Purdon. 2006. "Introducing Web 2.0: Social Networking and Social Bookmarking for Health Libraries." *Journal of the Canadian Health Libraries Association.* 67: 65-67.

Boulos, Maged N., & Steve Wheeler. 2007. "The Emerging Web 2.0 Social Software: An Enabling Suite of Sociable Technologies in Health and Health Care Education." *Health Information and Libraries Journal.* 24: 2-23.

Educause. 2005. "7 things you should know about social bookmarking." *7 Things You Should Know About Series.* Educause Learning Initiative <http://www.educause.edu/7ThingsYouShouldKnowAboutSeries/> (accessed March 25, 2007).

Google. 2007. *Existing Search Refinement Labels–Instructions.* <http://www.google.com/Co-op/docs/cse/labels.html> (accessed March 24, 2007).

Google. 2007. *Corporate Information–Company Overview.* <http://www.google.com/corporat> (accessed March 25, 2007).

Horrigan, John B. 2006. "Home Broadband Adoption 2006: Home broadband adoption is going mainstream and that means user-generated content is coming from all kinds of Internet users." *Pew Internet and American Life Project.* 28 May 2006. <http://www.pewInternet.org/pdfs/PIP_Broadband_trends2006.pdf> (accessed March 26, 2007).

Hungerford, Garrett. 2007. *Liszen: Library and Information Science Search Engine.* <http://libraryzen.com/blog/?page_id=61> (accessed March 24, 2007).

Hyman, Jennifer. 2007. "Create a Google Search Engine." *Librarian Central.* 22 February 2007. <http://librariancentral.blogspot.com/2007/02/create-google-custom-search-engine.html> (accessed March 26, 2007).

Jenkins, Henry et al. 2006. "Confronting the Challenges of Participatory Culture: Media Education in the 21st Century." *Building the Field of Digital Media and Learning Occasional Papers.* 19 October 2006. MacArthur Foundation <http://www.digitallearning.macfound.org/site/c.enJLKQNlFiG/b.2029245/k.CDF/Results.htm> (accessed March 26, 2007).

Jump Up: the Place to Start a Business 2007. <http://jumpup.intuit.com> (accessed March 24, 2007).

Rothman, David. 2006. *Consumer Health and Patient Information Custom Search Engine.* <http://davidrothman.net/consumer-health-and-patient-education-information-search-engine> (accessed March 24, 2007).

Zillmer, Nicole, & Bill Furlong. 2005. *The Emerging Opportunity in Vertical Search: A Review of Niche-Oriented Search Engines and Directories.* Updated Version. White paper–SearchChannel and Slack Barshinger <http://www.slackbarshinger.com/verticalsearch/pdf/0505_vertical_search.pdf> (accessed March 23, 2007).

A Squatter on the Fourth Estate: Google News

Jim Galbraith

INTRODUCTION

In any given week, advertisers place billions of advertisements on current events and global news sites. From April 2-8, 2006, advertisers placed 3,226,718,000 impressions (the number of times an ad is rendered for viewing) on news sites, ranking the genre fourth among the top ten genres. News sites fall behind e-mail (the leader during this time period with an impressive 29,234,591,000 impressions), general community, portal, and search engines sites, but ahead of sports, entertainment, and financial sites (Nielsen/NetRatings, 2007). That Google would venture into this market with Google News is not surprising. In 2006, 99% of Google's $10.6 billion in revenue came from advertising. Armed with a powerful search engine and a popular brand, Google had a competitive advantage.

Google News competes in a market segment described by Nielsen/NetRatings as "Current Events & Global News Sites." The leading sites in this segment can be divided into two categories: news services and news aggregators. News services include the sites of major news corporations like CNN, *The New York Times*, and MSNBC. All have roots in print or television news and hence editorial teams that report, write, and post original content; for these corporations the Internet is another, still relatively untapped, market. The second group, "news aggregators" such as Google News, Yahoo News, and AOL News thrive under the auspices of "Fair Use," using automated systems to crawl free news content on the Net and build news pages by linking to third party information. Some, Yahoo News for instance, also license content from traditional news organizations.

The difference between news services and aggregators is profound. News services practice journalism. They actively investigate and re-port stories; they are the fourth estate, the reporters in the gallery. Aggregators do not create content. They disseminate news gathered from diverse sources, relying on news services just as a retail store relies on manufacturers and suppliers. Google acknowledged in a *Los Angeles Times* editorial/press release that "Online content and web search engines exist–in fact, can only exist–as symbiotic partners, both of whom profit as technology enables more users to find the information they're looking for." It will be interesting to see how this symbiotic partnership is main-tained in the future. Should Google weaken news services financially by taking their audience and lowering their advertising revenue, content could be lost. Worse, a powerful societal check would be weakened.

Google would arguably be doing evil, which is literally against its company policy.

Google News is one of Google's lesser lights. Google News is not as slick as Google Maps or the focus of a copyright debate like Google Book Search. The site isn't discussed alternatively as a threat or boon to libraries as is Google Scholar, nor does it have the indulgent appeal of YouTube. In fact, Google News isn't even one of the most popular "Current Events and Global News Sites" on the Web. According to Nielsen/NetRatings (Figure 1), which tracks the number of unique users per month and visits each site receives, Google News ranks just outside of the top ten, behind aggregators AOL news and Yahoo News.

FIGURE 1. Nielsen/NetRatings (March 2007)

Top 20 Current Events & Global News Destinations for March 2007

Brand or Channel	Unique Audience [000]	Web Page Views [000]	Time Per Person (hh:mm:ss)
Yahoo! News	32,413	1,083,247	0:34:12
MSNBC	29,160	754,893	0:27:42
CNN	25,652	1,191,602	0:36:17
AOL News	17,426	538,695	0:41:46
NYTimes.com	14,547	504,532	0:33:48
Internet Broadcasting Websites	13,925	199,970	0:11:51
Tribune Newspapers	12,596	200,269	0:12:56
Gannett Newspapers and Newspaper Division	12,082	275,241	0:18:23
ABCNEWS Digital Network	11,545	99,565	0:08:54
USATODAY.com	10,943	171,376	0:17:50
CBS News Digital Network	10,913	70,838	0:06:54
Google News	10,803	185,486	0:12:06
Associated Press	9,370	80,576	0:09:11
McClatchy Newspaper Network	8,965	162,555	0:17:04
Netscape	8,715	263,988	0:23:40
Hearst Newspapers Digital	8,419	177,523	0:17:59
WorldNow	8,369	98,261	0:09:48
Fox News Digital Network	8,100	318,787	0:39:47
washingtonpost.com	7,935	144,356	0:18:02
BBC News	6,634	65,436	0:09:20

*All the numbers are in thousands.

Yet Google News has been successful, building a monthly audience of nine to ten million unique users since the beta site was launched in 2002. This is a strong performance for a news site without a foundation in television, radio, or print news. In part, Google News' success is due to its brand name. As Jarboe (2006) recently suggested, Google News is, in many ways, the "tail wagging the news search dog." The amount of press the site gets is disproportionate to its ratings and content. At the same time, it would be wrong to downplay the loyalty Google has gained by promoting simple, but powerful searching. Google News and its peers have broadened the scope of free news coverage and, in doing so, made a strong contribution to popularizing news.

Google News is remarkable, but it faces strategic and legal challenges. Most of the news services Google News competes against have well-known reporters, editors, and news personalities. They break news and offer insider commentary. Moreover, they can coordinate their presence across television, radio, print, and the Internet to gain and keep audiences. Google's "neutrality," its lack of editorial focus, narrows its potential audience to those who *don't* want their news to have an editorial perspective. Audiences are often drawn to news sources that expound a certain perspective. Conservatives turn to Fox News, Moderates/Liberals to MSNBC, and Liberals to *The Nation*. Google is also facing competition from non-traditional news sites such as Wikinews, Technorati, and Wikio, which are taking the popularization of news to a new level by creating news communities.

Google News has attracted its share of legal troubles. Agence France-Presse sued Google in 2005 for $17.5 million, alleging that it used AFP's stories on its Website without permission. AFP's lawsuit had not been adjudicated as of April 2007. More recently, a group of Belgian newspapers won a copyright suit filed in Europe, forcing Google to remove their content from its pages. Google plans to appeal the decision. Lawsuits directed against other Google properties may also impact Google News. Viacom's billion-dollar lawsuit over alleged copyright violations on YouTube will test Google's business model. Google has taken steps to prevent further lawsuits. In 2006, Google signed an agreement with the Associated Press to incorporate AP content in a future project. This move was seen by some as an effort to compensate AP for using its material, heading off a potential lawsuit without establishing a precedent for licensing content (Ellison & Lawton, 2006, A3).

Despite these challenges, Google News is growing. Recently the News Archive was rolled out, allowing readers to retrieve, often for a fee, news articles going back 200 years. Such innovations, coupled with

Google's continued exploration of new technologies, hint that the site has a strong upside.

GENERAL NEWS RESEARCH

Internet news sites are used widely by news researchers in news corporations as well as academic libraries. In corporate news libraries, expert researchers use the sites in conjunction with a panoply of other resources, proprietary and public, to answer questions for the news staff. In academic libraries, people use Google News in conjunction with library resources to do academic research or just to keep up with current events. The questions being asked and the resources used to answer them in these environments are not all that different.

In the news industry, competition to break stories and provide the best news coverage is fierce. Higher ratings, wider circulation, or a larger viewing audience mean more advertising revenue. News researchers/librarians track breaking news, gather background information on major stories, and do research for reporters who are developing news pieces. Researchers also respond to information requests. Questions range from the broad: "Why is peace in the Middle East so hard to attain?" to the specific: "Where do each of the space shuttle crew members sit during re-entry?" Requests always have deadlines. A researcher might have half an hour to explain why peace in the Middle East is difficult to achieve. Responding often requires a reference interview to determine what information is really needed or to refine a broad inquiry to an answerable question.

In academic libraries, people are often looking for similar information. Some people simply desire to keep up with current events; others are writing papers and articles, in-depth projects that require more specialized resources. As in a corporate news library, there is often pressure. Frequently, librarians are working with people who have due dates to meet or faculty who want to place their article in a prominent publication. Librarians face the challenge of guiding people to the best source for their needs, teaching users to discern questions that are best answered with databases like Lexis-Nexis and Factiva and those for which the Internet resources will suffice.

Resources in corporate news libraries vary depending on the size and financial wherewithal of the company. Most news organizations have access to either Lexis-Nexis or Factiva, often both, as well as subscriptions to major wire services: AP, Reuters, and Agence France-Presse. These databases are usually supplemented by more specialized sources like Congressional Quarterly, Facts on File, Jane's Online Research and Variety.com. News libraries use some specialized resources. "Locate and research" databases like Accurint and Autotrack are used to contact newsmakers (and perhaps their family and neighbors) for interviews and television appearances. Collaborative software like the Avstar Newsroom Computer System provides shared workspace where scripts and stories are written and edited, directors arrange elements of a broadcast, writers and reporters monitor newswires, and the staff communicate via email and instant messaging.

Academic libraries frequently have many of the same electronic resources, including Factiva, Lexis-Nexis, Congressional Quarterly, and Facts on File. Accurint, Autotrack, and Avstar are virtually unknown in academic libraries; they are too specialized. Academic libraries do tend to have substantially larger print reference collections, not surprising since they support in-depth research across many subject areas.

A key difference between corporate news libraries and academic collections is the subscription models they use. Academic libraries usually have campus-wide subscriptions with either unlimited access or a fixed number of simultaneous users. News libraries are more likely to "pay as they go" in order to save money. In a pay-per-search environment, professional news researchers often start by searching free Internet sources, falling back on paid searches when the information isn't available for free or they need the precision of a structured search engine. Using free resources saves money. Many academic library users work the same way, starting with Internet news sites and using subscription databases only when necessary. In this case, the "cost" isn't monetary, but rather the time and effort it takes to select and learn a new search engine. Why go through the trouble of searching Factiva or Lexis-Nexis when a simple Google or Yahoo search will suffice? As the Hull University's Contextual Resource Evaluation Environment (CREE) Focus Groups survey found in 2005, "There was a good awareness of the range of search tools and resources available to users, particularly amongst students. Notwithstanding this, there was a reluctance to actively seek out other search tools if known tools were perceived as doing the job" (Ingram, 2005, 8).

Choice of Internet news engines is largely based on experience and personal preference. Expert news searchers know the BBC is particularly good for international coverage, that local papers are good for info on the latest "if it bleeds, it leads" crime saga, or that Google News is wonderful for sweeping the Internet for stories that may have legs, but haven't been picked up. Less experienced news researchers may go to Google News because they like the Google search and get the results they need. All these reasons are valid as long as the questions can be answered satisfactorily using free Internet sources.

HOW DOES GOOGLE NEWS WORK?

Google describes its approach to news by contrasting the "traditional" way of looking for news, "picking a publication and then looking for an article that interests you," with the Google News approach:

> We do things a little differently, with the goal of offering our readers more personalized options and a wider variety of perspectives from which to choose. On Google News we offer links to several articles on every story, so you can first decide what subject interests you and then select which publishers' accounts of each story you'd like to read. (Google, 2007)

Google then goes on to explain how the site is put together:

> Our articles are selected and ranked by computers that evaluate, among other things, how often and on what sites a story appears online. As a result, stories are sorted without regard to political viewpoint or ideology and you can choose from a wide variety of perspectives on any given story. (Google, 2007)

Google's folksy "We do things a little differently" and its undocumented assertions tend to gloss over issues about whether or not Google's approach to news is really all that novel or even desirable. Lexis-Nexis and Factiva came up with the notion of aggregating news from diverse sources some time ago. As for "wider perspectives," run a few searches in Google News and you quickly realize that news organizations are already culling stories from other sources. A running joke among news researchers is that the Associated Press writes the news and everyone else just copies them. Indeed, a great deal of news is written by news syndicates. A headline search for "Martin Scorsese" may return 180 hits, but half may be republications or rewrites of a syndicated story.

Google News does not produce or license content. The site is computer-generated, employing crawlers to cull content from over 10,000 news sources, 4,500 of which are English language news sources. The stories are ranked according to relevance using an algorithm that uses over a hundred signals to evaluate each article, including the source and how often the story is linked to by other sites. Once ranked, the content is sorted into topical areas: World News, U.S. News, Business, Sci/Tech, Sports, Entertainment, Health, and "Most Popular" stories. The page refreshes at least every fifteen minutes and the search results are updated in real time. Articles are accessible via Google News for thirty days. The advantage of this approach is that it produces a wide-ranging, if eclectic, list of news stories; readers have more news to choose from. The disadvantage is that the site has a "slapped together" feel. At 2:11 p.m. on Saturday March 17, the lead story on the Google's "Top Stories, U.S." page was "Norway recognizes new PA gov't, to restore economic ties," reported by *Ha'aretz*, a story about Norway recognizing the new Palestinian government. Just below the story was a *Chicago Tribune* story titled "At War's Fourth: Bush v Democrats," a story marking the fourth anniversary of the War in Iraq. Interesting stories, odd prioritization.

The basic Google News search is very similar to the Google.com search. A few adjustments were made to accommodate searching news content. For instance, searchers no longer have the option of "Feeling Lucky" and going to the first web page returned for their query. The main difference is that Google News searches a 10,000 site subset of the entire Google search. For "competitive reasons," Google does not provide a source list. This leaves users to infer what is being searched from the results, a difficult, perhaps impossible task. The results may be misleading. A basic Google News query will return articles from *The New York Times*, *The Washington Post*, and the *Los Angeles Times*; the inference would be that the crawler is searching these sites. In reality, Google's crawler only searches the visible portions of these sites.

Google News' advanced search enables users to narrow their queries. Users can search for exact phrases, find at least one of the words (an "or" Boolean search), and exclude words. Searches can be limited to a particular date range, news source, location (a specific country or state in the United States), or to specific parts of an article (headline, body, URL). Over the weekend of March 10, 2007, President Bush visited South America in an effort to counter Venezuelan President Hugo Chavez's growing influence in the region. To find background information on his trip, one could have run a basic search for "Chavez Bush" that returned 5,000 hits. An alternative was to run an advanced search using the same terms, but specifying March 9-10 as the date range and *The New York Times* as the source and return eight. Google always links to related stories, so if an article is insufficient, finding others is easy.

Google recently unveiled its News Archive, which spans over 200 years and contains a combination of pay-per-view and free content. Paid content includes historical articles from *The Washington Post, The New York Times, The Hartford Courant,* and the *Chicago Tribune.* Free content includes articles from CNN, *Time Magazine, The Guardian,* and *The Harvard Crimson.* Income from article sales goes to the newspapers, not Google; access is generally through Proquest or Readex. When newspapers contract with Proquest or Newsbank, they usually retain the rights to their content in the consumer space. Nevertheless, Google is taking on the role of vendors like Factiva and Lexis-Nexis. Part of Google's appeal is that the service is "free." How will Google's audience react to features that are primarily fee-based? The Archive also poses a challenge for library educators: how do we let our users know they can get this content for free?

Google offers several options for getting news as it happens. Google users can create RSS or Atom feeds based on their searches, set up "Google Alerts," have stories sent to their email account, or receive news on their personal computing device through Google Mobile. All are effective ways of keeping up with current news.

A common critique of Google is that its lacks transparency. Google has stumped the best of reviewers. In reviewing Google Scholar, Peter Jacso (2005) conceded that "It will be no surprise that I can't provide my usual overview about the content, composition and dimensions of the database. No one can with a software like this, and with the secrecy of Google." Google's "black box" construction is problematic. Google News boasts of searching over 10,000 sources, a claim that cannot be verified without a source list. This is a practical concern when trying to search by sources; the engine does not search partial names effectively. Typing "Houston" instead of "Houston Chronicle," for instance, confuses the system. Finding local news is particularly problematic; how many people know the names of local papers?

Google's crawlers are also noted for their inability to distinguish between reputable sources and "stories" put out on the Internet by publicists, marketers, and hoaxers. In one famous incident in March of 2006, a fake press release appeared on Google News which claimed that Will Ferrell had died in a hang-glider accident. Dotinga got to the heart of the issue in a recent article: "Are these 'aggregators' providing the news–or are they diluting it with the fakery, hucksterism, and puffery that affects the rest of the Internet?" (2006, 1). Major news services labor under journalistic ethics and standards; aggregators do not. Aggregators do not distinguish between reliable and unreliable sources; they do not debate what does and doesn't constitute news. If the Google algorithm can be gamed by publicists and marketers to blur the distinction between news of record and promotional material, is it truly, as claimed, a neutral news service?

GOOGLE NEWS AS A REFERENCE AND RESEARCH TOOL

By its nature, news research is shaped by timing as much as the nature of the questions being addressed. Some research is done in the moment: tracking news as it happens, reacting to breaking stories. Other research is done within the context of daily/weekly news cycles: fact-checking, developing background information on an active story, and keeping up with current events. Finally, there is research that is independent of news cycles: putting together background material on upcoming elections, preparing obituaries in advance for major celebrities, writing reference guides for major topics. Google News is not uniformly useful for all types of news research; its utility as a reference and research tool is largely determined by the parameters of its search algorithm.

An anecdotal account of tracking a "breaking" news story illustrates why Google is not the best source for breaking news. On February 22, 2007, at 8:09 p.m. EST, the Associated Press posted a story on its Washington Dateline wire entitled "Senate Dems move to limit Iraq mission" (Espo, 2007). Timing wire stories can be tricky. Wire stories are continually updated as they develop; each rewrite has its own time stamp. In this case, the story was posted by 8:09. The story appeared on Yahoo News via the AP newswire almost as soon as it hit the wires. By 8:15, MSNBC.com and Foxnews.com had also picked up the story, featuring it as "breaking news" on their site. By 8:31, MSNBC's "Count-down" television show had already reported the story twice and Keith Olbermann, the host, had promised a wrap-up before the end of the hour. As of 8:35, the story had not reached Google's "Top Story" or "U.S. News Page." The most recent features on the pages were 42 minutes and one hour old, respectively. In fairness, CNN had not yet reported the story either.

Google News had, in fact, picked up the story, via the *Houston Chronicle* site, which reported the AP story. Google's automated system however did not "notice" the story and post it to "Top News" or even the U.S. news site. As the breaking news was being broadcast, the story was still buried. The fact that CNN had not yet reported the story is an indication that the story was not headline worthy to all editors. How would Google handle a story guaranteed to be the headline of its news cycle?

On March 6, 2007 the AP released a story at 11:40 a.m., EST, indicating a verdict had been reached in the I. Lewis "Scooter" Libby trial. MSNBC,

CNN, FoxNews, AOL News, and Yahoo had all posted the news by 11:45 a.m.; Google News had yet to report the news on its "Top Story" page. Minutes later, at 11:50, a search for the word "Libby" still returned no stories on the verdict (the results were sorted by date). Google's automated search finally picked up the story between 11:50 and 11:56 from secondary sources; other sites were already offering live video coverage of the verdict. By 12:07, MSNBC, FoxNews, CNN, and Yahoo had announced that Libby had been found guilty on 4 of 5 charges. The verdict reached Google's "Top Story" page by 12:11, but only as a related story. The headline still read "Libby Juror Questions Indicate Possible Confusion."

The Google News algorithm relies on other sites to tell it if a story is headline-worthy. Lacking editorial discretion, Google News lags behind other sites in covering breaking news. For casual news readers, delays of a few minutes may not be problematic, but for professionals or newshounds, 10-15 minute delays might as well be hours. When timing matters, Google is not the best option.

Google News is much more useful for keeping up to date on current events, doing background research on current news stories, and fact-checking. In answering these questions, Google's broad 10,000+ site reach can be used to its fullest. Moreover, since news tends to run in daily/weekly cycles and current news is syndicated broadly across the Internet, Google's limitations (not searching the invisible web, the 30-day content window and the lack of transparency) are less likely to be an issue. If a story is out there and it is not an exclusive, Google's search engine will pick it up.

Browsing Google News' broad topical areas is an effective way of keeping up with current events. The site will have the top stories of the day, but also a serendipitous mix of other stories. Browsing Google News on April 3, 2007, I found the following stories: "US House Speaker arrives in Damascus for talks" (from the People's Daily Online with 619 related stories), "Tussle Over Iraq Bill Reminds Many of a Bitter 1995" (from *The New York Times* with 1,343 related stories) and an interesting article on Keith Richards, "Richards: I snorted my dad's ashes, and they went down well" (from *The Independent* with 443 related articles). Many "related stories" are simply updates/rewrites of developing Reuters or AP wire stories. On April 3, 2007 a shooting occurred at CNN plaza. As of 9:41 p.m. EST, Google News had links to *The Baltimore Sun* (the 7:12 p.m. update of the AP story), Forbes.com (the 7:27 p.m. AP update), and *The Toronto Star* (the 8:27 p.m. AP update). When using Google News to follow developing stories, sorting by time to get the most recent rewrite is important. An unintended consequence is that Google News is a very good resource for studying the development of stories.

One of Google News' strengths is that it links to Google's suite of sites. On March 9, 2007 Brad Delp, the lead singer of the band Boston, died at the age of 55. Boston peaked commercially in the 1970s, so Delp's passing, while sad, was not major news. For those who were interested in the story, however, Google News offered a cornucopia of information: 300+ related news stories, at least 40 blogs which reported his death (reached through Google Blogs), hundreds of images of Delp (via Google Images), and videos by the band Boston (found on YouTube). Google News' coverage of a relatively minor entertainment story was in-depth and used multimedia.

Google News' advanced search is good for fact-checking. For instance, to find the number of troops in Iraq, one could search commonly-used phrases like "soldiers in Iraq" or "troop levels" to find articles on the subject. For television news researchers, Google News is a terrific resource for finding stories to mine for "Factoids," the facts seen at the bottom of the screen or in the "crawler" while news stories are being aired.

In arguing for the role of librarians as providers of value-added content via the invisible web, Egger-Sider and Devine wrote that "There are myriad questions that can be answered in a better way or with more reliable sources than those that Google will find" (2005). Google News is not an adequate search engine for in-depth news research. If a researcher wanted to put together comprehensive biographies of potential Supreme Court nominees, including case histories, the researcher would need a wider range of resources. Used in conjunction with Google, Google Scholar, and Google Book Search, Google News is, however, a decent finding aid. A Google search on "Supreme Court Cases" leads to the Cornell University's Legal Information Institute, a very good source of information on the Supreme Court.

Google News is not the best resource for tracking breaking news, nor is it yet an ideal resource for more in-depth research. However, Google News is a fine resource for keeping up with current events, researching stories within the current news cycle, and finding background information.

ALTERNATIVES TO GOOGLE NEWS

News fans have a variety of sites to choose from. Google's competitors in the "Current Events and Global News Site" category offer a combination of original news stories, wire stories, and news video. In addition to these sites, a new wave of community journalism sites are marrying traditional hard news coverage with social software. The following are just a sample of the sites available, chosen because they are prominent and illustrative of the different news sites available.

Yahoo News, the leading Internet news site, employs a hybrid approach to gathering news. Yahoo gets its main content by licensing content from over 100 news organizations including Reuters, Associated Press, the *Chicago Tribune*, *Los Angeles Times*, and *The Christian Science Monitor*. Yahoo also uses crawlers to cull news from "over 7,000 news sources in 35 languages." Like Google News and other sites, Yahoo allows users to customize their own news page, create feeds, and set up news alerts. Yahoo employs an editorial team that oversees its news coverage. As a result of its active editorial control and licensing partnerships, Yahoo News tends to be nimble at reporting breaking news, but also has a great deal of depth to its coverage.

MSNBC.com, a joint venture of Microsoft and NBC Universal News, offers MSNBC news coverage and features the Newsbot Beta. Newsbot is an automated news system "built on advanced computer algorithms to determine which stories and photos are most relevant," that searches over 4,800 sites. Newsbot's sources are listed, demonstrating the remarkable coverage offered, but also the lengths to which a search engine must go to reach 4,800 sources. The 4,800 sources include *ChessBase News*, the Seinfeld Blog, and both the "Ski Club of Great Britain" and the "Ski Club of Great Britain (UK)." Newsbot has a "bias" in its search protocol; content from MSNBC is given priority. The MSNBC site also offers podcasting, newsletters, alerts, and Desktop Weather.

The next phase in the evolution of Internet news will involve community journalism, the application of social software like blogs and wikis to hard news. The challenge for established news sites will be to incorporate these features while still maintaining the integrity of their reporting.

One incarnation of this is Wikinews, an offshoot of Wikipedia. On Wikinews people post and collectively edit news stories, essentially doing the work of news companies. The result is a refreshing mix of headline news, colorful local news, and a lot of pop culture. On March 17, 2007, headlines included "Warmest global winter on record according to NOAA" (sourced from the NOAA web site and Reuters Canada), "Friendly fire killing of Lance Corporal Matty Hull deemed unlawful" (sourced from BBC News Online and Guardian Unlimited), and "Richard Dean Anderson in Stargate Continuum" (sourced from the GateWorld fansite). As with Wikipedia, the community is self-policing and expected to maintain high editorial standards. All of the articles cite original sources which, in the main, are unimpeachable (who can argue with GateWorld?).

Wikio may be the most progressive in terms of combining the social web with hard news. Wikio, which premiered in April 2006 and is still in the beta stage, is an effort to create an "authoritative news site" by combining the news gathering capability of aggregators like Yahoo News and Google News with the social interaction offered on sites such as Digg, Wikipedia, and Technorati. While the capture of news is automated, Wikio employs a team of editors who "optimize the sources before posting to improve the quality of the pages and to optimize the requests of the users." Wikio focuses on "hard news," avoiding the proliferation of pop-oriented material found on other sites. Wikio claims that its selection of news sources is independent, but excludes sites "with racist, homophobic, sexist or generally intolerant content; those with no value added in editorial terms; those propagating spam." Wikio allows users to personalize their news page by adding additional "tabs" to the main news page and adding comments at the bottom of news stories.

Google News faces stiff competition from established news sites, and the addition of new players should make the market a very interesting one to watch over the next few years.

CONCLUSION

Google News is a powerful news search engine, useful for keeping up with current events, fact-checking, and light news research. The search engine falters when research becomes specialized: following breaking news, doing in-depth research.

Surprisingly, Google News feels generic compared to its peers. The site lacks the personality of the MSNBC, Yahoo News, or *The New York Times* sites and looks old compared to Wikinews, Wikio, and Technorati. One can't help but wonder if Google News' automated crawler is really a copacetic way of getting news. Do we really need to search 10,000 sites to find information about Nancy Pelosi's trip to Syria or get the latest on American Idol? How many articles do you need to retrieve before hitting the point of diminishing returns? To whom is Google News meant to appeal?

In an article entitled "Is Google News Really News?" Richard Wiggins laid out a series of steps Google could take to improve its news service, including listing the criteria for a news source's inclusion, listing all the sources included, noting when sources are added or deleted, and providing users with filters so they can screen for newspapers, magazines, and blogs (Wiggins, 2006). I would add partnering with a handful of news services to facilitate speedier handling of breaking news, introducing some editorial control so that big stories are not buried, and linking the Google News Archive search to academic libraries' holdings. Google may have to tweak its philosophy to adopt some of these measures, but they would give the site more personality.

Google News is very good at news aggregation, but aggregation isn't where news sites are heading. Google News' successors and even some of its older rivals are creating virtual news communities in which finding articles is not an end, but the first step in synthesizing and discussing news. For its part, Google has indicated it is "optimistic" about the potential of online communities. It remains to be seen how the concept will be worked into Google News. Without innovation, Google News may very well start losing ground to social news sites like Wikinews and Wikio and may never gain ground on reliable sources with personality like MSNBC and CNN.

REFERENCES

Delaney, Kevin J. 2005. "Yahoo 'Hybrid' Now Dominates News Web Sites." *Wall Street Journal (Eastern Edition)*, April 14.

Dotinga, Randy. 2006. "When Computers Do the News, Hoaxes Slip In." *Christian Science Monitor,* March 29.

Egger-Sider, Francine & Jane Devine. 2005. "Google, The Invisible Web, and Librarians; Slaying the Research Goliath." In *Libraries and Google,* ed. William Miller & Rita M. Pellen, pp. 89-101. Binghamton, NY: Haworth Press.

Ellison, Sarah, & Christopher Lawton. 2006. "Google to License Content From AP For New Service." *Wall Street Journal (Eastern Edition),* August 4.

Espo, David. 2007. "Senate Dems Move to Limit Iraq Mission." *Associated Press, Washington Dateline,* February 23, Friday 4:00 a.m. GMT.

Gaither, Chris. 2005. "Web Giants Go With Different Angles in Competition for News Audience." *Los Angeles Times.* April 11.

Eun, David. 2006. "Google isn't the boogeyman." *Los Angeles Times.* Nov. 26. <http://www.latimes.com/news/printedition/suncommentary/la-op-eun26nov26,1,1467-502.story?coll=la-headlines-suncomment> (accessed April 16, 2007).

Google. 2007. "A Novel Approach to News." Google. <http://news.google.com/intl/en_us/about_google_news.html> (accessed April 4, 2007).

___. 2006. *10-K For The Fiscal Year Ended December 31, 2006.* <http://www.sec.gov/Archives/edgar/data/1288776/000119312507044494/d10k.htm> (accessed April 8, 2007).

Ingram, C., C. Awre, V. Arora, T. Brett, & G. Hanganu. 2005. "CREE Focus Groups Results and Comment." University of Hull. April. <http://www.hull.ac.uk/cree/downloads/CREEfocusgroupreport.pdf> (accessed March 7, 2007).

Jarboe, Greg. 2007. "Is Google News the Tail Wagging the News Search Dog?" *SearchEngineWatch.com* February 13. <http://searchenginewatch.com/showPage. html?page=3624977> (accessed April 9, 2007).

Jasco, Peter. 2005. "Google Scholar (Redux)." *Péter's Digital Reference Shelf* June. <http://www.gale.com/servlet/HTMLFileServlet?imprint=9999&region=7&fileName= reference/archive/200506/google.html> (accessed April 6, 2007).

Nielsen/NetRatings. 2007. "Top Site Genres." <http://www.nielsen-netratings.com/ resources.jsp?section=pr_netv&nav=1> (accessed April 16, 2007).

Pfanner, Eric. 2006. "Google Defies Order That It Publish Adverse Belgian Ruling." *International Herald Tribune,* September 23.

Walker, Leslie. 2004. "Microsoft Deploys Newsbot To Track Down Headlines." *The Washington Post,* August 1, F6.

Wiggins, Richard. 2006. "Is Google News Really News?" *Searcher,* May, v.14, n 5: 39-44.

York, Maurice. 2005. "Calling the Scholars Home: Google Scholar as a Tool for Rediscovering the Academic Library." In *Libraries and Google.* ed. William Miller & Rita M. Pellen, p. 117-133. Binghamton, NY: Haworth Press.

Index

Numbers followed by t indicate tables; those followed by f indicate figures.